IKE'S LAST BATTLE

IKE'S LAST BATTLE
The Battle of the Ruhr Pocket April 1945

Charles Whiting

LEO COOPER

First published 1989 by Leo Cooper

Reprinted in 2002 by
LEO COOPER
an imprint of Pen & Sword Books Ltd
47 Church Street
Barnsley
South Yorkshire
S70 2AS

ISBN 0 85052 914 X

A CIP catalogue for this book is available
from the British Library

Printed and bound in England by
CPI UK

CONTENTS

ILLUSTRATIONS

The photographs not credited above came from the author's collection.

AUTHOR'S ACKNOWLEDGEMENTS

I ought to name them, but they are really too many: the ordinary men and women in Germany who helped me with this book. However, I should like to mention two, Herr Heinrich Bastian (now deceased) and *Brigadegeneral* Hans-Georg Model, son of the Field-Marshal.

In the USA, I should like to thank Calvin Boykin, late of the 7th US Armored Division, for his kindness and assistance over many years; and, in particular, Tom Dickinson of the New York Public Library System and formerly of the 70th Infantry Division. As always T.D. turned up trumps.

Thanks, all of you.

'Clearly Berlin is the main prize. There is no doubt whatsoever in my mind that we should concentrate our energies and resources on a rapid thrust to Berlin.'

Eisenhower, September, 1944

'That place [Berlin] has become, so far as I am concerned, nothing but a geographical location, and I have never been interested in these.'

Eisenhower, March, 1945

Prologue

'The real trouble with the Yanks is that they are completely ignorant as to the rules of the game we are playing with the Germans. You play so much better when you know the rules.'

Field-Marshal Montgomery, 1945

In the spring of 1955 a small group of Germans made their way a little uncertainly through the great woods belonging to the noble von Spee family, looking for a certain oak tree. They were a mixed bunch: a couple of foresters in their grey-green uniforms and slouch hats, with hunting rifles slung over their shoulders; a few labourers, in peaked black caps dating from the war, carrying shovels; and a sombre middle-aged man who had the look of an undertaker about him — appropriately enough, for that is what he was. Leading them was a slight young man aged twenty-eight, whose postwar career had not particularly prospered under the new 'economic miracle' —*das Wirtsschaftswunder* — which had swept West Germany in these last few years.

The woods were remote and silent. It was hard to believe that they were located in the heart of Germany's greatest industrial region, the Ruhr, the workshop of the Reich ever since old Gustav Krupp had opened his first factory in nearby Duisburg back in 1811. Now, after being released from the Allies' prisons, to which they had been sentenced for war crimes, the old coal and steel barons were back at the helm once more, transforming the bomb-shattered Ruhr into the powerhouse of Europe. But here all was peace and pastoral tranquillity.

The very remoteness of the woods seemed to enhance the solemnity of the mission. After the initial chatter and bustle of the introductions, the men had lapsed into a brooding silence, aware that they were delving into one of the mysteries of that haunted, unholy, recent past. They moved cautiously, wordlessly skirting the odd bomb and shell craters from that time, being guided in curt undertones by the slight young man.

He, for his part, was wrapped in a tight cocoon of his own thoughts. For the young man, who bore a name that ten years before had been famous (for some, infamous) throughout Western Europe, was engaged in nothing less than a search for his long vanished father.

It was ten years since the son had seen the father. In January, 1945, as a young officer-cadet of barely eighteen, he had been summoned by his divisional commander and told he was being given a leave. The reason for this unexpected event, he later learned from no less a person than General von Manteuffel, commander of the Fifth Panzer Army, was that a surprise visit from him should help his father celebrate his fifty-fourth birthday. With another officer, the young cadet set off to cross war-torn Germany, heading for the remote border area where his father had been stopping the might of the US army for nearly four months. He had bled the Americans white, first in the Hürtgen Forest, then in the Ardennes, and now this January he was making them fight for every square metre of ground they captured in the Eifel. It was a tremendous feat for an Army that everyone had thought had been beaten back in the summer of 1944.

The birthday had been a great success. The young man had gone on inspections to the nearby front with his father; had seen him 'make a sow' of some of his unfortunate commanders (for his father's temper was notorious and he was feared by his officers); had gone skiing with him; had indulged with him in one of those tremendous drinking bouts for which the German Army was famous; and had watched his father and his senior commanders, generals to a man, snowballing each other outside the HQ like excited schoolkids just released from school on a winter's day.

But the time passed all too quickly. The young cadet had to report back to his training unit. Both he and his father knew that they faced a long hard fight before the battle for Germany was over. That snowy morning his father rose even earlier than usual to see him off; he stood with a group of his staff officers on the steps of the hunting lodge that was his headquarters, while the driver of the car revved the engine, flooding the dawn air with exhaust fumes. Their farewells over, the young man's car started to move off, squeaking over the hard-pressed snow of the drive. He took one last look back at the figures on the steps and thought his father seemed 'very serious, almost lonely, as he stared after our departing car. Suddenly the realization seized me — I would never see my father again.'

The young man was right. He had fought his little war with the Grossdeutschland Division in North Germany, had been captured by the British, finally to be released to an uncertain future in a defeated Germany, left to fend for his widowed mother and two sisters. His father was officially listed as missing but the family knew he was dead; they had already received a few of his personal trinkets from various officers on his staff. But they had done nothing to inform the authorities. After all, Father was a 'war criminal' . . .

It was years before the family learned of his fate. Even if they had known earlier about the hurried grave in the woods, they could have done very little about it. All of them were far too busy trying to keep body and soul together in this terrible, new, defeated Germany. Throughout the 'cigarette-end' summer of 1945, the 'cabbage winter' of 1946 and the continuing deprivations of 1947 and '48, their battle was with a new foe: hunger. As Field-Marshal Montgomery himself announced, the average German was living off 800 calories a day, fewer than had been received by the inmates of their former concentration camps.

Gradually life became easier. The currency reform of 1948 led to brighter economic prospects. The black market disappeared almost overnight. In 1949, with the Cold War raging, the Americans saw to it that their recent enemies formed their own independent state, the Federal Republic of West Germany. The boom had commenced. The Korean War increased the pace and output of the once shattered Ruhr industry. Now there was no more talk of turning Germany into an agricultural state, as the American Morgenthau had proposed in his controversial plan, for the new Germany was a valuable ally of the Americans. By the mid-fifties there were urgent talks going on in Paris, Washington, London and Bonn about re-arming Germany and creating a new German army — the Bundeswehr. Germany would no longer have to be ashamed of her old soldiers.

The time had come to dig up the dead man.

The son, piecing together what little information he had, knew that the grave was here, in these woods; here, on that terrible April day in 1945, the father's body had been given a hasty burial by two staff colonels, even as the American trap was closing in on them. Here, among all these trees, stood one that bore the tell-tale sign — and there it was. There was no mistaking it: the carved 'M' on the trunk of the oak, now overgrown a little by moss. This was the spot. The workmen in their peaked caps began to dig.

One of the dead man's staff had once expressed his admiration of him by quoting from Goethe: *'Den lieb' ich, der Unmögliches begehrt*' (I love him, who craves the impossible). Then he had been at the height of his fame, the soldier of whom even Hitler himself had been a little afraid. 'Did you see those eyes?' the Führer had breathed after one audience with him. 'I wouldn't like to serve under him.'

What was now revealed by the spades of the workers gave no clue to the dead man's former greatness. Even thirty-one years later the son, now a pensioned-off general of the German Bundeswehr, was reluctant to talk about what they found that day. Time and nature had taken their course. All that remained were the tattered rags of what had once been the uniform of a Field-Marshal in the Greater German Army, a skeleton, and a shattered skull — but he had been expecting that.

Hurriedly the pitiful remains of the soldier who had been Nazi Germany's youngest Field-Marshal were collected from his wartime grave. The party had to move fast, suspecting that those brash young reporters from the *Stern* and *Spiegel* would find this bizarre little scene *'ein gefundes Fressen'* (a set feast), as they called it: a scoop, in other words. After all, the dead man was still considered a war criminal. The contents of the grave were swiftly removed and carried back through the forest to the waiting vehicles which would now transport the dead man to his last and more dignified resting place.

The small convoy of vehicles swept across the gleaming new bridge over the Rhine, which the dead man had once tried so desperately to defend. Passing through the industrial district, with its smoking chimneys and booming factories, they soon entered a rural Germany which had not yet benefited from the new 'hard D-Mark', where the narrow fields were still worked on the medieval strip system and the peasants ploughed with oxen. On and on they drove through the villages, past bomb-damaged houses whose roofs were repaired with tin plating, past fields in which lighter patches revealed where they had been saturated by shells in that terrible winter and spring of ten years before, past roadside embankments where once the Wehrmacht's vehicles had sought refuge from Allied bombers. Here in the countryside the scars of wartime were a grim reminder of that last great battle the dead man had fought.

Gradually the terrain began to slow them down as the convoy followed the winding hill roads through shell-shattered fir forests, for they were now entering the Hürtgenwald — the 'Death Factory' the GIs had called it a decade ago. Here the Field-Marshal's soldiers had stopped the Americans — dead. One American division after another had been fed into these wooded heights to be felled by

German guns. Their casualty figures were appalling: up to sixty per cent in some rifle companies. After two weeks in the Hürtgen Forest, whole companies had surrendered, battalions had refused to fight, generals had been sacked for lack of courage. With a scratch force of second-rate infantry the Field-Marshal had held off the whole might of the US Army for months, saving the front from collapse as he had done four times in Russia previously. Furthermore, in the middle of the battle for the Hürtgen Forest, he had even found time to inflict a stinging defeat on the British at Arnhem!

They drove through Kleinhau, a village which had been totally flattened in the fighting. Once Hemingway had reported from here that he had seen a 'half-roasted Kraut' being eaten by a 'Kraut dog'. But now the convoy was approaching its destination: the *Ehrenfriedhof* (Cemetery of Honour) at Vossenack.

The *Ehrenfriedhof* had been created by the German authorities to honour their own dead. For years after the war, once the mines were cleared, the dead of both sides had been collected — in this area, thousands of Americans as well as Germans — and transferred to more appropriate graves. The Americans were taken over the nearby border to Belgium and France to be re-buried there. No American soldier killed in combat against the Germans would ever lie permanently in the soil of the enemy; in death, as in life, these young men would remain segregated. In 1955, however, and for years to come, there was precious little honour accorded to the men buried at Vossenack, the men who had died for 'Folk, Fatherland and Führer'. Postwar Germany, the 'land of the economic miracle', wanted to forget her embarrassing past — including those young Germans who had fought for the wrong cause.

But the young man who had come to bury his father in a worthy grave at last had little time for such considerations. Here were the men his father had once commanded: row after row of small stone crosses, barely protruding above the lawns, many of them marked 'Unknown German Soldier'. Here his father would be buried too. So it was done.

In due course, another of those unobtrusive gravestones would be erected. It would bear the simple legend: '*Walter Model —F.M.*'

It is still there today, thirty-odd years later, marking the spot where the mortal remains of Otto Moritz Walter Model, the youngest Field-Marshal in Hitler's Wehrmacht, were reburied so secretly, without any pomp or fanfare, that day in 1955. It bears, perhaps, the only witness to the tragic mistake that was made that April of 1945 when Model, realizing that there was no way out, shot himself. For the dead, the several thousands of German soldiers and civilians and their American enemies, that resulted from that mistake have been scattered to the winds. Victims all, their deaths served no purpose save to perpetuate the enslavement of Central Europe under another name.

It was a mistake made by Adolf Hitler in the first place, but one that was later compounded — surprisingly enough — by his most bitter foe, Dwight D. Eisenhower, the Allied Supreme Commander. The one had ordered the German Ruhr defended to the last, thus bringing yet further death and destruction to the great industrial area inhabited by 10,000,000 civilians and defended by Model's 400,000 soldiers. The other — the American — had ordered the place should be attacked, caring apparently little about the useless sacrifice of his soldiers' lives, the local civilians, or the future of Germany which depended on keeping this vital industrial area in working order.

But then, as far as the ordinary soldiers of both sides were concerned — the *landser* and the doughboy — mistakes on the part of their leaders were all to common in these last months of the war in Europe. In the end, they became resigned to the bitter fact that (with the exception of Walter Model) the Top Brass would die safely tucked up in their own warm beds. But for them, the mistakes of the Top Brass would, all too often, be paid for in blood — their blood.

On the American side, the first mistakes of the campaign in Europe were seen on the D-Day beaches. General Omar Bradley's refusal to use the specialized British tanks known as 'Funnies', which elsewhere helped to clear the beaches, turned the landing of the 1st and 29th American Infantry Divisions into 'Bloody Omaha'. Many of his men must have shared the opinions of Patton — Bradley's one time boss — that he was 'a man of great mediocrity'. For that was not the last of Bradley's mistakes, made with the connivance of the Supreme Commander.

To ensure that the armies of his Twelfth Army Group played a full role in the battles of 1944/45, they were allowed to involve themselves in bloody sideshows which contributed little to the winning of the war. Patton, for example, was able to go barrelling off into his headline-winning jaunt into Brittany, which had no strategic importance whatsoever. The error was compounded when Bradley ordered that the Breton ports, which Patton had failed to capture, should be taken. Brest alone cost him 10,000 casualties. Thereafter Bradley left them alone and they surrendered tamely in May, 1945. It was no different with Bradley's other army commander, General Hodges, who led the US First Army. Instead of driving straight for the Rhine, he was allowed to divert nearly ten divisions to engage in the bloody and totally useless fiasco of the Battle of the Hürtgen Forest.

The Battle of the Bulge was another grave mistake, costing Hodge's First and Patton's Third Armies some 80,000 casualties in all and delaying the end of the war by a further six bloody weeks. Prestige and honour were hurt by the surprise attack in the Ardennes, but still these top American generals continued to handle their huge armies with the same unthinking carelessness with which they had once led companies and battalions only five or six years before.

The Rhine was reached and again Bradley, with Eisenhower's approval, allowed his subordinate commanders to indulge themselves in prestige adventures — 'ego trips' we would call them today — which had little relevance to the real business of winning the war as economically and efficiently as possible. American generals vied with each other to cross the great river at a dozen most unlikely spots so that they could be recorded as having their ceremonial 'piss in the Rhine'.

Then, on 28 March, 1945, Eisenhower himself made an unprecedented move. Without the approval of his own superior commander, General Marshall, or the two Allied political bosses, Roosevelt and Churchill, he sent a telegram to Stalin announcing that he had made a major change in Allied strategy for the rest of the war. Instead of advancing on Berlin, as his subordinate commanders and their men expected him to do, now that the Germans were virtually defeated in the West, he would 'encircle and destroy the enemy forces defending the Ruhr', then halt his troops on the Elbe. There he would wait for the Russians, while Patton's Third Army would plunge south into the bucolic scenery of Bavaria and the delights of the Austrian Alps. Berlin, 'a mere geographic location', as Eisenhower now phrased it, would be left to the Red Army.

This was to prove the greatest mistake of all. After eleven months of the bloody campaign in North-West Europe, a campaign that had cost over 750,000 casualties among his own men, the Supreme Commander of the Western Allies was handing the ultimate political prize to Soviet Russia. And if wars are conducted for political advantages in the future, as well as solutions to the old problems which occasioned those wars, then for what real purpose did all those young men die? What purpose had their supreme sacrifice served?

Right into the 1980s, Eisenhower's apologists have maintained that the Supreme Commander made this tremendous mistake of concentrating on the Ruhr area while leaving 'the main prize' of Berlin — as he himself had once called it — to the Russians because he had been politically naive about the Soviets; because he had been in the dark about their military buildup and intentions in East Germany; or simply because he had just been carrying out President Roosevelt's orders.

But none of this was true. To take the last claim first, by March, 1945, Roosevelt was a dying man. When Eisenhower sent his astonishing message to Stalin, Roosevelt had a mere two weeks to live. The President had no part, direct or indirect, in Eisenhower's decision to leave Berlin to the Russians. Nor had General Marshall, Eisenhower's immediate military boss. It was Eisenhower's own decision, pure and simple. Nor is it true that Eisenhower was unaware of Russian military intentions in East Germany. As his own grandson admitted in his book, *Eisenhower at War*, published in 1986, the Supreme Commander had irrefutable evidence of Soviet Army forces assembling for an assault on Berlin. That evidence came from the Germans — thanks to Ultra, the decoding operation at Bletchley Park in England, where German Army signals were being intercepted and read by the British and Americans. Via Ultra, the Wehrmacht's appreciation of Red Army strength and intentions was in the hands of Eisenhower's intelligence.

Moreover, there is reason to suppose that Eisenhower's knowledge came from an even more direct source: the Russians themselves. Although for obvious reasons the fact has never been publicized, the Bletchley Park operators were probably also reading the signals of Russia, the supposed ally! Why else should Ultra have remained shrouded in such obsessive, almost pathological, secrecy right up to the 1970s, nearly three decades after the operation officially ended?

It was not until 1974, when Group Captain Winterbotham published his book *The Ultra Secret*, that the great decoding effort became public knowledge. Only then was it clear that many hundred of people, perhaps thousands, both British and American, had known the secret of what went on in Hut Three, the rusty Nissen shelter at Bletchley Park; and all of them had kept their knowledge to themselves. In post-war years, some women even refused to undergo medical operations in case they inadvertently revealed the secret while under the influence of anaesthetics. The man who could have claimed to have built the world's first computer in connection with the Ultra operation went to his grave, allowing the world to believe the first one — the Univac— had been constructed two years later. Another scientist closely connected with Ultra was not honoured for his work at Bletchley until thirty-five years later, after Winterbotham's book had come out.

Naturally, the British kept the secret because they were bound by the terms of the Official Secrets Act and could be punished if they revealed it. As late as 1973, when British author Charles Whiting visited Winterbotham at his remote Devonshire farmhouse and urged him to 'go public' on Ultra, the eight-year-old former SIS man objected, 'But the boys'll put me in the Tower if I do!'

But the Americans who knew the great secret were *not* bound by the British Official Secrets Act. Why is it that none of them revealed it? There were several ex-journalists close to the secret, such as Ingersoll on Bradley's staff (he guessed it) and Butcher on Eisenhower's (who revealed pretty well everything else in his book *Three Years with Eisenhower*), who would have known they had a bestseller on their hands. So why didn't they spill the beans in the immediate post-war years?

The answer is obvious. Pressure was put on them not to do so because Ultra had been used to read Russian signals during the war — and was still being used for that purpose after the war had ended. Russian signals were notoriously lax, as historian and wartime Bletchley operative Peter Calvocoressi has recently pointed out:*

From 1941 we exchanged a certain amount of intelligence with Moscow, with a mutual lack of complete candour. They (if I remember right) gave us a copy of the German Army code table which we called the 'Bird Book'. We sent them, via our Ambassador, intelligence derived from Enigma, but without telling them where we got it (because their cypher security was so abysmal that they seemed likely inadvertently to give our secrets away to the Germans).

But how did the British code experts know that Russian 'cypher security was so abysmal'? There can only be one answer to that. The British were tapping the Soviet signals traffic all along.

*In a letter to the *Daily Telegraph*, dated 4 January, 1988.

So if Eisenhower was not as uninformed about Russian intentions in March, 1945, as his apologists have since maintained, what was the real reason for his decisive change in strategy? What was it that led him to fight a purposeless battle for the Ruhr and leave Berlin to the Red Army? There are those who argue that Eisenhower's new strategy was prompted by a commendable desire to keep casualties to a minimum. As support for their argument, they usually quote General Bradley who told Eisenhower in March that it would cost the US Army 100,000 casualties to take the German capital – 'a pretty stiff price to pay for a prestige objective'.

But this argument got short shrift from General Simpson, whose US Ninth Army would have led the attack on Berlin. 'Ridiculous!' he asserted on his sickbed nearly forty years later:* 'We really had no opposition at all. Anybody who suggests otherwise doesn't know what he is talking about. There was practically nothing ahead of us except German troops pleading to be made prisoner!' And his Chief-of-Staff, General Moore, agreed with him. Four decades on, Moore remembered that among the Germans who retreated into the Ninth's lines was General Walther Wenck, Commander of the German Twelfth Army — the only real force opposing Simpson at the time — and that Wenck had told him: 'General, we Germans have been fighting the Bolsheviks for four years. You Americans are going to have to fight them next. Don't you think it would be better if we joined forces and fought them together right now?' This was the kind of opposition which was going to cost the US Army 100,000 casualties on the road to Berlin!

So why did Eisenhower order his armies to stop on the Elbe? What induced him to make the greatest strategic blunder of any American general in the Second World War, a blunder that has determined the political situation in Central Europe right up to our own time and probably way into the twenty-first century? Why was Berlin sacrificed for the bomb-shattered, useless Ruhr? Why were eighteen American divisions employed from 25 March to 17 April, 1945 in the Battle of the Ruhr Pocket, a battle that should never have been fought?

*General Simpson died in 1982 in his late eighties.

PART I

A Trap is Set

'If you want to have a decent war, the first thing you do is get rid of your allies.'

US General Fox Connor, First World War

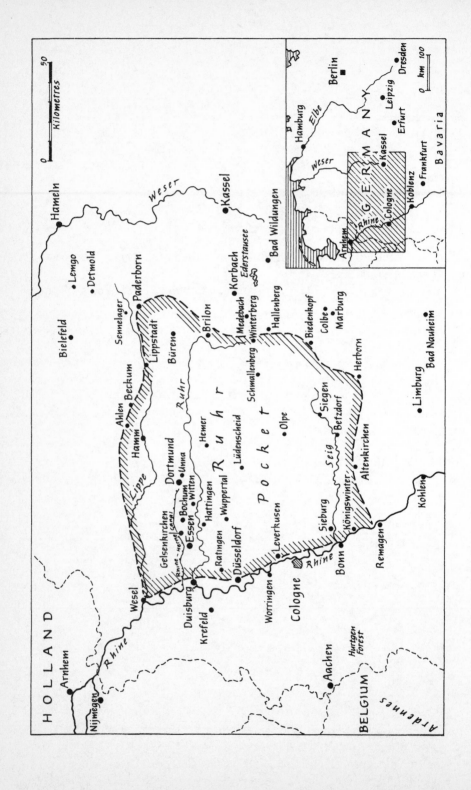

ONE

'Nice chap — no soldier'

For the General, this would be the last time he'd ever be able to escape from the public eye. From now onwards, for the remaining twenty-odd years still left to him, virtually every minute of his day would be recorded for posterity. Soon the Great American Public would know just how many cigarettes he smoked a day (sixty), the state of his heart (poor) and rate of his blood pressure (high), even the fact that his underpants were silk and that he required his valet to hold them out for him so that he could step into them. This undemocratic habit he had acquired as a humble major during his pre-war days in Manila.

But the third week of March, 1945, offered him a rare chance to escape from the pressures of his high office. After ten gruelling months, day after day making the decisions that sealed the fate of millions, he had set off in his private train for Cannes in the South of France, together with his servants, his 'personal assistant' — the tall green-eyed Irishwoman Kay Summersby, a former model and divorcee — and a batch of poker-playing, hard-drinking fellow generals. An opportunist American millionaire, who had perhaps guessed that the General might one day become the 'Father of the Nation', now the war was virtually won, had offered him his luxurious villa rent-free. The villa, romantically named 'Sous le Vent' and into which the owner had poured three million dollars, was located at a secluded spot directly on the coast; and the General could have it, if he wished, for five long days. It would be his first real vacation since 1943.

Of course, the break in this remote 'hideaway', as the General's staff called it mischievously (the word had salacious associations), had to be kept top-secret. With the last major battle — on the Rhine

— still to be fought in North-West Europe, the Great American Public would have been shocked to discover where the General was spending these last days before the battle. Soon thousands of young men would be springing into action while their Commander relaxed in a villa which Kay Summersby thought 'the most luxurious place I have ever seen'.

Not that the General did not need a rest. A few days before, General Arnold of the US Army Air Corps had visited his head-quarters in France and had noted that the war 'had taken a whole lot out of him, but he forced himself to go on and would until [the] whole mess was cleaned up'. He was indeed in a bad physical state. He had a touch of flu; his 'football knee' was acting up again and was badly swollen; and a cyst on his back had just been cut out by his personal doctor, leaving a deep and painful wound which required a number of stitches.

In fact, his immediate staff and cronies thought the General was on the verge of a nervous breakdown. Only the week before, his Chief-of-Staff had rounded upon him in exasperation at the General's refusal to take a break: 'Look at you!' he had snorted. 'You've got bags under your eyes. Your blood pressure is higher than it's ever been, and you can hardly walk across the room.' Kay Summersby felt the same. As she later wrote, 'When the General was out in public, he pulled himself together by sheer willpower and looked healthy and vigorous and exuded his usual charm. But the moment he got back to the office or the house, he slumped. And every time he had to take more than twenty or thirty steps, that knee put him in agony.'

But now he had submitted to the demands of his staff. For the first two days of the five-day break, he simply slept. He would wake up solely to eat, on the terrace overlooking the sea, and have a few glasses of wine, then return to his bedroom to sleep again. Once Kay Summersby suggested a game of cards, for the General was passionately devoted to poker and bridge. But he shook his balding head; he could not even find the energy to read one of the 'Western' pulp magazines which were his favourite reading.

'All I want to do is sit here and not think,' he told Kay Summersby on the third day. 'I just can't concentrate. My mind is fuzzy.'

She realized he was in danger of sinking into a depression. 'You're simply exhausted,' she told him. 'You can't push yourself the way you have and not feel it.'

'I suppose so,' he answered. 'But the way I feel now, I don't think I'll ever be able to concentrate on anything again.'

Mrs Summersby knew better than anyone, even his doctor, just how exhausted the General was. A year ago, long before the hard wearisome campaign in Europe had begun, the General had returned to London after a flying visit to Washington. On that first night they had found themselves alone. The General's staff was always discreet and would remain so about his private life long after he was dead. There had been drinks, several of them. 'Inevitably,' as she recalled decades later, 'we found ourselves in each other's arms in an unrestrained embrace. Our ties came off. Our jackets came off. Buttons were unbuttoned. It was as if we were frantic. And we were.' But it was no use. The General was unable to perform. He snuggled his face into the hollow between her neck and shoulder and said miserably: 'Oh God, Kay, I'm sorry. I'm not going to be any good for you.'

The General was suffering from chronic exhaustion; that much Kay Summersby knew. What she didn't know was that these sunny few days on the French Riviera would be the last she ever spent in intimate contact with the General. There would be no baby that she so desired from the General. No marriage either. Even as the two of them rested on the sun-dappled terrace, the General with his trousers rolled up to display his skinny legs, their relationship was being discussed by members of his entourage. All were agreed: there was no future in it. For there were those in Washington, and in Europe too, who had plans for the General, now that the war was nearing a successful conclusion. They were political plans and an Irish divorcee, half the age of the General's wife back in the United States, played no part in them.

On the third day of his vacation the General started to feel better. The rest, the sun, the white wine were beginning to have an effect. That evening after supper he snorted: 'Goddamnit, I'm tired of going off to bed every night while the rest of you do God knows what! How about staying home and playing a little bridge with the old man tonight?'

His old cronies — 'Big John', 'Beatle', 'Brad', all of them generals — obliged and the General and his partner, Kay Summersby, won. As she recorded long after her partner of that night died, 'It was a good evening . . . There was nothing fuzzy whatsoever about his concentration on the cards.'

It was about now that Brad — tall, gangling, bespectacled and lantern-jawed, who somehow seemed out of place among these hard-drinking, cynical, wenching fellow generals — started to broach the subject that had been uppermost in his mind for the past two months.

Back in January, 1945, Brad felt he had been publicly humiliated by 'Monty' — in this chummy cosy world of the Top Brass everyone was known by his nickname. The undersized, cocky Britisher, had made it appear that he alone had defeated the Germans in the Ardennes Battle. Now Brad wanted to prevent Monty from gaining the kudos of winning the final victory in Central Europe. In his opinion, the last battle with the Nazis would have to be seen by the world, and the Great American Public in particular, as being fought by *Americans* under the leadership of *American* generals. Naturally! Now it was up to the General to make the decisions that would shape the final strategy of the last campaign. He, Brad, was not scheduled to go to the Pacific to fight the 'Nips'. He wanted to end his long career in the US Army with a tremendous victory which would go down in history.

Two weeks earlier Brad had called a meeting for his four army commanders: 'Georgie', 'Big Simp', 'G' and 'Courtney'. Swearing them to secrecy, he told them he did not want the US Army to become a supporting force for Monty's full-scale crossing of the Rhine in the north. Naturally they agreed. As Georgie noted in his diary afterwards, 'It is essential to get the First and Third Armies so deeply involved in their present plans that they cannot be moved north to play second-fiddle to the British-instilled idea of attacking with sixty divisions on the Ruhr plain.'

Now Brad wanted the General's authorization to change the current strategy laid down in Washington and London. For their political bosses, British and American, they would still pay lip-service to the notion that Monty would be making the main effort. In fact, Brad wanted the whole direction of Allied strategy changed. First Big Simp's Ninth Army and Courtney's First Army would cut off the Ruhr by a gigantic pincer movement. Then the Ninth and First, together with Georgie's Third Army, would form up for a massive drive through Central Germany to halt on the River Elbe where they would link up with the Red Army. This would mean, as Brad wrote later, that American forces would be placed 'at center stage' and Monty's reduced to 'a supporting role' in the north. Both he and the General knew, of course, that 'neither London nor Monty would like it ... that for prestige and political reasons the British would howl to high heaven'. Why? Because Berlin would be left to the Russians and everyone at the top knew that, for political reasons, 'Winnie' (i.e. Churchill) burned to capture the German capital before the Red Army did.

We do not know the General's reaction to Brad's suggested change of policy made that spring day in Cannes, for his thoughts at the time were not recorded. The war was nearly over; he was sick, bone-tired, anxious about his own future — and now he faced a critical decision about the final strategy of the war in Europe. Yet, writing home to his wife that March, he seemed merely concerned to placate her worries. She was constantly harassing him in her letters about the supposed high living and loose morals of the US Top Brass in Europe. She suspected, rightly in fact, that the General's relationship with his green-eyed 'personal assistant' was not as platonic as he made it out to be. Only a couple of months before she had accused him of 'dirty tricks' and he had written back:

You've always put your own interpretation on every act, look, or word of mine, and when you've made yourself unhappy, that has, in turn, made me the same . . . . Don't forget I take a beating every day . . . . Please try to see me in something besides a despicable light — and at least let me be certain of my welcome home when this mess is finished.

Now, after two and a half years of separation, the General was about to return home. He had left the States an obscure major-general, known only to the older members of the regular Army. Now he was the most powerful military man in the Western world — albeit as hen-pecked as the humblest of his soldiers. But before he returned to the States he had to make this one last major decision.

'Ike', for that is how the rest of the world knew the General, had to decide this third week of March, 1945, whether or not his armies would go for 'the main prize'. Was it to be Berlin . . . or not?

That same March day, even as General Omar Bradley was persuading General Eisenhower to accept the new strategy, five hundred miles to the north another senior soldier — German this time — was also being asked to change his plans.

Field-Marshal Walter Model, Commander of the German Army Group B, looked like the typical Hollywood stereotype of a Prussian officer, run somewhat to seed: arrogant in manner, with his cap cocked at a jaunty angle and a monocle screwed into his left eye. In fact, he was the scion of three generations of music teachers, pious Protestants and middle class; the community into which he was born was utterly remote from those vast East Prussian estates of the serf-owning *Junker* caste, which had traditionally produced the aristocratic officers who had staffed the Prussian and Imperial Armies for nearly three centuries.

But if Model's background was not that of the traditional upper-class Prussian officer, he still had all the military virtues and habits, good and bad, of that class. Unlike most of the American generals against whom he would soon fight the last battle, he had seen much of war. He had been wounded in combat four times, twice in the First World War and twice in this war. Once a bullet had passed right through his body; the surgeons pronounced him a 'medical wonder', for it had failed to injure a single vital organ and soon the patient was making life hell for the doctors and nurses who attended him.

He was as ruthless as those old Prussians, too, and much feared by his long-suffering staff. Once when he left on one of his rare leaves, his Chief-of-Staff gave out the signal: '*Schweinfurt*' — a pun on the German city of that name, but which could also be translated as 'the swine has gone'. More than one senior officer, on hearing that he was being posted to Model's staff, asked to be relieved. When Colonel Wilck, the defender of the Imperial German city of Aachen, asked for permission to break out with what was left of his men, Model signalled him arrogantly to fight 'to the last bullet' and then: 'let yourself be buried in the ruins!'

One day in 1942, when the German Ninth Army had reached breaking point on the Eastern Front, Model arrived unexpectedly at the Army HQ. Wearing a fur-collared greatcoat that reached his ankles and a pair of old-fashioned earmuffs covering his ears, he stalked in, threw his cap on a chair and, ignoring the salutes of the staff officers, strode to the situation map and studied it for a moment. 'Rather a mess!' he snapped, then barked out a string of orders. The staff officers stared at each other in open-mouthed amazement; where, in the name of three devils, was Model going to get the men for the bold counter-attack he was now proposing?

Finally Colonel Blaurock, the Ninth's Chief-of-Staff, ventured, 'And what, *Herr General*, have you brought us for this operation?'

Model surveyed his new Chief-of-Staff through his monocle before answering 'Why — myself!'

That was typical of Model. His arrogance, his overweening vanity, his biting sarcasm and restless energy made him feared, even hated, by his staff, whom he constantly threatened with a court-martial. Once, for instance, during the Battle of the Bulge, his command car was blocked by a snowbound road. Model didn't hesitate. He got out and began shovelling snow with the rest of the common soldiers. A little later he came across an elegantly uniformed captain and demanded to know where he had been when the shovelling was going on. The unhappy captain was forced to confess that he had been sitting in his vehicle. Model flushed purple. 'So,' he rasped, 'you would let a field-marshal clear the road for you while you sit comfortably in your car. As from today, *Kamerad*, you are a private.' Whereupon he ripped the stars from the unfortunate officer's epaulettes.

But if Model was unpopular with some of his officers, he was liked by the 'stubble-hoppers', as the infantry called themselves. Every day he spent at least eight hours at the front, sometimes taking over the command of battalions, even companies, in action, when the situation became tricky. Time and again in Russia he had saved the front from breaking down at the very last moment.

In the summer of 1944, when transferred to the West — a post he did not want — he had rallied what was left of the beaten German Army streaming out of France, chased by the victorious Allies who thought the Germans were finished and the war about over. Model soon showed them their mistake. At Arnhem in September he inflicted a grave defeat on Montgomery. One month later he held the Americans in the Hürtgen Forest, on the German border, and turned that battle into a 'Death Factory' for the GIs. Then, in December, he commanded the great German counter-attack in the Ardennes which cost Bradley's armies nearly 80,000 casualties and gave the US Top Brass their greatest scare of the war in Europe.

Now, in March, 1945, Model found himself commanding his shattered armies on the other side of the Rhine and waiting for the all-out Allied attack over Germany's last natural bulwark. At Remagen the Americans were already across and had been for over two weeks. But Model did not regard them as much of a threat. The main threat, he reasoned, would come from Montgomery in the north. Once the 'Victor of El Alamein' crossed the Rhine in force, Model guessed, Montgomery would launch a major attack in the Duisburg—Düsseldorf area.

And it was his flanks that worried Model. He was fairly confident about holding his front along the Rhine, but the situation on both flanks was precarious and he had virtually no panzers and absolutely no reserves to launch a counter-attack when the Anglo-Americans crossed the river. But at this stage of the war, with defeat staring Germany in the face, what was the value of fighting on? If he did so, Model knew, the *Ruhrgebiet*, Germany's greatest industrial area, could well be turned into a vast wasteland. Germany's means of production for the future, even after defeat, would be totally destroyed — and what would become of her people then?

Twelve days before, Field-Marshal Albert Kesselring had arrived from Italy to take up his post as Model's new Commander-in-Chief West, greeting his worried staff with the light-hearted remark, 'Well, *meine Herren*, I am the new V-3!'* But that kind of statement was typical of a too optimistic soldier, who was always smiling his gap-toothed smile and was known to his troops as 'Smiling Albert'.

Model's sombre Lutheran temperament would not allow him to make easy, off-the-cuff remarks of that nature. Back in February when he had last seen his wife (after the destruction of their home in the great raid on Dresden) she had noted that he remained 'unchanged, optimistic'. Even at this late stage, it seems, Model was presenting an outwardly confident front to the world — particularly to his staff and soldiers, of course. But with the chain of command breaking down everywhere so that he was becoming virtually his own master, without interference from the Führer, would he be justified in continuing the hopeless fight which would bring so much suffering to the civilians?

He knew what the Minister of Armaments, *Reichsminister* Speer, now on his way to visit him here at his HQ in the Hessian village of Altenkirchen, wanted him to do. He had already mentioned the subject to him two days before. Now he would urge Model to give his full acceptance to his plan. Speer, clever, ambitious and once Hitler's greatest protegé, wanted him to disobey the Führer's orders to fight to the last, turning Germany into a wasteland. But if Model accepted Speer's plan, in the end it could mean only one thing — surrender.

On the day that Eisenhower was travelling to Cannes in his special train, Speer visited Hitler at his HQ. His former patron received him coldly. Speer, sensitive and astute as he was, could see the Führer was angry at the memorandum he had given him a few days earlier stating that 'the final collapse of the German economy could be expected with certainty within four to eight weeks' and after that the war 'could not be continued on the military plane'.

*i.e. As a follow-up to the two previous terror weapons, the V-1 and V-2.

It was Speer's fortieth birthday, but the interview with Hitler gave him no cause for celebration. He realized now, for the first time, just how unpredictable his one-time friend had become. Hitler told him he could expect a written reply to his memorandum; then, after an icy pause, continued:

If the war is lost, the people will be lost also. It is not necessary to worry about what the German people will need for elemental survival. On the contrary, it is best for us to destroy even these things, for the nation has proved to be the weaker and the future belongs solely to the stronger, eastern nation [he meant Russia]. In any case, only those who are inferior will remain after this struggle . . . for the good have already been killed.

It was the true voice of National Socialist nihilism. The Götterdamerung was fast approaching and what did lesser mortals matter? Speer was glad to escape into the night air, away from the madman who controlled what was left of the battered 'Thousand Year Reich' and its destiny.

Speer's unease only deepened that night. Driving along the deserted *autobahn* with Field-Marshal Kesselring, who had also been visiting the Führer, attempting to cover the 300 miles to Kesselring's HQ at Bad Nauheim before dawn, he knew the dreaded *jabos* — the Allied fighter-bombers — could well appear at any moment; they seemed to be everywhere these days, shooting up trains, trucks even individual peasants working in the fields. Kemptka, their SS driver, had switched on the car radio, and the three occupants of the big tourer listened anxiously to the broadcast warnings of approaching Allied bomber squadrons: '*Night fighters in grid number . . . Several Mosquitoes in grid . . .*' Whenever they came too close for comfort, Kemptka would switch on the parking lights and the car crawled along the edge of the road until the bombers had droned away in the distance. Then, flicking on the high beam, with the supercharger howling, Kemptka once again took them hurtling down the empty *autobahn* at 130 kilometres an hour.

Even then Speer's thoughts were uncomfortable. Kesselring, the new Commander-in-Chief West, was a disappointment. Speer saw him as 'a soldier pure and simple' and 'not inclined to discuss Hitler's orders'; this was not the man to halt the senseless destruction of what was left of Germany.

On reaching Kesselring's HQ they paused to eat — their meal interrupted by the howl of diving *jabos* and the chatter of machine guns, as the enemy attacked the area. Then it was off again on the dangerous 125 mile journey from Nauheim to Model's HQ at Altenkirchen. Surely, Speer told himself, Model would see sense. Everyone knew that the Field-Marshal was afraid of no one, not even the Führer. He was probably worried about the safety of his family, of course: his wife, son and two daughters. These days, the loved ones of anyone who opposed the despot could be imprisoned without trial, even executed, under the system of *Sippenhaft* (roughly: 'arrest of next-of-kin'). But Speer knew Model was totally disenchanted with the unrealistic leadership at the top. The last time he had met the Field-Marshal, two weeks before, Model was in a furious temper at the orders coming from Hitler's HQ. He had been commanded to counter-attack the Americans at Remagen with certain specific divisions and re-capture the bridge across the Rhine there. He snorted to Speer: 'These divisions have lost their weapons and have no fighting strength at all. They would be less effective than a company! It's the same thing all over again. At headquarters they have no idea of what is going on . . .. Of course, I'll be blamed for the failure.'

Speer had sensed the Field-Marshal might be receptive to his proposal, that Hitler's new 'scorched earth' policy should not be applied to the Ruhr under his command, and he was right. 'Model promised him that in the fighting in the Ruhr area he would spare the indispensable bridges and especially the railroad installations'.

Now, tired as he was after two days on the road, Speer began to hope again as the big car edged its way down secondary roads, cutting through the forests and hills of the Sauerland, dodging the *jabos* circling overhead. Model would listen to his proposals, he was sure.

The big tourer drove into the white-painted village with its half-timbered medieval houses and onion-towered church, set in a background of the surrounding hills with the firs marching up their slopes like spike-helmeted Prussian grenadiers. Altenkirchen seemed like another world, peaceful, remote, far from the war raging only miles away. Nothing indicated that this was the headquarters of an army group, consisting of three armies; there wasn't an officer or soldier in sight, not even a motorcycle dispatch-rider. Model had learned this lesson after his previous headquarters in the Eifel had been bombed by the Allied air forces. At his HQ not a single vehicle moved during daylight hours.

Model received the civilian in the village inn and Speer promptly launched into his proposals, beginning with the need to preserve the infrastructure of the Ruhr, vital for the future of any post-war Germany. But the discussions had hardly begun when a staff officer appeared, bearing a teleprint. Model peered at it momentarily through his monocle. Then, looking both embarrassed and perplexed, he handed it to Speer.

Speer sensed it was bad news, and it was. This was the Führer's answer to his memorandum of two days before, rejecting every point he had made and insisting that 'all military, transportation, communications, industrial and supply facilities, as well as all resources within the Reich' were to be destroyed. This meant 'the death sentence for the German people', Speer told himself dejectedly, and there was nothing he could do now to prevent it. For in the signal Hitler had stripped him of all his powers. The Führer would now rely on his *Gauleiters* to carry out his policy. If nothing were done, Germany was going to be 'thrown back', as he later wrote, 'into the Middle Ages'.

Model was a disappointment too, since their last meeting. The Field-Marshal knew, of course, that he had the power of life or death over some of Europe's major industrial plants — the world-famous Bayer chemical and pharmaceutical works at Leverkusen, the Krupp works at Essen, the M.A.N. works at Duisburg, and many more. But he also knew that any action he might take to prevent these plants being destroyed under the terms of the new 'scorched earth' policy would be instantly reported to the Führer by the five *Gauleiters* located in the Ruhr area.

Moreover, Speer now realized that Model's attitude towards him had changed; he was more aloof and declined to discuss Speer's plan to safeguard the Ruhr industries. The Field-Marshal was going to fight on; he would carry out Hitler's orders to the bitter end, even if it did mean plunging Germany back into the Dark Ages.

Speer gave up, rejecting in disgust that Model lacked the 'moral courage' (*Zivilcourage*) to do what he knew was right. Worn out and dispirited, he found himself a bed in a nearby farmhouse and lay down to sleep for a few hours before returning to Berlin. But his sleep was unsettled and in the end he rose and went for a walk, across the dew-damp fields and up one of the nearest hills. From there he gazed down at the village below, eerie in the dawn mist, which the sun was trying to burn away. Then he turned his attention to the vista:

I could see far out over the hills of Sauerland, the land lying

between the Sieg and Ruhr rivers. How was it possible, I thought,
that one man wanted to transform this land into a desert.

Of all the Top Brass concerned with the last battle to come, Field-Marshal Montgomery was the most sanguine in that third week of March, 1945. He had just moved his Tactical Headquarters across the Meuse into Germany, to a former riding school not far from the village of Straelen. It was located near some pine woods, scored by a large anti-tank ditch which had been intended — and failed — to keep the British Army out of Germany. As a delighted Montgomery wrote to his mentor 'Brookie' (Field-Marshal Sir Alan Brooke) that week: 'My HQ are now in Germany. I have waited a long time for this moment, and have travelled a long way before bringing it to pass. It is a great thrill.'

Now the sun shone and Montgomery was back to his famous caravan and the wandering farmyard that accompanied it: one cow, four geese and ten chickens, all of them laying well. Every night there were large omelettes made of goose eggs available for the handsome young men who made up his 'eyes and ears' — and plenty of looted schnapps and wine, too, when the 'master' had gone to bed.

Already his Pioneer Corps was at work on the vast smokescreen, along a sixty-six-mile length of the Rhine between Nijmegen in Holland to below Wesel in Germany, to hide his activities from prying German eyes. Behind this screen he had massed his armour and infantry, British, Canadian and American, thousands of tanks and hundreds of thousands of men. Behind these in turn were the guns, more than he had used in the initial barrage of his first victory at El Alamein two years before. They stood wheel to wheel, waiting for the order to open fire. And in England and France two whole parachute divisions were alerted to drop on the other side of the Rhine, some 30,000 men, British and American. All was planned down to last .36 grenade for the infantry and tiepin for the Bailey bridge which would soon span the 1,500-foot breadth of the great river. Months of planning had gone into the operation to come: the greatest assault crossing of a river in the whole of the war. Montogmery was satisfied at last. Nothing could possibly go wrong. Everything was perfect.

Once the Rhine was crossed the way ahead was clear. As he had written to his intimate 'Simbo' Simpson on 20 March, 'One man must be in general command north of the Ruhr.' Naturally Montgomery intended to be that man.

As usual, however, Eisenhower was threatening to throw a spanner in the works. Four days before, after the months of preparation, Eisenhower had suggested a change of plan. Once Montgomery's attack over the river to the north of the Ruhr had proved successful, the thrust to the Elbe and then on presumably to Berlin would be subdivided. Eisenhower proposed that Bradley's Twelfth Army Group should operate in that area together with Montgomery's own Twenty-first Army Group.

He, Montgomery, was not having that. It would clutter up the battlefield, make it too untidy, something to which he had always strongly objected. One always needed a 'tidy battlefield'. As he wrote at the time, 'The whole thing is complete nonsense; the employment of two Army Groups round the *north* of the Ruhr is not only unsound tactically, it is quite impossible administratively.' Besides, he wanted to be in sole charge north of the Ruhr. For it was to the north that the most important victory of this final battle would be gained — Berlin.

In response to Eisenhower's suggestion, Monty proposed to Supreme Headquarters that Bradley should remain where he was to the south of the Ruhr. Talking the matter over with a member of Eisenhower's staff, he recommended that 'Twelve Army Group should get a good large bridgehead from Bonn to Mainz and then strike north-east, joining me east of the Ruhr.' Thereafter, with one American Army (Simpson's Ninth) under his command, and 'ten to twelve American divs' to be attached to him when required from Hodges' First US Army, he would set about capturing what Ike called 'that main prize'.

So far, however, Monty had heard nothing directly from the Supreme Commander on his counter-suggestion. Ike was absent from his headquarters (naturally Montgomery did not know that he was holidaying with Kay Summersby in his Riviera 'hideaway'). But he was confident that this time he could persuade Ike of his point of view.

Had Montgomery only remained silent and accepted Bradley's new role to the north of the Ruhr, overlooking the tactical and administrative problems of two Army Group HQs working side by side, the whole course of the last stage of the war in Europe would have been changed. Bradley would have ensured that Berlin remained the Western Allies' main target and the face of Central Europe — right into our own time — would have been vastly different.

But, opinionated and egocentric as he was, Montgomery had never learned to curb his tongue. He simply had to have his way.

And he did — with disastrous results. Relegated to the south at Montgomery's own suggestion, Bradley saw to that.

The first time Montgomery had met the future Supreme Commander he had characterized him scathingly to his long-suffering Chief-of-Staff, Freddie de Guingand, as 'Nice chap — no soldier.' Now, as Montgomery waited, apparently relaxed and confident, at his remote tiny tactical HQ, the American Top Brass were already working flat-out to repay 'the little fart' for all the snubs and insults they felt they had suffered at his hands. Soon the British Field-Marshal would learn that not only was Ike 'no soldier', he was not a 'nice chap' either.

TWO

'You must have faith'

It was dawn on Palm Sunday, 25 March, 1945. Tension was in the very air. For two weeks the American soldiers huddled in this tight bridgehead, across the Rhine from Remagen, had been waiting for this moment. Now, with Patton's Third Army already across the Rhine to their south and Montgomery's Twenty-first Army Group battling its way across to the north, the three corps of Hodges' First Army were finally going to make the break-out. Five infantry and two armoured divisions were about to launch the first offensive on Model's Army Group B.

All of them were veterans, though admittedly their depleted ranks were now filled up with 'wet noses', green soldiers straight from the 'ripple-dipples' or Replacement Centres. They were the hard-core infantry divisions, which had been in the fighting right from the beginning on D-Day: the 1st US Infantry, for instance, known as 'the Big Red One' (motto: *'No mission too difficult, no sacrifice too great'*), or the 3rd Armoured Division, which had lost over 3,000 men in its long bloody trail from the beaches. Others had served their lethal apprenticeship in the Ardennes and the battles of the German frontier, like the 78th Infantry or the 9th Armoured Division, which had captured that original bridge across the Rhine at Remagen on 7 March, 1945, and made it, for a week at least, 'the most famous bridge in the world'.

They had a score to settle, too, for many of them had been through the 'Death Factory' of the Hürtgen Forest. From September, 1944, to February, 1945, they had suffered horrendous casualties at Model's hands, especially the infantry. In the end, after the breakthrough, the US Top Brass had declared it a victory; but the veterans knew differently. Model hadn't been beaten. He had simply retreated when he saw there was no more advantage to be gained by fighting on, leaving the shattered forest to the dead and the handful of exhausted American survivors. Now the time had come to make Field-Marshal Model pay the 'butcher's bill' for a change — and no one knew this better than General J. Lawton Collins, commanding the US VII Corps which would spearhead the break-out from Remagen.

It was Collins who had persuaded his Army Commander Hodges, to move into the Hürtgen Forest in the first place. The son of Jeremiah Collins, an Irishman who had enlisted in the Union Army at the age of sixteen, he had fighting in his blood. To his chagrin, he had missed combat in the First World War. Instead he had served two years in the very same area from which he was now going to attack, as an officer in the US Army of Occupation based at Coblenz — 'our own home town', as he was wont to call it to his wife Gladys who he had married there at the town hall. A nervous and explosive man with hard blue eyes, who looked much younger than his forty-eight years, he was a ruthless driver of others; he would never hesitate to sack anyone who he felt had failed him. It was only four years ago that he had seen action for the first time, as commander of the 25th 'Lightning' Infantry Division, helping to drive the Japanese from the Pacific island of Guadalcanal. He had distinguished himself there for his bravery under fire and earned himself the nickname that would stick with him for the rest of his combat career: 'Lightning Joe'.

As commander of Hodges' VII Corps Collins had swept through northern France in a campaign lasting only twenty days, which culminated in the capture of Cherbourg. At the time Bradley had stated: 'Nobody's going anywhere until Joe gets Cherbourg.' Thereafter he had driven into Belgium, capturing Mons, Namur and Liège as well as the first German city of any size — Aachen. The Ardennes and the Hürtgen had followed, but 'Lightning Joe' had then redeemed his reputation by playing a major role in the capture of Germany's fourth greatest city, Cologne.

Now, with his divisions poised ready for the attack, Collins briefed his commanders at his command post on the Rhine at Koenigswinter, where once as a young man in love he had journeyed on the gaily painted paddle seamers, drinking those Rhenish white wines he liked so much. Collins, who had the ear of Hodges and was admired by Bradley, knew that there was something in the wind. Like Bradley, he was not going to sit back and allow this new operation to develop into a sideshow, a kind of flank guard for Monty's drive to the north. As he emphasized to his assembled commanders, the coming operation was destined 'to crush Germany'. There was to be no hesitation, no concern about keeping casualties down.

In particular Collins addressed his remarks to General Rose, the tall, immaculate martinet whose 3rd Armored would kick off the attack, together with a regiment of the 104th Infantry. The former cavalryman, who had enlisted as a private at sixteen and risen to become a general, had a reputation for independence. That month, for instance, Rose had written a letter, which had reached Eisenhower himself, criticizing American equipment and maintaining that German tanks and guns were far superior to their own. So Collins stressed that Rose should advance with all possible speed, emulating Patton's famed 4th Armored Division, which had recently fought and driven all the way from the German—Luxembourg border to the Rhine in less than fifty hours — a tremendous feat.

General Rose's comments are not recorded. But from now onwards Maurice Rose, the son of a New York rabbi, would be in the forefront of his Division, as if his pride had been stung. Within five days Rose would be dead, killed in action.

Now, as Sunday dawned fine and dry over the front, the guns began to rumble. The infantry gripped their rifles tighter in hands that were suddenly damp with sweat. Behind them, the drivers of the Sherman tanks gunned their engines, filling the air with blue smoke. Officers called out their orders. NCOs shrilled their whistles. Over the German lines beyond the Sieg River red flares started to shoot into the still air. The time for attack had come.

Hurriedly the 'Timberwolves', the GIs of the 104th Infantry Division, clambered up onto the decks of the 3rd Armored's tanks. They would ride into battle with the 'Spearhead Division', as the 3rd was known. Whenever a strongpoint was encountered, it would be their job to drop off and go into action. On their flanks the doughboys of the 78th and 1st Infantry Divisions tensed for the counter-attacks that Intelligence predicted would come their way once the drive had started.

The tanks began to roll. In front of them were miles of winding, hilly roads that led to their first objective — Altenkirchen, where a few days ago Speer had pleaded with Model to stop the senseless destruction of the Ruhr. But it was too late for that now. The Ruhr had already become a battlefield.

The American tactics were simple but lethal. At the point would be the lead tank, rumbling forward, its crew tense and nervous, ready for the first bright flash that would indicate a German anti-tank gun firing or the blinding bright red, followed by a flurry of fiery sparks, that meant they had run into some suicidal youth with a *Panzerfaust*. Once hit, the lead tank would radio the details to the second Sherman crawling behind at some 500 yards' distance. It would roll to a stop and, while its machine-gunner blazed away to the front, the infantrymen of the 104th would dismount and go into action.

By mid-morning the 3rd Armored Division had covered two miles. Behind it were left the smouldering wrecks of a dozen or more Shermans and the fragile-looking bundles of rags which had once been men. But 'Big Six', as General Rose was codenamed, brooked no slackness, no hesitation, no pause. That morning he was up front as usual, urging, encouraging, cajoling, threatening, jeeping from outfit to outfit, accompanied only by his driver Glen Shaunce and his aide Major Robert Bellinger. At one stage Collins discovered Rose with his command post located in an exposed house at the very edge of a small town, under enemy fire. 'Maurice,' he snorted in exasperation, 'do you *always* have to have your CP in the last house in town?' Whereupon the Divisional Commander drew himself up and replied: 'General, there is only one way I know to lead this Division and that's at the head of it.'

But Collins was still not satisfied with the First Army's progress. That day he sped from one CP to another, urging his divisional commanders to ever greater efforts. The US Army's premier division, 'the Big Red One', had beaten off four counter-attacks reinforced by tanks; but Collins rounded on its commander, calling for more haste. Then it was Rose's turn. Collins was determined to show the world that his boss, Hodges — regarded among his contemporaries as a slow, plodding infantryman — could outclass even the dashing Patton. Back at Army HQ, Hodges' Chief-of-Staff had just announced to the press that 'The General [Hodges] is today showing the public that when it comes to using armor he is second to none.' But, as Collins now reminded Rose, Patton's 4th Armored Division had reportedly advanced at the rate of twenty or thirty miles a day; the 3rd's rate of progress fell far short of that.

Rose remarked soberly that whenever the 3rd Armored wanted to make a dash they found all available German armour flung in to stop the Division. But the goad worked. Rose resolved that on the morrow he would urge his commanders on to even greater feats. It was like a deadly game. Win or lose, the result would mean death for many of the players — including some of the Top Brass.

While their young men died on the other side of the Rhine, the Top Brass went to church. After all, it was Palm Sunday. In a captured German church beside the great river, Montgomery and the Chief of the General Staff, Sir Alan Brooke, attended a church parade. With them was no less a figure than the Prime Minister, who, against the objections of both Brooke and Montgomery, had insisted on coming to see the battle for the Rhine. As Jock Colville, Churchill's private secretary, recorded in his diary, 'I think it is the first time I have known the PM go to church.'

The army padre, a member of the Church of Scotland, preached a good sermon and Sir Alan Brooke liked the hymns because they were Presbyterian. After the service, wearing the uniform of a colonel of his old regiment, the 4th Hussars, Churchill presented Good Conduct Certificates to some of the soldiers present, 'bulled up' in spite of the battle raging less than a mile away; then proceeded, as Colville recorded, to 'more or less preach a sermon' himself to the troops, on his favourite theme 'of an Influence, supreme and watchful, which guides our affairs and of the Almighty's Great Design into which all our human actions fit if we do our duty'.

In high good humour, waving his cigar at the cheering troops and giving them his V for victory sign, Churchill then set off with Brooke to the Rhenish town of Rheinsberg. There, at General Anderson's HQ, Simpson, Bradley and Eisenhower were waiting for them.

Anderson, one of Simpson's Corps Commanders, quickly briefed his august guests on the situation on the other side of the Rhine, before Brooke sat down to have a talk with Eisenhower. They discussed the question of the coming German surrender and Eisenhower's plans for the future. The latter asked whether Brooke agreed with his intention to push south for Frankfurt and Kassel. Brooke said he did. Thereupon, according to Eisenhower,* Brooke said warmly: 'Thank God, Ike, you stuck by your plan [the attack on a broad front to the Rhine]. You were completely right and I am sorry if my fear of dispersed effort added to your burdens. The German is now licked. It is merely a question of when he chooses to quit. Thank God you stuck by your guns!'

Brooke, however, denied this. He later wrote: 'I am quite certain that I never said to him, "You were completely right", as I am still convinced that he was completely *wrong*.'

*In his book *Crusade in Europe*, published in 1948.

But it was later. On this sunny Sunday, with the war almost over, they had a light *al fresco* lunch on the lawn of a house commandeered from a German colliery manager. Brooke joked with Bradley, while Churchill chattered with Eisenhower, and Montgomery — to whom Eisenhower was barely speaking by now — did the same with Simpson and Anderson. On the surface it all seemed very warm and friendly. The press photographers had a field day, taking snaps of them for their papers back home. The British and American Top Brass presented, or so it appeared, the very picture of Allied solidarity in this moment of victory on the Rhine.

Then Eisenhower excused himself; he had to confer with Bradley. The Supreme Commander had not seen Montgomery since before Christmas (nor would he see him again until the war was over). But at no time during this brief meeting on the Rhine did he mention to Montgomery — or the two other most important personages in the British politico-military hierarchy, Brooke and Churchill — that he was considering a radical alteration to Allied strategy for the remaining course of the war in Europe. As yet Eisenhower was not ready to explode his bombshell. He knew, however, that when he did he would need the backing of his chief, General George Marshall, in Washington. The President was dying; although he was Commander-in-Chief of the US Army, the real power over military affairs now lay in Marshall's hands. But Marshall would back him up to the hilt; only two days earlier he had sent Eisenhower a cable complaining of 'the overdose of Montgomery which is now coming into the country' in the form of newspaper coverage of Monty's forthcoming attack across the Rhine. Like Bradley, Marshall was exceedingly conscious of the prestige of the US Army and wanted it to have a major share of the imminent victory.

To keep his chief happy, Eisenhower sent him a deliberately low-key message:

The dash and daring of First and Third Army sectors have gotten us two bridgeheads very cheaply which can be consolidated and expanded rapidly to support a major thrust.

Even Marshall, it seems, was being kept in the dark over Eisenhower's astonishing new strategy.

At that meeting in Rheinsberg, Churchill had shown Eisenhower an abusive letter from Molotov, the Soviet Foreign Minister, accusing the British and Americans of negotiating with the Germans behind the backs of the Soviet Union. From Eisenhower's angry reaction,

Churchill gained the clear impression that not only did the Supreme
Commander see the Russians as the new threat, now the Germans
were virtually finished, but also shared the British Prime Minister's
eagerness to seize Berlin before the Russians could get there.
Meanwhile, Eisenhower — content, no doubt, to leave Churchill
thinking what best pleased him — left Rheinsberg for his discussions
with Bradley.

Of those discussions neither Eisenhower nor Bradley left any
written record. We shall never know, therefore, whether it was
at this meeting that Eisenhower put the final touches to his radical
new policy — a policy that contradicted the one agreed upon by
London and Washington. But it is curious, as Montgomery later
remarked, that Eisenhower and Bradley waited till Churchill and
Brooke were back in England before springing their surprise: 'All
very dirty work, I fear.'

That Sunday, however, the British were still happy and confident.
Churchill did not yet know that his concept of victory in Europe,
with its effect on his post-war plans for the Continent, was no
longer valid. Soon his own strategy for dealing with the Russians
would be in ruins, thanks to Eisenhower. Now Churchill was intent
on enjoying himself. As soon as Eisenhower had gone, he turned to
Montgomery and chortled: 'Now *I'm* in command. Let's go over.'
He wanted to cross the Rhine.

To his great surprise, Montgomery snapped back: 'Why not?'

Together with Simpson and Brooke, they found their way to a
nearby railway bridge, its iron girders twisted and wrecked. With
snipers' bullets and shells still falling, Churchill scrambled across the
shattered bridge; oblivious to the danger, he was enjoying himself
hugely. Indeed, Simpson virtually had to order him back.

Watching the Prime Minister's antics, Brooke was reminded of
something that Churchill had once said to him: 'The way to die is
to pass out fighting when your blood is up and you feel nothing.' As
Brooke later wrote to his wife, 'I rather feel he [Churchill] considers
that a sudden and soldierly death at the front would be a suitable
ending to his famous life and would free him from the never-ending
worries which loom ahead.'

About the same time that Eisenhower departed for his mysterious
conference with Bradley, some fifty-odd miles away on the other
side of the Rhine, Model realized that he had lost contact with
his Fifteenth Army, attempting to stop the American breakout

from the Remagen bridgehead. All morning the reports had been flooding into his headquarters: the *Amis*, as the Germans called the Americans, were breaking through everywhere. Intelligence had clearly underestimated the enemy's strength. Already the American armoured divisions were advancing on Altenkirchen, Weilburg, and Limburg and a dozen other smaller places.

By midday Model's communications were breaking down. He could no longer contact the HQ of General von Zangen, who commanded the Fifteenth. Hastily he despatched his own staff officers to the crumbling front to report on what was happening. Those who made it back brought bad news: there was enemy armour everywhere and the sky was full of US *jabos*. Frantically Model tried to re-establish contact with his front on the Sieg by means of the artillery commander's own radio network. There were also brave, patriotic civilians who, at the risk of being shot as spies by the *Amis*, reported on the enemy's progress over the civilian telephone network, and telephonists at the local exchange who did the same.*

Eventually Model learned that General von Zangen had disappeared. Some of his corps commanders, too, were on the verge of fleeing. One such was General Hoehne, who with about thirty staff officers was on the point of abandoning his shattered 276th Infantry Division and leaving what was left of the 6th SS Mountain Division to fend for themselves. 'Corps HQ,' Model said later, in something of an understatement, 'was no longer in a position to exercise effective command.'

It was into this chaos that Speer found himself driving as he ventured into the Ruhr once more in another attempt to stop the senseless destruction of German industry ordered by the Führer. In some places the troops had already fled. A curious, expectant mood hung over the silent streets and squares. At one intersection, however, the *Reichsminister* came across one solitary 'stubble-hopper', armed with two *panzerfausts*. He looked at Speer in surprise as the latter braked and asked what he was waiting for.

'For the Americans,' he replied.

'And what will you do when the Americans come?' Speer asked.

The man hesitated only momentarily, before growling, 'Get the hell out of here!'

---

*After the campaign was over, the Americans boasted that they used the local telephone network to talk to the burgomaster of the next town in their line of advance into surrendering. What they overlooked was that the Germans were using the same system to report on *their* progress.

It was a reply that pleased Speer. He hoped that everyone would be as sensible; now that the war was hopelessly lost, there was no longer any point in attempting to fight. It would only increase the misery of the average German's lot after the war.

That afternoon, however, Speer realized that the local *Gauleiters* still believed in the *Endsieg*— the final victory. He discovered that they were preparing to flood the local coal mines and prevent their restoration for years to come by destroying the lift machinery. Barges loaded with cement were to be sunk in the area's canal network, to block Europe's greatest inland port, Duisburg. Any surviving factory would be blown up. Hitler's *Gauleiters* were finally going to finish off the destruction that the RAF had inflicted on the Ruhr over these last two terrible years.

Speer was determined to put a spoke in the *Gauleiters'* plans — and he knew he would have the support of the Ruhr's industrial barons. Back in the early 1930s the Krupp family, the Thyssens and the like, had helped Hitler in his rise to power, providing him with the armaments with which to conquer Europe. But survival was their watchword; just as they had survived the impositions of the Weimar Republic, so they intended to survive now. When Speer alerted Dr Rohland, their representative, he immediately went into action. Summoning twenty reliable men from the coal industry to the former Thyssen castle at Landsberg, he told them to gather up all the available blasting caps, dynamite and fuses and throw them into the sumps of the local mines, in order to prevent the *Gauleiters* getting their hands on them. If they met any resistance, Dr Rohland told the men, they would have fifty machine guns — supplied by Speer — with which to counter it. They were to defend their place of work against all attempts by the *Gauleiters* and their minions to wreck the key installations.

The police and party officials had already given up their weapons to the Army. They would be powerless to enforce the *Gauleiters'* demands. As Speer well knew, his action was tantamount to open revolt.

But Speer had reckoned without Field-Marshal Model.

In 1919, shortly after the First World War, Germany had been racked by violent division and dissent, with uprisings on all sides, both left-wing and right-wing. The Ruhr, in particular, had been the scene of outright rebellion against the policies of central government in Berlin, with a force composed of workers and ex-soldiers attempting a local communist revolution.

And it was here in the Ruhr that the young Captain Model, newly returned from the trenches, had been forced to fight against his fellow Germans. Marching into the great industrial centre, Model's battalion had confronted the rebels, who refused to back down. Severe fighting ensued, and 1920 the battalion was forced to retreat all the way to Cologne, which at that time belonged to the British Army's Zone of Occupation. Model and his men thus had to surrender their weapons to their erstwhile enemy, the men against whom they had so recently been fighting in the trenches.

It had been a bitter time for Model. Interned by the British in Cologne, while his future adversary Collins was wooing his bride-to-be in nearby Koblenz, Model (who was also to find his future wife, Herta, in the Ruhr that year) had plenty of time to reflect on the results of rebellion. In the fight against their own people, Model's battalion had lost two officers and twelve men, with about one hundred wounded. From that day forward, Model had been a die-hard opponent of revolt in any shape or form.

It is not surprising, therefore, that Model refused to support Speer's plans. When Speer called on him that Sunday in March, 1945, Model agreed merely 'to keep the fighting as far from the industrial area as possible and thus reduce the destruction of any factories', though he also promised to keep in touch with the Ruhr industrialists over the next few weeks. There was no discussion about bringing the war to an end.

Perhaps Model saw the civilian *Reichsminister*, who had once been a promising young architect, as a traitor to his former patron the Führer and as a rat who was preparing to abandon the sinking ship. Or perhaps he saw Speer for what he really was: a born survivor, who would be alive long after Model was dead, surviving even twenty years of imprisonment in Spandau as a convicted war criminal. At all events, Model did not reveal his personal thoughts to Speer. He was not a man to share his feelings with anyone — even his own son, now serving as an officer-cadet in the elite *Grossdeutschland* Division, fighting against the British in northern Germany.

Model's attitude puzzled Kesselring, his superior, who visited him several times at this stage of the war, before the Ruhr pocket was finally cut off. For Kesselring, who had successfully fought a holding action against the Allies in Italy for the last two years, the Ruhr presented tremendous possibilities for defence and surprise. But Model's proverbial energy had vanished. Model 'agreed with my views but took no action', Kesselring wrote after the war; 'to this day even, the operation of Army Group B remain incomprehensible to me.'

A closer, more sensitive observer was the Chief-of-Staff of Model's Fifth Panzer Army, Major-General von Mellenthin. Like Model, von Mellenthin was an 'old hare', a veteran of the front line, with personal experience of the difficult day-to-day decisions facing a commander in the heat of battle. He felt that Model was 'wrestling with himself to find a solution to some inner conflict':

Like all senior commanders he was faced with an insoluble dilemma: as a highly qualified officer he saw the hopelessness of further resistance, but on the other hand he was bound in duty and honour to his superiors and subordinates.

In von Mellenthin's presence Model had several times raised the question of surrender, only to reject it on military grounds.

'After all,' von Mellenthin wrote after the war, 'the Field-Marshal knew no more about the general situation then the simplest company commander in his army group.' Model's ignorance sprang from 'Führer Command No 1', dated 13 January, 1940, which laid down that 'no officer or authority must know more than is absolutely necessary for the execution of his particular task'. Model and von Mellenthin reasoned that the Führer might still have something up his sleeve, some plan of action unknown to them which would make a continued struggle worthwhile. He might have a new war-winning weapon; or perhaps he was secretly negotiating with the Western Allies, persuading them to redirect their efforts and fight at Germany's side against the Russians. The latter suggestion had been disseminated by the Minister of Propaganda under the direction of Dr Josef Goebbels, and a surprisingly large number of Germans of all ranks and classes believed it to be true.

There was also talk of a German national resistance movement — *Der Werwolf* — on the lines of the large-scale Russian guerrilla *apparat* or the French *maquis* which had been the bane of Model's life in those two countries back in 1943–44. A group called the *Alpenfestung* (known in Western Allied circles as the 'National Redoubt') was being established to the south in the German-Austrian Alps. There, according to the rumours, elite Germans troops, well equipped and provisioned behind their fortifications, would hold out either until the Western Allies offered better terms to Germany or until the unholy alliance between Russia and the Anglo-Americans broke down, as Goebbels confidently predicted it would.

Model already knew something of this secret resistance movement. Only last year it was two of his own intelligence officers who had selected the first training camp for the young volunteers, both male and female, at the remote fifteenth-century castle at Hülchrath not far from the Rhine. When the area was overrun, the volunteers were moved further north to the edge of his Army Group B in the Hessian hills.

Perhaps all was not as black as people such as Speer painted it, he reasoned. Hadn't the Führer himself stated this March: 'You must have faith! I still have ways and means of bringing this war to a victorious conclusion.' And even if Hitler were merely whistling in the dark to keep his own spirits up, even if all was really lost, then there was still one other alternative to surrender.

Back in 1943, when Model first heard the shocking news of Field-Marshal von Paulus's surrender, together with his Sixth Army, in Stalingrad, he had declared, 'A German Field-Marshal does *not* surrender!' He was wrong, of course; in a mere six weeks' time when Germany finally capitulated, German field-marshals would surrender by the dozen, including his present chief 'Smiling Albert' Kesselring and his predecessor von Rundstedt who had once called Model contemptuously '*der Bubi-Marschall*' (the Boy Marshal). But that evening, as Model swallowed more of the pills that kept him going with such restless energy, the thought must have entered his mind that he might be forced to choose that other alternative.

In Roman times the defeated general had fallen on his sword. In the German Army, if an officer disgraced himself, traditionally he was left alone with his pistol — and one bullet.

Aachen, the old Imperial German city on the Dutch-German border, had been captured in October, 1944, after a six-week siege by Collins and his VII Corps. In the months that followed the city had regained some of its normal function, though it had been terribly damaged in the bombing and the street-fighting of the siege. Water, gas and electricity had been restored. A newspaper, the first non-Nazi newspaper in Germany since 1933, had been established. The military government had set up shop and weeded Nazis out of all official posts. There was even an elementary postal service. While the rest of the Reich was still under fire or close to the frontline, Aachen seemed a modest haven of peace.

The victorious Americans decided that such an important city needed a German *Oberbürgermeister* or senior mayor. They were fighting this war for democracy, weren't they? Well, then, Aachen needed a non-Nazi mayor, courtesy of the 'Big Red One'. The man they picked (US democracy couldn't be stretched to popular elections as yet) was a balding forty-two-year-old Catholic lawyer, Franz Oppenhoff, who had a record of opposing the Nazis during their eleven years of control in Aachen.

Oppenhoff knew he was taking a risk in accepting the job. Even at his swearing-in ceremony he told the US cameramen not to take his picture, in case their photographs fell into Nazi hands; for the sake of himself and his family he asked the town commandant 'to ensure that no names are mentioned and no photographs taken during the ceremony'. For five months now he had lived with his fear, often telling his wife: 'They've already cast the bullet with my name on it . . . I know their Gestapo methods [he had once been arrested by that organization] — they'll get me in the end. Somewhere or other there is already one of their paratroopers assigned to the job of murdering me.'

He was wrong. There were six of them, led by an SS officer named Wenzel. Three of the others also belonged to the SS: Leitgeb, an Austrian and long-time Nazi, and two border policemen by the names of Hennemann and Heidorn. The other two were Erich Morgenschweiss, a sixteen-year-old from the Hitler Youth, and Ilse Hirsch, a pop-eyed, sulky, pasty-faced member of the Hitler Maidens who would prove more determined than the rest.

Ever since Oppenhoff's appointment by the *Amis*, this little group had been undergoing special training for their murderous task, in an operation code-named 'Carnival'. In the second week of March, 1945, the operation began. A captured Flying Fortress, flown by a Luftwaffe pilot, managed to dodge Allied radar and night-fighters to parachute the team into Holland. They landed in wooded country — but were met by a welcoming party from the Dutch border guard. During the ensuing firefight, the team became split up and disheartened. What was the point of going on, some of them asked; after all, the Allies were already across the Rhine. But Ilse Hirsch rallied them. Operation Carnival would go ahead.

Franz Oppenhoff lived at 251 Eupenerstrasse, a detached house on the outskirts of Aachen backing onto open fields and woods. On Palm Sunday, after attending morning service in church with his wife and two daughters, he was relaxing at home, free for a few hours from the stress that had caused him to age so noticeably in the past few months.

After lunch the Chief Burgomaster enjoyed a cup of 'real' bean coffee — acquired by Frau Oppenhoff through the black market — into which he stirred three tablespoons of sugar; he had an extremely sweet tooth. Then he and his wife spent the warm spring afternoon working in the garden, something they would never have dared to do before the war for fear of condemnation from the strict Catholic community in which they lived. At six that evening they packed their children off to bed, with a slice of bread and black treacle as their supper. Then, with the children safely asleep, the Burgomaster put on his official US armband, which indicated to roving military patrols that he was allowed to be out after curfew, and took his wife to their neighbours, the Fausts, for a drink.

Some two hours later the pleasant Palm Sunday get-together was disturbed by the arrival of the Oppenhoffs' maid, twenty-one-year-old Elisabeth Gillenssen. Looking frightened, she said a strange American had just knocked on the door of Number 251 and had demanded a pass. Puzzled that an *Ami* should want a pass from him, but still not suspicious, Oppenhoff accompanied the maid back to his house, where she fled inside and left him to face the man standing in the shadows.

It was Wenzel, the mysterious SS officer who commanded the hit squad. 'We're not *Amis*,' he told Oppenhoff. 'We're German airmen.' For the first time Oppenhoff saw the others crouching in the background; but still he felt no fear as the SS officer continued: 'We were shot down near Brussels three days ago. Now we're trying to make our way back to the German lines. What about getting us passes, *Herr Bürgermeister?*'

Oppenhoff shook his head. 'I can't do that,' he said. 'You should report to the Americans and give yourselves up. The war's nearly over anyway. It's only a matter of days.'

Suddenly Leitgeb, the Austrian, snapped to attention and barked: 'Heil Hitler!'

Oppenhoff's expression soon changed. He realized that none of these 'German airmen' wore uniform and that one of them had a pistol poking out of his pocket. Hurriedly he said: 'But let me get you something to eat.' He backed into the house and calmed the maid, telling her to cut up some bread for the fugitives.

When he had gone, Leitgeb hissed to Wenzel, 'When he comes again . . .'

In the light of the moon Wenzel's face looked pale. 'Yes — now,' he croaked, drawing his pistol with the big silencer. His hand trembled and Leitgeb saw he was afraid.

Oppenhoff started walking back down the corridor towards them. Wenzel hesitated.

'Do it!' Leitgeb urged.

Wenzel didn't reply.

'You cowardly sow!' the Austrian exploded. He grabbed the pistol from Wenzel's nerveless fingers.

'What —' Oppenhoff opened his mouth to protest. But it was too late. Leitgeb thrust the pistol to the Burgomaster's head and fired. Oppenhoff was dead before he hit the steps.

From the Faust house there came sounds of doors being opened. 'There's somebody coming,' Wenzel exclaimed. 'Let's go!'

'Wait a minute, you pig,' Leitgeb snapped. 'We've got to have proof.' He bent down and tugged off the dead man's official armband.

Just then there was a sudden volley of shots. A patrol of the US Signal Corps had discovered a break in their wire where the murderers had cut it beforehand, and now they spotted the murderers themselves. But their shots were wild; the hit squad got away. Operation Carnival was over.

Oppenhoff, the first Allied-appointed burgomaster, had been assassinated: the news was soon being flashed around the world. The *New York Times*, whose headline was 'Non-Nazi Mayor of Aachen Killed by 3 German Chutists in Uniform', commented: 'Hitler often has threatened retaliation against Germans who cooperated.'

And as the 'chutists' fled northwards through minefields and Allied patrols, the German papers too announced the news. According to Goebbels' Press Agency, Oppenhoff had been executed at the orders of the 'German People's Court' for 'collaboration with the enemy'. Hitler's own paper, *Der Völkische Beobachter*, called Oppenhoff 'a dishonourable, treacherous creature [who] deserved the fate he brought upon himself'. And it went: 'In future, anyone who infringes the highest law of the land, the law of national honour and loyalty, will inevitably meet the same fate.'

But the most ominous result of Oppenhoff's murder was not publicized in the newspapers of March, 1945; indeed, it did not become widely known until long after the war. For the burgomaster's death, together with Goebbels' 'Radio Werewolf' which went on the air six days later, was used by the American Top Brass to support Eisenhower's new strategy.

The Americans had been expecting for some time now to encounter a last-ditch upsurge of German resistance. Here, it seemed, was evidence that it had begun. They argued that this area of Germany was now so obviously dangerous that the Allies' original strategy *must* be changed.

By coincidence, that same Palm Sunday saw the completion of a policy study by the Twelfth US Army Group; its subject was 'Re-orientation of Strategy'. In an appendix to the study documents, the Army Group Commander, General Omar Bradley himself, warned of 'guerrilla warfare' and referred to the Werewolves who would — he confidently predicted — lead the German people in a last defiant response to the Allied advance. This fact alone, he claimed, rendered the Allies' original objectives 'obsolete'. And Bradley was not alone in his fears. In the map room of the Supreme Commander's HQ at Rheims there hung an Intelligence chart bearing the legend 'Reported National Redoubt'; it was covered with a rash of notations detailing enemy installations in the German Alps.

But the National Redoubt did not exist. It was a propaganda device, a product of Josef Goebbels' fertile brain. He saw the advantages of playing on the Americans' fears, and his 'Radio Werewolf' was designed to do just that. His broadcasts to the 5,000-odd German boys and girls who made up the Werewolves encouraged the Americans in their belief that an organized resistance movement was about to sally forth from its National Redoubt and attack the Allied supply lines.

It was absurd, of course, as General Siegfried Westphal, Kesselring's Chief-of-Staff, told his interrogators at the end of the war: 'As if,' he sneered, 'what the Wehrmacht had failed to do could be accomplished by . . . mere rabble of boy scouts!'

And yet, according to General Bradley, this sequence of events was a decisive factor in the Supreme Commander's radical change of strategy.

THREE

'Go!'

'*I've got bags—bags on my mind*!' Bradley declared happily, as he entered his office this dry sunny Wednesday morning, beaming at his staff. Enthusiasm of this kind was foreign to the General, who looked more like a schoolmaster than a soldier. He was normally reserved and unemotional. But the news from the front this morning gave him good reason to be excited.

The German Rhine front had broken down completely. Patton's Third Army had just linked up with Hodges' First Army at Giessen, and on Collins' front enemy resistance was weak and disorganised. The German Fifteenth Army defending the area had apparently vanished. The Ruhr seemed to be wide open. No wonder the General was so pleased with himself.

'*The General is now after bags!*' his staff chuckled to one another as they hurried about their business, while the telephones rang, typewriters clattered and the clerks, male and female, carried out their little romances. '*Bags of surrounded prisoners . . . Heaps of captured Krauts . . . The General wants the SACK . . .!*'

What Bradley and his excited staff officers meant was the envelopment of the Ruhr in the classic *Kesselschlacht* manoeuvre, so beloved by the German General Staff: a 'pocket battle' effected by surrounding the enemy with a pincer movement. In the last few days prisoners had come streaming into American lines in large numbers, for the Germany Army was in the process of disintegration. Even in Model's best divisions there was little will left to fight. But Bradley wanted more. According to his Intelligence sources, Model had 150,000 troops under his command (in fact, he had twice that number). What an impact it would have in the papers back home, Bradley thought, if he could 'bag' those Germans in a pincer movement executed by his First and Ninth Armies! It certainly would outscoop Monty, who was still grabbing the headlines with his Rhine crossing and subsequent break-out. The fact that the capture of large numbers of German prisoners no longer had any significance did not enter Bradley's head that morning; nor did he stop to consider that the encirclement of the Ruhr might well entail a long siege and cause the war to be prolonged. His mind was full of 'bags' and he was going to have them, however unimportant. A quarter of a century later, the same sort of purposeless strategy would dominate the mentality of America's generals in Vietnam, with their persistent demands for even higher 'body counts'.

Bradley gave out his orders. Collins' VII Corps would head for the German town of Paderborn, while III and V Corps wheeled north-east to protect 'Lightning Joe's' drive. At the same time Simpson would send his 2nd Armored Division towards Paderborn too, where the two Armies would link up and create the pocket. Apparently it never occurred to Bradley that Simpson's Ninth Army was still under Monty's command. Simpson was an American general, commanding an American army. Therefore, Bradley as Army Group Commander had a right — and a duty — to give Simpson his orders; to hell with Allied solidarity!

Thus was born the concept of the Ruhr Pocket, which could be said to have prolonged the war by three unnecessary weeks. The Commanding General wanted his 'bags', and, in the general confusion of that last week of March 1945, nobody in the American camp seemed to notice the total irrelevance of the strategy. A few days later the American Secretary of War, Henry Stimson, would warn the US Army chief in Washington, General Marshall, that this destruction of the Ruhr would harm the economic future of Europe. But Marshall took no action. He told Stimson he had no views on the matter and anyway he didn't want to bother Eisenhower at this stage of the war. 'I think,' he said, 'the fat is probably in the fire and whatever the political conclusions it is too late, too impracticable, to take any action.'

Obviously 'bags' for American generals were more important than bread for European bellies.

In the Ruhr it was a crazy day. Later they would call it 'the rat race', the time when the American armour broke loose. The 3rd, 7th and 9th Armored Divisions surged forward on parallel roads, bypassing towns whenever they could, leaving the infantry to mop up behind them; to the left and right of the roads they took there were still vast tracks of the countryside left in German hands.

Everywhere the armour's progress was cheered on — and hampered too — by mobs of civilian and military ex-prisoners making their way home, looting, raping and killing while doing so. There were hundreds of thousands of them: men and women who had been snatched off their farms and cottages in the heart of Russia, Greece, France, Holland and half a dozen other European countries to work in the Ruhr's once teeming war factories and mines. Others were soldiers, men who had been behind German barbed wire since Dunkirk, newly freed by the Allies but fearful that they might still be killed by their own planes. For the skies were full of American fighter-bombers, accompanying and protecting the advancing armour.

At Limburg 1,000 British and US prisoners-of-war, who had already suffered eight dead, killed by their own planes, took off their shirts and formed up into a huge SOS, as the Thunderbolts came barrelling down out of a perfect sky, their guns already blazing. One man cracked and ran for cover. But the others stood fast. At the very last moment the pilots recognized the signal. They swerved away, dipping their wings in salute. And there the prisoners would stand for a further six hours, until nightfall when they felt safe once more.

Of course, it wasn't only the DPs — displaced persons — and the newly liberated prisoners who looted, killed and raped. During the 'rat race' discipline was breaking down and the officers were finding it difficult to control their men. Whenever they stopped the GIs set off on 'walkabouts', breaking down the doors of likely-looking houses with their rifle butts so that they could search for loot, while the terrified civilians huddled outside, weeping and wailing. Soon looting became so widespread that not even the military police could be relied upon to remain honest; indeed, the cynical frontline troops took to calling the MPs 'the lootwaffe'.

In one picturesque village in the Americans' line of advance, Private Lester Atwell watched his comrades breaking into the thatched and timbered cottages. Up front as a medic, he wanted no part of the looting. He went into the kitchen of an old German woman's house and sat down. Moments later, two infantrymen battered down the door — which was open anyway — with their rifle buuts.

'Has this place been looted yet?' they yelled at Atwell.

The old woman began to cry, throwing her apron up over her wrinkled face.

'Hey, get her the hell outa here!' one of the men yelled. 'What'ya bitching about anyway? Go on, ya old bitch, get out!'

As the old woman fled in panic Atwell went out into the yard, suddenly overwhelmed with misery. 'God, I'm tired of this,' he thought, 'tired of the war, of human beings — of everything.'

As their advance gathered momentum the men were seized with a sort of hysteria. In the wild confusion of the battlefield it became impossible to separate fact from rumour. One story that spread like wildfire among the frontline units concerned the 6th SS Mountain Division.

The SS mountaineers were part of the German 89th Corps, now disintegrating under pressure from the US First and Third Armies. But they were still maintaining their discipline; they were a vigourous and determined group of young men, mostly in their early twenties, and many of them had spent the war fighting in the barren tundra of Finland and northern Russia. They were used to fending for themselves in the rugged countryside in which the Americans now seemed to have trapped them. Some 2,000 of them had set off on foot, carrying only personal weapons, taking to the woods and hills as they sought to regain their own lines.

During the course of their wanderings some of them came across a US field hospital just behind the lines. They captured the place without difficulty and spent the night there, feasting on US rations and smoking American cigarettes — even enjoying what the GIs called 'Hitler's secret weapon', the standard-issue chocolate bar that the Americans claimed gave them 'the shits'. The SS troopers conducted themselves very properly, however, and at dawn they left in captured trucks carrying as much food and supplies as they could manage.

But the news of their night in the field hospital soon reached the American combat units, and somehow became twisted into a totally unfounded rumour which passed from unit to unit in the strange grapevine of the front. In essence, the rumour was that the young SS fanatics had first murdered the doctors and orderlies, then spent the night raping the female nurses, systematically, one after another.

The rumour reached the ears of General 'Red' Irwin, commander of the American 5th Division, who promptly sent his men out to find the wandering SS troopers and round them up. Naturally his orders did not include the killing of any prisoners; but his men had minds of their own — and they were out for blood. Veterans of the battle for Metz, the fighting on the Siegfried Line and now the race through the Rhineland, they set out on a ruthless hunt for the fugitives.

Some were allowed to surrender, but of the surviving 1,300 SS mountaineers in that rugged forest area it is estimated that 500-700 were slaughtered in cold blood by Irwin's men.

Only hours later a similar fate befell the SS Westphalia Brigade at the hands of the 3rd Armored Division. The Americans captured and then shot 120 prisoners, most of them teenage recruits and some still wearing their own civilian shoes. The majority were killed by a slug at the nape of the neck. Their bodies, the Americans told the locals, were not to be touched; they were to lie where they died in village street or field, exposed as a warning to other SS youths of just how terrible the Americans' revenge could be. So the corpses lay in the open for five days, plundered of their few possessions by passing DPs, until finally the American authorities relented and allowed them to be buried.*

Amid all the looting and wanton savagery, however, there were instances of great sacrifice and nobility of spirit. Some American soldiers continued to risk their lives for their comrades' sake, even now when it was obvious to all that the war was nearly over. Some American medics, indeed, braved German artillery fire to go out and rescue wounded enemy soldiers. And despite the widespread breakdown of discipline, some young American officers did manage to control their men, risking unpopularity by forbidding their soldiers to indulge in looting and unnecessary destruction of German property.

After the war four individual soldiers from the 1st, 7th Armored and 97th Divisions were awarded their country's highest honour — the Congressional Medal — for the valour in combat that they showed over the first few hours and days of the 'rat race'. All but one had died as a result of their brave conduct.

One of them, Staff Sergeant Petersen of the 'Big Red One', was going into the attack with his battalion when it came under heavy German mortar fire. His platoon was given the mission of trying to outflank the enemy who were now pinning down his company. Petersen was hit almost at once; wounded in both legs and bleeding heavily, he fell to the ground. But he refused to give up. He crawled down a shallow depression, with machine bullets cutting the air just above his head, towards one of the

---

*After the war the German authorities attempted to prosecute the unknown GIs who carried out these killings, but without success.

enemy's machine-gun emplacements, and flung a grenade at the German crew.

That silenced the fire from that direction. But a second machine-gun crew had spotted him. They swung the MG 42 round and sent a hail of slugs in his direction. Calmly Petersen tossed a second grenade. The machine gun disappeared in a ball of fire and the four-man crew reeled back, dead and dying.

Petersen started to crawl again. An enemy rifleman spotted him. He fired, hitting Petersen in the arm. But still he continued crawling. As the official citation put it later: 'By almost superhuman effort, weak from loss of blood and suffering great pain, he again raised himself to his knees and fired a grenade from his rifle.' This finished off the third machine-gun crew. At last Petersen could relax — though not for long.

The company aid man had just begun treating his wounds when Petersen saw one of his men stagger and fall, hit by shrapnel as a mortar bomb exploded nearby. He wrenched himself away from the medic, ignoring his warnings, and started to crawl through the mortar barrage towards the seriously wounded soldier. Bombs exploded all around him, sending up black mushrooms of smoke and flying earth. Red-hot shards of jagged metal pierced the air. He had almost reached the prostrate soldier when it happened. A burst of machine-gun fire ripped into his chest. He collapsed and died on the spot.

Not far away, that same afternoon, Lieutenant Walter Hill of the same company bore himself just as bravely, rescuing two of his wounded soldiers under fire before charging a line of enemy machine guns at the head of his platoon. One by one, the enemy picked them off. Hill, too, was wounded; but he — like Petersen — pushed on alone and managed to destroy three machine-gun posts. Returning to his platoon, he led his men on another fearsome charge. The Germans reeled back in panic, and this time their defences collapsed in confusion. But Lieutenant Hill did not survive to see the end of the day. Wounded again, but this time mortally, he died as bravely as he had fought.

Joe Hastings, of the 97th Infantry Division, also died a valiant death — two weeks later, on 12 April, 1945, almost within sight of victory. Like Petersen and Hill, like the fourth recipient of the Congressional Medal of Honor, Corporal Thomas Kelly of the 7th Armored Division (who survived), Hastings had displayed almost superhuman courage during the battle for the Ruhr pocket. All four had been prepared to sacrifice their lives — little knowing that the cause for which they fought would ultimately prove worthless.

*

Far away from the front and the scenes of death and destruction, the Supreme Commander had now returned to his headquarters at Rheims. That morning he had flown back from a conference in Paris, with Kay Summersby, and found two signals waiting for him on his desk marked with the highest security rating: 'For Eisenhower's eyes only'.

The Rheims HQ had been established in the old *College Moderne et Technique*, a technical school for boys, just opposite the shell-pocked main station of the town. Eisenhower's office was on the second floor, overlooking the main street which was usually crowded with military trucks, jeeps and motorcycles and just beside the station's shunting yard. The room was almost spartan; his desk stood on a raised platform, flanked only by flags.* He sat there now, reading the two top-secret documents in blue leather folders, smoking his favourite Luckies cigarettes.

One of the signals was from Marshall. Now that the German front seemed to be collapsing, he had a suggestion to make. In order to prevent a last-ditch stand by the enemy in the area of the Bavarian-Austrian Alps, wouldn't it be wise — Marshall asked — to advance on the line Nuremberg—Linz or Karlsruhe—Munich?

The other signal was from Montgomery, and it made Eisenhower feel 'like a horse with a burr under the saddle'. For Montgomery wasn't asking; he was *demanding*. His message contained nine terse paragraphs setting out his intentions. In his view, the Anglo-Americans lacked the supply and maintenance capacity for two major drives from the Rhine; he wanted there to be only one. 'If we attempt a compromise solution,' Monty warned, 'and split our maintenance resources so neither thrust is full-blooded, we will prolong the war.' Eisenhower knew what he was getting at, of course; Monty wanted to concentrate on a single thrust — at Berlin. And, naturally, Monty wanted to lead that thrust. This was the same old tune he had been playing ever since the previous September, when it first seemed that the German resistance was crumbling.

In characteristic fashion, Monty concluded his signal: 'Time is of such vital importance that a decision is required *at once*.'

Still fuming at Monty's autocratic manner, Eisenhower sat back in his chair, lit another of his Luckies and pondered on the two signals.

*The desk is still the⁻ ⁚⁖⁖ as Eisenhower left it in May, 1945.

Three years before when he had first come to London as an obscure major-general, appalled by the stink of Brussels sprouts which seemed to be everywhere, Eisenhower had been a 'Johnny-come-lately', an unknown American officer who had never even commanded a platoon in action. He was dealing with officers who had shed blood for their country on battlefields all over the world, men who had led armies into battle. Understandably he was deferential to those British officers, so self-assured, so knowledgeable about war, who bore the scars of battle on their bodies. Hadn't Montgomery lain for dead on the battlefield for six hours in the 'Old War' before he was finally picked up? Why, even Churchill had charged with the cavalry in battle and, as an escaped prisoner-of-war, had been on the run with every man's hand against him and a price on his head!

But Eisenhower had been a paper-shuffler for most of his career, an office boy, a staff officer, who in thirty years in the Army had never heard a shot fired in anger. Suddenly he had been thrust into the limelight, given command over these other officers who had seen and done so much. At first he had bent over backwards not to offend them, his deference to them so marked that Patton sneered: 'Ike is the best general the British have.' But gradually, over the months and years thereafter, Eisenhower's confidence had grown. Time and time again he had been forced to take decisions on which many young lives depended. His experience in Africa and in Europe had hardened and matured him, making him more resistant to the carping criticism of the envious, the inferior, the politically and militarily impotent.

And yet, with all his hard-earned experience, the Supreme Commander of a force nearly 5,000,000 strong knew that his character was still flawed by a fatal weakness. Once he had made a decision he seemed incapable of sticking to it. Over and over again he had wavered, backed off, modified, weakened, toned down, allowed himself to be swayed by the opinions of those around him. So what decision was he going to make this day? What response should he make to the two signals?

All morning the staff officers came and went as he pondered his decision. The pile of butts in the ashtray grew ever higher. Outside, the trucks roared off to the front, with MPs shrilling their whistles and yelling at the grinning black drivers when their driving seemed too reckless. It was a day like any other day in a busy headquarters.

Around midday General Bradley arrived for lunch with Eisenhower. Ever since Cannes, Bradley had kept very close to the

Supreme Commander, almost as if he didn't want Ike to be subjected
to any other opinion than his own. Constantly 'buttering him up', as
Montgomery would call it later, Bradley kept reminding Eisenhower
that he was an *American* general, that he owed a loyalty first and
foremost to the United States Army.

Afterwards Bradley maintained that he told Eisenhower that
day that any main thrust to Berlin (led naturally by the hated
Montgomery) would cost the Allied force 100,000 casualties. It
would be much better to wait on the Elbe for the Russians to
link up with their own troops there, while the US Twelfth Army
Group concentrated on driving south-east and reducing the 'Alpine
Redoubt' before the fanatical Nazis and their 'Werewolves' dug
themselves in there. And this was the reason that Eisenhower
later gave to justify his decision. The 'butcher's bill' would be
too high for a prize which really wasn't of such great strategic
importance. Privately he knew, however, the decision was based
on more personal matters. Bradley and his subordinate commanders
— Patton in particular — felt that they were being neglected while
Montgomery was hogging the glory. Why should that be when for
every British soldier in the field there were three American?

Besides, Eisenhower had his own position and personal future
to consider. As he told the writer Cornelius Ryan after the war,
Montgomery 'had become so personal in his efforts to make sure
that the Americans — and me, in particular — got no credit, that in
fact we hardly had anything to do with the war, that I finally stopped
talking to him'. Why should he now go in to bat for Montgomery
against the opposition of all his senior generals?

After that last lunch with Bradley he must have mulled over
the problem, wondering what the verdict of history would be if he
gave Montgomery his head: wouldn't the wrong people be gaining
the credit for the final Allied victory in Europe? Hadn't Bradley told
him that the 'prestige of the US Army' was involved? What would
history's judgement be on him if he made a decision in the British
favour now? He no doubt knew that Patton was going round telling
people that Ike would one day run for president. Even if this met
a sceptical response from his staff, it was a matter of fact that
virtually every successful American general — from Washington
through Jackson and Grant, right up to old 'Black Jack' Pershing
— had been offered the highest political office in the land once the
battle had ended.

By three that afternoon Eisenhower had smoked nearly forty
cigarettes and had approved the draft of the first cable he would

send, detailing his new strategy for the final battle on the other side of the Rhine. It had been a lot of work. But now it was up to his staff to deal with the three cables that must be sent off before the day was out: one to Montgomery; one to Marshall; and one to a man the staff all called jokingly 'UJ', short for 'Uncle Joe': Joseph Stalin. He, for his part, could relax for a while. The decision had at last been made.

It had been a long day for the men of Collins's 3rd Armored Division, a very long and bloody day. It began with an attack on the German university town of Marburg. They had started out full of energy and enthusiasm, as the Divisional History noted: 'There was expectancy in the air, and victory. It was something like the breakthrough in Normandy, the same dust in the air — billowing clouds of it, pungent and stinging, laced with the stink of burning vehicles.' So the excited tankers raced forward, taking casualties and inflicting them, aiming to cover over twenty-four miles before nightfall. Rattling by in their Shermans and half-tracks, the troopers tried not to notice the wrecked tanks, each surrounded by a circle of freshly dug graves.

Naturally General Rose was up front with them as well. As the Divisional History phrased it in the tough confident prose of the time:

Talk about pride of organization! These men, from their general down to the guy who loaded K-rations on a supply truck, were all of the same opinion — they belonged to the first team. This was the big bowl game and there wasn't a shadow of doubt as to who'd take home the goal posts.

Rose, together with his aide and driver, stepped into a fire-fight with some Germans hiding in a roadside cemetery. There was the angry snap-and-crackle of small-arms fire for a while. Then the Germans — twelve of them — surrendered and the Commanding General, in his immaculate uniform and gleaming boots, was observed walking back down the battle-littered road, herding the 'Krauts' in front of him with aid of his big drawn .45.

Other pockets of resistance were left behind. Now the roads were crowded with newly released French prisoners cheering and yelling '*Vive l'Amerique!*' The local villagers, hearing the thunderous roar of armoured columns approaching, opened their windows and hung out white flags, shirts, grandpa's underpants, anything white to indicate they would not fight. They knew that Hitler's 'Thousand Year Reich' was doomed, even if the Nazi *Prominenz* didn't. At one point, one of the columns — Task Force Lovelady, named after its commander — observed a German supply column, obviously unaware that there were any *Amis* in the area, driving straight towards the US rear. But Colonel Lovelady told his men to let the Krauts get on with it — they hadn't time for lost Germans. The advance must continue. 'Big six' (Rose) was yelling for progress. They rolled on, eating up the miles.

They were taking ever more prisoners — too many for the Division to cope with. At one village a group of German soldiers tried repeatedly to surrender, and found themselves just as repeatedly ignored, until finally a trumpeter took pity on them. Others were simply disarmed, looted of anything important or interesting, given a kick in the rear and sent off to find the POW cage by themselves. By the end of the day, a spot check would indicate the Division had taken about 3,000 prisoners in all, the equivalent of a full regiment of infantry.

At noon the leading elements of the Division were entering the outskirts of Marburg. A sizeable town of 25,000 inhabitants, Marburg was the site of no fewer than seven military hospitals, presently tending 6,000 German wounded. Because they had not been subjected to the same intensity of Allied air raids as other parts of the Ruhr, Marburg's citizens were well housed and fed. As a result, perhaps, they seemed to the victorious GIs to be arrogant and supercilious. But not for long. Yelling at them in broken German, the GIs burst into their homes and any suspected Nazis were rudely turfed out to be herded down the cobbled street with blows and kicks. Then the looting started. China, pictures, furniture were tossed out of windows. Beds were sprawled upon and soiled by dirty combat boots. Fine wines and liqueurs were swilled down gleeful American throats.

It was no different at the village of Herborn, also captured by the 3rd Division's roving columns that afternoon. As the Divisional History records:

The people of Herborn were amazed. They had been told that the Americans were meeting defeat on the Rhine and here, many miles from the 'sacred' river, they woke to find the streets crowded with those cocktail-drinking, night-clubbing, jitter-bugging degenerate Yankees whom their beloved Führer had so scornfully dismissed as incapable of waging total war.

But soon the 'degenerate Yankees' were worn out, or drunk. It had been a long hard day. They had covered nearly twenty-five miles this Wednesday, fighting all the way, with not only General Rose but also his staff officers engaged in the confused fighting (on the morrow Rose's G-I Colonel Jack Boulger would be ambushed and captured by the Germans while travelling from one command post to another). They bedded down in their new 'homes' and prayed that they'd be allowed to sleep a long time.

That wasn't to be. For now the signal that Bradley had sent that morning finally reached Colonel Robert Howze, commander of the 3rd Division's Combat Command Reserve. Howze immediately summoned Lieutenant-Colonel Walter 'Rich' Richardson, one of his tank commanders. He had a mission for him, *right from the top*!

Richardson was not impressed. He had been fighting for over a week; he'd lost a lot of sleep and now he guessed from Howze's tone that he was going to lose some more. But despite being disgruntled by the summons, Richardson was interested. The tough Texan, who had made many enemies during the Division's period of training in the States, was an ambitious reserve officer who had spent his weekends studying tactics. Serious, intense, he wanted to become a top tank commander. Perhaps the new mission might help his reputation.

At Howze's CP he met Colonel Sam Hogan, a fellow Texan with whom he had fought in France, the Ardennes and the Rhineland. Hogan was slow-talking and relaxed (he reminded Richardson of a young Will Rogers); he had studied at West Point and was a Regular Army officer, given to flamboyant gestures such as flying the flag of the 'Lone Star' state on his jeep.

The two Texans chatted a while, then Howze got down to business. This Wednesday the usually calm commander was excited: 'We'll move,' he told the two lieutenant-colonels, 'to here!' He pointed to the city of Paderborn on the situation map. 'We'll really go!' He looked meaningfully at Richardson and the other man knew why. The German city was more than a hundred miles away.

'You mean,' Richardson stuttered, 'get to Paderborn — in one day?'

Howze nodded. 'Tomorrow morning you leave for Paderborn. Just go like hell! Get the high ground at the Paderborn airport.' He then turned to Hogan and ordered him to cover the Richardson task force, slightly echeloned to the left. Task Force Welborn, from another of the 3rd's three combat commands, would drive up on the right. The rest of the Division would follow the best it could.

Now Rose entered the CP and joined in. He told his two colonels, 'Get to Paderborn — don't stop!' He explained that the 2nd Armored Division from General Simpson's Ninth Army would also be driving for Paderborn, where, if everything went well, the two Armies, the First and the Ninth, would link up. This would 'bag' the whole of the Ruhr — over 150,000 German soldiers under Model's command would be in the sack! It was the kind of mission the ambitious Richardson liked: one for which armour was specially suited. Now at last they'd be able to show Patton and his boastful 4th Armored Division just how quickly the 'Spearhead Division' could move.

Swiftly the plans were made. Two combat commands, those of Howze and his friend Boudinot, would drive on Paderborn abreast. Each combat command would advance in two columns, separated from each other by three to five miles, with the divisional reconnaissance regiment leading the way and seeking out any danger points. General Hickey's third combat command would follow in the centre, prepared to assist either flank if necessary. Just behind the leading elements, General Rose would follow in his jeep with a small escort, plus Colonel Fred Brown, the artillery commander, and Colonel Wesley Sweat, the Division's G-3. With them they would have an armoured car packed with radios so that the General could communicate with his widely extended force.

It was going to be a bold and dangerous operation, reminiscent of the tremendous armoured drives the Germans had made in France and Russia in 1940 and 1941. But none of the officers present that night in the tightly packed CP felt any fear as they made their hurried preparations to move out on the morrow: excitement and tension, yes, but not fear. For this was going to be the greatest armoured drive ever carried out by an American formation in the whole of the Second World War. *One hundred miles or more in a single day*!

None of them was more excited that Maurice Rose. He knew that this was going to be the high point of his career. It had taken him nearly thirty years to get this far, ever since he had joined the US Army at the age of seventeen and been sent to fight on the Mexican border. The First World War (in which he was wounded) had given him the chance to become an officer, and thereafter he had worked steadily up the ladder of promotion. Standing well over six feet, erect, dark-haired and fine-featured, he was a martinet who brooked no opposition. When the Second World War broke out and he was sent to fight first in Africa, then Italy and now north-western Europe, he had tolerated no interference by man, events or conditions. For this stern, introverted commander bore a secret with him. He was a Jew, and he knew only too well how anti-semitic the pre-war US Regular Army was; 'Kikes', 'Hebes', 'Yids' didn't serve as officers in the American Army. Now, at the age of forty-six, he was going to fight his last battle and all these excited officers present this night would learn only after his death that their commander, with whom most of them had a love-hate relationship, had been a Jew all along.

But Rose had no inkling that he was going to die soon. He had promised General 'Lightning Joe' Collins that same evening: 'I'll be in Paderborn at midnight tomorrow.' And Maurice Rose always kept his word. The time for talk was over. What counted now was action.

It was the same thought that animated Colonel Richardson as he reached his own command post and instructed his men on their mission. He told them that they were going to move out at six the following morning. Howze had stated that the tankers were free to move anywhere and anyhow — off the road, on trails, across the fields, on the main highways, up railroad tracks — as long as they got to Paderborn in one day. The Combat Command chief had given him, Richardson, just a single order.

It was 'Go!'

Not so many miles away, while Richardson's mechanics and armourers sweated over their Shermans and White half-tracks, preparing them for the great push tomorrow, loading ammunition, fuelling the tanks, piling up the heaps of jerricans to be carried by the trucks, Field-Marshal Model was in despair. He knew that his flank had been virtually turned by the link up of two enemy armies, the First and Third at Giessen, and he suspected that there was worse to come.

Model knew too, that he was hampered now by his limited sources of intelligence. Von Zangen, commander of his Fifteenth Army which had borne the brunt of the fighting so far, had disappeared. Those officers of his staff who had managed to visit the Fifteenth's former area of operations had indicated that the situation was critical. One of them told Model that he had come across a section of the front which was manned solely by a 'Volunteer Wounded Battalion', made up of wounded soldiers from all branches of the service and commanded by a one-armed lieutenant. Another reported that he had found a position defended by sixteen-year-old schoolboys, who had been conscripted into the anti-aircraft service. A third came across some *Luftwaffehelferinnen* (female auxiliaries in the Luftwaffe) bearing rifles and prepared to do battle with the advancing Americans, despite the Führer's edict that a woman's place was in the home.

Model's best source of information now was General Florke. Florke was a corps commander without a corps; he had been ordered to form a 'stop line' to halt the American advance, but he could find no troops. Searching the thick fir-tree forests of the area, however, he found signs of the Americans everywhere. He saw the distant glow of their fires; their voices drifted towards him on the breeze. He met fleeing civilians who told him the *Amis* were just behind, they had broken through, they would catch him if he went any further.

In due course the despondent General radioed his information back to Model. The best they could hope for, Florke told Model, was either that the Americans would now rest after their rapid advance of the last three days, or that they would turn east and attack the neighbouring army group, leaving Model's Army Group B a chance to sort out the mess in relative peace.

It was a pious hope and Model knew it. The Americans might well turn west and link up with Montgomery's armies. Then Model would be trapped. His mobile reserves were sadly depleted, amounting to only a couple of shattered armoured divisions. The best chance for Army Group B, he reflected, would be if it could break out from the Ruhr and head east to continue the battle there. But such a move would have to be authorized by either Hitler or Kesselring, and such authorization was not forthcoming. The alternative was to keep the army group here, to dig in and form fortified positions, loosely linked together — 'hedge-hopping' they had called it in Russia — and then fight the *Amis* to the bitter end. But that, as Speer had warned, would mean the destruction of the Ruhr, the final economic ruin of Germany's industrial heartland.

Model was facing the same dilemma that confronted all thinking German commanders that week. Loyalty demanded that they fight on to the last man and the last round of ammunition. It would be cowardice and betrayal not to do so. They had asked so much of their soldiers at the front and the long-suffering civilians back home; after four and a half years of war, how could they meekly surrender now? Yet if they didn't, the bloodshed would continue — and likewise the destruction of all the factories, farms, roads, bridges and everything else that Germany would need to build a future.

What was Model to do?

In the end he did very little. His usual aggressive decisiveness seemed to have deserted him. Instead of choosing one of the two obvious options, to break out or surrender, he temporized. He ordered the one corps of van Zangen's army with which he was still in touch, Lieutenant-General Bayerlein's 53rd, to withdraw from the line of the River Sieg and to prepare for a counter-attack on the Americans' flank, in the general direction of Limburg.

But Bayerlein, a big burly man and a veteran of the African desert campaign and the Normandy battles, knew just how weak his corps really was. He considered Model's order to be 'impossible . . . entirely hopeless . . . insane'. Miserably he began to prepare his corps for their counter-attack, knowing that this would be the end. One day soon he would take matters into his own hands, and try to bring about an end to this senseless battle for the Ruhr.

FOUR

'Bradley will be responsible'

Colonel Richardson rose at four o'clock that Thursday morning. It was typical of him. His men were still asleep; reveille for them was in another two hours. But Richardson wanted to know what the way ahead would be like for them, once the great drive for Paderborn commenced. Together with his driver, he set off in his jeep on his lone reconnaisssance.

The morning was quiet. The guns had ceased thundering; far off on the horizon he could see vague pink flashes, but there was no sound. It was almost as if the world were already at peace. Richardson knew that somewhere out there in the darkness the enemy would be waiting for his men; they surely couldn't cover the hundred-odd miles to Paderborn without encountering some sort of resistance. But the countryside seemed empty. Even the cattle had vanished.

Richardson decided he had seen enough. The first stretch of the road ahead was clear. He ordered his driver to turn and head back to his CP, noting as he did so that there was a hint of rain in the air and the new day now dawning might be overcast; that might mean that his armoured columns would have to go without air support. He shrugged and dismissed the thought. Back at his CP he concentrated on inspecting his vehicles, checking whether every tank commander had stacked extra cans of gas on his vehicle.

At 0600 hours precisely on this Thursday, 29 March, 1945, Richardson gave the order to move off. The drivers thrust home their gears. In the half-tracks the infantry clutched onto stanchions for support. The dawn air filled with the cloying stink of gasoline. The long column creaked forward. In the lead there was a half-track and several jeeps. Behind them came Richardson's own jeep, its long wireless aerial lashing back and forth like a silver whip, accompanied by three Shermans stripped of equipment.

Now came the 'muscle' of the long column: seventeen Shermans laden with infantrymen and three of the new top-secret Pershing tanks, equipped with great overhanging 90mm guns. Ironically General Rose, who had complained to Eisenhower three days before about the weakness of American tanks, would now go into his last battle supported by the only US armoured vehicle really capable of tackling the feared German Tiger.

Another break in the column. Then followed Richardson's staff, plus a battery of self-propelled 105mm guns, seventeen more Shermans, a handful of the light reconnaissance tanks called Honeys, and a long line of trucks filled with men, ammunition and rations bringing up the rear. Task Force Richardson was a highly mobile, battle-tested outfit; in spite of the fact that the men were tired this dawn, almost every man was as enthusiastic and as eager as was their colonel himself. For they knew that if they pulled off this attack it would go down in history as the longest armoured thrust of the Second World War.

Richardson waited till every vehicle of the long column was moving and then gave the signal the drivers had been waiting for. They stamped on their throttles, gripping the controls impatiently as they watched the speedometer needle quivering ever further to the right. Their top speed was thirty-two miles an hour, and it took all a man's strength to keep a thirty-ton Sherman on the road safely at that speed. Behind them the infantry relaxed; if the column bumped into a strong roadblock, their orders were to avoid a fight and go cross-country. They wouldn't be needed.

Roaring down the empty German roads,the tanks skidded round bends as their frantic sweating drivers fought the metal monsters round, the infantry on their decks holding on as best they could. In the trucks other men poked funnels through the side of the canvas hoods and urinated through them. For on this drive there was going to be no stopping. If anyone was hungry he'd have to eat his rations cold, straight out of the can.

The hours passed. As Richardson had suspected, he had no air support; but it didn't matter. The only Germans they had so far spotted were those who wanted to surrender; the prisoners were added to the rear of the long column for Major Kapes and his MPs to deal with. Otherwise the only people on the roads were DPs and former prisoners-of-war limping south in their thousands, some in strange striped pyjamas which Richardson would soon learn to recognize as the uniform for inmates of the concentration camps.

At the column's point, the tanks of the 83rd Armored Reconnaissance Battalion now turned off the roads and went cross-country to avoid the villages and towns in their path. Still they met no opposition to speak of. To their rear, the unfortunate divisional G-I Jack Boulger was ambushed by marauding Germans and taken off to the 'cage', where he would remain almost to the end of the war. Otherwise all was quiet. The German armies appeared to have vanished. The Americans' great armoured thrust was turning into nothing more than a kind of peacetime motorized march.

Twenty-odd miles away, at Model's new HQ in the small, half-timbered town of Olpe, Lieutenant-General Bayerlein was confused and angry. The HQ, he thought, 'was like a madhouse. Reports came flooding in all the time, the one contradicting the other. It was just the same with the orders and counter-orders being issued from the HQ.'

Model didn't seem to notice. He told Bayerlein to use his two armoured divisions — the once-famed *Panzerlehr*, which he himself had once commanded, and the 9th Panzer — plus his 3rd Panzergrenadier Division and the 3rd Parachute, assembled around the town of Schmallenberg, to launch an attack in an easterly direction towards Bad Wildungen. As Model snapped, 'With this operation we intend to break out to link up with the troops of Army Group G to the east. You must do everything you can, Bayerlein, to carry out the mission successfully.'

For the first time Bayerlein realized that the Field-Marshal feared his Army Group was being trapped in a pocket. It was clear, too, that Model thought a successful breakthrough to the east would allow him to withdraw his troops to fight another day in Central Germany. And indeed that was exactly what Model intended; he had signalled Kesselring asking for authorization.

Bayerlein asked if he would receive any help from what was left of von Zangen's Fifteenth Army. Model, who still did not know the whereabouts of the missing Army Commander, said he hoped that the Fifteenth would be ordered to attack from the direction of Kassel. With luck the two attacks, Bayerlein's from inside the pocket and von Zangen's from outside it, would converge and cut off the *Ami* armoured columns which were at this moment obviously heading for Paderborn.

The news appeased Bayerlein a little. Model then told him that the Fifteenth's artillery commander, who was with them at the HQ in Olpe, had already been ordered to throw up an emergency defence line from Siegen to Brilon. This line — manned by the *Volkssturm* (German Home Guard), Luftwaffe anti-aircraft gunners, and anyone else who could be scraped together — would hold the Americans long enough for him to go into action.

Half an hour later, Bayerlein left the HQ feeling a little more optimistic. The weather cheered him up, too. It had now begun to drizzle, which meant he could drive back to his own headquarters without risk of attack by the enemy *jabos*. Ever since he had barely managed to escape from the dreadful slaughter of the Falaise Pocket in the summer of 1944, Bayerlein had had a healthy respect for Allied fighter-bombers; but today the cloud cover was too low for them. He climbed into his grey Mercedes and told his driver and escort to start. On the way he pondered on Model's orders, wondering how he was going to get sufficient tanks and men to launch a major counter-attack. Both his panzer divisions were down to the strength of a battle group and the morale of the men was not particularly good. All the divisions of his Corps had been in action constantly ever since D-Day; and there were only a handful of his veterans left.

Suddenly, west of the village of Küstelberg, the Mercedes and its escort came to a halt. Down below, those tanks moving along the village street were clearly *Ami*; there was no mistaking the high superstructure and turret of the US Sherman. Bayerlein cursed. The village was supposed to be defended by over 200 *Volkssturm* men. Old buffers and unfit they might be, but they had rifles and machine guns. They should have been capable of holding off the *Amis* till he was through, at least. Little did Bayerlein know that, only an hour before, the victorious Americans had disarmed them and packed them off home as harmless.

Bayerlein's mood slumped again. Even before he could gather his troops together to launch the vital counter-attack, upon which so much apparently depended, the *Amis* appeared to have cut him off from his command.

Bayerlein was not the only one cut off that Thursday. General von Zangen was also trapped, A burly, heavy-jawed man with dark hair combed straight back, von Zangen had watched in despair as his Fifteenth Army began to crumble in the face of the enemy armoured columns. Time and again, he himself had just escaped capture by the skin of his teeth. Then, two days ago, he and his entire signals staff had realized they were trapped in the little village of Biedenkopf, with the rattle of tank tracks getting ever louder.

Von Zangen knew the approaching tanks could only be enemy. His own armour had vanished days before. What was he to do? Should he surrender? Hastily he dismissed the idea, though his group did contain women clerks in uniform. He made a swift decision and rapped out his orders. They'd make a run for it.

His drivers needed no urging. While everyone else flung themselves aboard, grabbing with them little bits of kit and weapons, they gunned their engines into life. The noise of the tanks was coming nearer and nearer. It wouldn't be long now before they were visible. The lookout posted in the steeple of the old church came pelting towards the little convoy. The Americans were just round the next bend!

'Los!' an officer cried. 'Losfahren!' The drivers let out their clutches. The column of German vehicles, all 120 of them, tightly packed together, moved off in low gear.

Up front, von Zangen surveyed the hills around the village, wondering where they could hide until darkness fell; the vague outline of a plan was forming in his mind. Behind him there was the sudden chatter of a tank machine gun, like someone running an iron bar along some railings. White tracer flashed past him harmlessly. The *Amis* were scared, he told himself. They were wasting ammunition already, even though no one had fired at them — but then, they did have the ammunition to waste.

Suddenly the General spotted a hiding place. To the south-west of the village there was a wooded area big enough to hide his little column. He jerked his fist up and down three times in rapid succession: the infantry signal for advance at speed. Despite his situation, von Zangen smiled to himself. Here he was — a soldier of thirty years, who had once commanded a whole army — giving signals like a subaltern to a command which was little larger than a company. But there was no time to ponder that thought at the moment. The first group of American tanks was beginning to nose its way into the village now. They had to get undercover soon.

Ten minutes later they were. All their vehicles were safely hidden among the trees, with broken-off branches covering their decks. Just in time, too, von Zangen, told himself. For not only were the *Ami* Shermans everywhere, there was also a lone plane circling lazily above Biedenkopf, as if it had all the time in the world and its pilot had never even heard of the Luftwaffe. The General lit a cigarette to soothe his nerves. So far so good. Now all they had to do was to kill the long hours till night fell and avoid being spotted. After that, he'd put phase two of his plan into operation.

Moodily he puffed at his cigarette and watched the little metal beetles scuttling by down below. There were scores of them and they were taking absolutely no precautions now. He frowned. It was as if the war were already over and they had won.

For over twelve hours the British reaction to Eisenhower's cable of the 28th had smouldered, then finally broken into a burning rage. Right at the top, Churchill was furious with Ike for the very first time since they had met back in 1942. What right had Eisenhower — a soldier — to address Stalin directly, without using channels? Even Supreme Commanders did not communicate personally with the Soviet dictator unless they were given permission to do so by their political bosses; and President Rooosevelt had certainly not given Eisenhower that permission. Also, this sudden change of strategy had caught the Prime Minister completely off balance. Only the day before, he had received Montgomery's signal announcing his drive to the Elbe and 'thence by *autobahn* to Berlin, I hope'. Now Berlin seemed to be out.

If Churchill's anger was tempered a little by bewilderment, Montgomery's fury was unconfined. Eisenhower's new strategy was plain enough to him. One paragraph of his signal said it all:

As soon as you have joined hands with Bradley in the Kassel—Paderborn area, Ninth United States Army will revert to Bradley's command .... Bradley will be responsible for mopping up and occupying the Ruhr and with the minimum delay will deliver his main thrust on the axis Erfurt—Leipzig—Dresden to join hands with the Russians. The mission of your army group will be to protect Bradley's northern flank.

Bradley now would win the kudos of final victory, even if he would not capture Berlin.

Looking back now, Montgomery was sure that Eisenhower had known he was going to revise the Allied plan at that meeting in Rheinsberg on 25 March; yet he had made no objections at the time to Montgomery's own plan to advance from the Rhine to the Elbe. Monty felt betrayed. In his opinion, Eisenhower's dramatic change of strategy had nothing to do with military reality. It was designed to curb him, to put him in the position of being a mere flank guard for Bradley. It was a matter of personal prestige, and Monty couldn't see why Bradley wanted to waste time and troops now mopping up the Ruhr. For him 'the main business' lay to the north and east; it would be quite sufficient to send one corps of Simpson's Ninth Army round the north face of the pocket soon to be formed in the Ruhr. The most important thing for him was to get to the Elbe.

Despite his rage that morning, Montgomery harboured the hope that everything would turn out well in the end. He felt that Churchill and his mentor Brooke could bring their influence to bear on Eisenhower so that he would change his strategy again and firmly place Berlin (to be captured under *his* command, of course) as the Western Allies' primary objective. In the meantime, he wrote to his confidante in the War Office, Major-General Simpson, he was 'making no change in my plans or orders'. As far as Monty was concerned, the race for Berlin was still on.

That afternoon the British in London did bombard their opposite numbers in Washington with calls and cables demanding that Eisenhower be forced to reconsider his decision. Churchill, in particular, did not want to leave Berlin to be captured by the Russians. By now he saw them as the main enemy. In his opinion, 'Soviet Russia had become a mortal danger to the free world' and he believed 'that a new front must be immediately created against her onward sweep ... that this front in Europe should be as far east as possible ... that Berlin was the prime and true objective of the Anglo-American armies.'

What Churchill, Brooke and Montgomery failed to see was that a change was taking place in Anglo-American relations. The anglophile section at Supreme Headquarters, and at lesser headquarters such as Patton's and Bradley's, had a much slighter influence on Eisenhower than any of them supposed. Perceptive Americans were realizing that once the British Empire collapsed, which most of them thought it would after the war, Britain would be a small third-class power. America, on the other hand, must emerge as a world superpower, one whose actions could not be dictated by any smaller nation. That would be like the tail wagging the dog.

Meanwhile, the US Army lacked control at the top. Roosevelt, the only American capable of overruling any decision made by his generals, was a dying man. In these last crucial weeks of the war, it was his generals who were making the decisions, both military and political. Eisenhower was concerned not only with the prestige of the

US Army but also with ensuring that after the war (American public opinion played a great role here) there was harmony with Russia. Why risk American soldiers' lives capturing Berlin and Germany east of the Elbe, when that territory could only become a source of friction between Russia and the United States?

Let Churchill thunder all he liked, Eisenhower and his superiors, the Joint Chiefs of Staff, did not see Russia as a menace to the peace of Europe. The American public demanded the total destruction of Nazi Germany and, thereafter, a brave new world, filled with sweetness and light. They would not tolerate any new war or threat of another conflict. And these American generals and admirals, who four years before had been contemplating a slippered retirement on colonels' and captains' pay, were very mindful of the need to keep American public opinion on their side. If anyone decided to let Bradley have his head and leave Berlin to the Russians that March, it was 'Joe Blow' — the Great American Public.

As dusk was falling on Thursday, 29 March, a weary, dirty Colonel Richardson checked his milometer: it registered seventy-five miles. His men had broken the 4th Armored's record from Bitburg to Andernach on the Rhine the previous month. No other American division had driven so far in one day. But fog was beginning to roll in across the fields, nestling onto the hills to his front like a silent grey cat. Richardson was having trouble with his radio, too. So he decided to keep on going.

The Task Force had already captured Mengeringhausen and Obermarsburg. Now Richardson's forward elements seemed to have captured Brilon as well. Richardson decided to have a look, but just as he reached the edge of the pretty little tourist town, a pre-war ski resort, his radio crackled into life. It was 'Big Six', General Rose. He ordered Task Force Richardson to clear Brilon of any remaining enemy before proceeding.

Richardson had a mind of his own. During the Battle of the Bulge, Rose had threatened to court martial him for some now forgotten misdemeanour; but Richardson had managed to dodge it. Now he stuck to his original orders from Howze. Bobby Howze had told him to get to Paderborn with all speed, avoiding pitched battles, and that was what he was going to do.

Taking a few vehicles with him, he set off to reconnoitre the way ahead, trying to find the best route to Paderborn now only thirty miles away. An hour later he came across an obliging civilian who gave him directions. But by now the fog had really come down, and it was very dark as well.

Richardson decided to get out of his jeep and lead the column on foot. Just as he did so he heard the rumble of tanks: it was the main body of his force catching up from Brilon. Idly he wondered what had kept his men so long in Brilon; he had heard no sound of firing. A young lieutenant dropped from the first tank and came across to his CO. Even in the gloom Richardson could see that he was scared, and Richardson didn't blame him. 'Follow me,' he ordered and began walking down the road alone, feeling both scared and foolish, a bit like one of those fellows with a red flag leading an automobile in the old movies that he'd seen as a kid.

The Shermans, their headlights obscured by blue tissue, rumbled behind him, getting closer and closer all the time. Richardson cursed. It was bad enough risking being shot by some last-ditch Kraut, but he didn't want to be run over by one of his own goddam tanks. He began to walk faster. The lead tank increased its speed. Now the monster was right behind him. When it gave him a hefty nudge in the back, he sprang to one side and dropped into the ditch. Like a faithful dog, the tank did the same.

Puzzled, angry, frightened, Richardson scrambled back into the centre of the road and waved his flashlight frantically at the tank. What was going on? Still the tank was bearing down on him. Peering back, Richardson saw that the second and yes, the third tank were skidding all over the place in their attempts to follow the leading Sherman. And just behind them was the boxlike shape of an ambulance. 'Jesus Chr-rist!' he cursed; what the hell was an ambulance doing up here so close to the point?

Suddenly the first tank creaked to a shaky stop, rearing back on its bogies. Next instant there was the sound of steel striking steel as the second Sherman slapped into it, followed by the third.

Richardson yelled at the stalled tanks, then turned to the young lieutenant, 'What the hell happened to the tank commander?' he demanded. The lieutenant clambered up onto the turret of the first tank and peered into the green-glowing gloom. 'Something's wrong, sir,' he called. 'There's champagne all over the floor.'

'*What!*'

Richardson doubled across and sprang up the side of the Sherman. Inside he saw the tank commander in his leather helmet, sitting on the metal floor, looking decidedly glassy-eyed and clutching two bottles of German *Sekt*. Richardson realized that there was no time for disciplinary action. He had seen this sort of thing before; during the drive across France, the men had lived off champagne and calvados. Dropping to the road, he ordered: 'Guide the tanks up the road — and *keep* them on the road.'

'Yessir,' the lieutenant said smartly.

'Throw the champagne out and keep all hatches open,' Richardson continued, reasoning that it was cold and damp; the night air would sober up his drunken tankers.

Now the CO set off to discover what an ambulance was doing at the 'sharp end' of his column. He soon found out. A familiar figure shuffled up to him: it was one of the medical orderlies, known to the men as 'Doc Scattergood'.

'We ought to go back to Brilon, Colonel,' the medic said mysteriously.

'Scat, what the hell is going on?' Richardson demanded.

'Colonel, I have to tell you the truth,' the other man answered a little thickly, then confessed that he was the one who had found the warehouse full of champagne in the ski resort.

Richardson wasted no time. He knew his 'Spearheaders'. He went back to his jeep and radioed his executive officer immediately. He was to get the rest of the damned task force out of Brilon *tootsweet*, even if he had to shoot them out!

While Colonel Richardson set off again, leading his column on foot, von Zangen took advantage of the fog to escape — aided, of course, by the general confusion of that crazy drive for Paderborn. Carefully he threaded his 120 vehicles in groups into the long column of US tanks and trucks that now packed the highways heading north. His lead drivers hung onto the faint rear convoy lights of the American vehicles in front of them while von Zangen desperately studied his map, searching for a suitable place to turn off. He knew that the *Ami* drive would take him away from Olpe and Model's HQ, so he had to ensure that every now and again his vehicles broke out of the unsuspecting enemy convoy and picked up a new one heading generally in the direction he required.

It was a tricky, nerve-racking business. It needed only one *Ami* 'snowdrop'* to step into the road and halt them, perhaps to let another vehicle pass, and they would be discovered. More than once they escaped checks of this kind by a hair's breadth. On other occasions they fought their way through mud and gravel

---

*German name for a US military policeman, on account of the MPs' white helmets.

where the *Ami* tanks before them had crossed ploughed fields in their determination to avoid built-up areas. Some time that confused night, two of their vehicles were challenged and the occupants of the trucks were discovered to be German. But, in the end, the others made it, dropping out of the enemy convoy for one last time and reaching Army HQ where a begrimed, unshaven, weary von Zangen reported immediately to Model.

The Field-Marshal was his usual brisk, nervous self. The fact that von Zangen had escaped the *Ami* trap by the skin of his teeth was barely commented upon. Wasting no time, Model filled in the weary General on the events of the day and the counter-attack he had planned for the morrow, while the two men sipped one of the sweet liqueurs that Model favoured.

So far, Model informed von Zangen, his Fifth Panzer Army had not been attacked by the enemy. With it, he hoped, he might be able to exploit the gap to the east which the counter-attack of the 30th should open. But as yet he had not received Kesselring's permission for the Bayerlein counter-attack or the break-out of his Army Group. As Model saw it, his mission to contain the *Amis* at Remagen and stop a broad-front advance over the Rhine had failed. To stay in place and defend the Ruhr was 'absurd, as such a defence could not even pin down enemy forces'.* Time was rapidly running out; the pocket around the Ruhr had almost closed. Now everything depended on 'Smiling Albert'.

Von Zangen was too tired to argue, but he knew Model was wrong. It wasn't Field-Marshal Kesselring but that madman in Berlin who made the final decisions. His fate, Model's fate, the fate of the lowliest 'stubble-hopper', was in the hands of Adolf Hitler. If only Model would act independently, he could bring the whole sorry mess to an end while there was still time.

Midnight. Richardson checked his milometer and found that he had travelled an amazing 109 miles through enemy territory — and his only immediate casualties (there had been others to the rear of which he didn't know) were hangovers.

He yawned and rubbed his weary eyes. He and the men had had enough for this Thursday. Paderborn was only five miles ahead; he would set about capturing it in the morning. He

---

*Model was wrong in this respect. His defence of the Ruhr pinned down eighteen divisions, more than in the whole of Montgomery's Second British Army.

stopped the column and told the drivers to 'gas up', while the rest got a few hours of sleep. They needed it, especially the drunks from Brilon who were now nursing king-sized headaches. Why American soldiers thought they could drink continental wines like they drank 3.5 percent Budweiser back home, he'd never know.

Minutes later, like most of his men, Richardson was asleep. Ahead of them shrouded in fog was the ruined cathedral city of Paderborn. All was silent. The barrage, the permanent background music to war, had ceased. Not even the usual flares sailed into the night sky. The front, it appeared, had gone to sleep and Paderborn seemed theirs for the taking.

But the front had not gone to sleep. All that afternoon, alarmed by the rapid advance of the 3rd Armored Division, Model's staff officers had been frantically trying to obtain permission from SS Headquarters in Berlin to use the last reserves available in the Paderborn area.

Finally it had come through and *Obersturmbannführer* Hans Stern had gone to work with the typical arrogant energy of an officer who wore the feared silver skull-and-crossbones on his rakishly tilted cap. Stern, a heavy-set tankman of thirty-eight, was an 'old hare'. He had served on virtually every front since 1939, had won the Knight's Cross of the Iron Cross for bravery in Russia, had then fought that long bitter campaign in the east before being promoted, in January 1944, to take over the SS Training School at Sennelager just outside Paderborn.

Within the space of a few hours, Stern had organized the staff and recruits at his training school into a new brigade, the 'SS Brigade Westfalen': 3,000 men comprising both ageing instructors and young trainees of seventeen or eighteen — 'greenbeaks', as the rookies were called, who although trained as tankers had not the slightest idea of infantry tactics — supported by the thirty-two tanks used at the school for training, many of them mechanically unreliable. But in reserve Stern had a further twenty-five Royal Tigers of the 512 Tank Destroyer Detachment. Each of these huge 60-ton tanks was armed with an enormous 125mm cannon, which could knock out a Sherman at a range of 3,000 metres; by contrast, the American tank had to get within a range of 800 metres before it had even a hope of tackling the enemy.

Now Stern prepared to tackle the Americans with his new-born brigade. The men had no mortars, radios, anti-tank guns or supporting artillery, though they did have sufficient *Panzerfausts*. They lacked any form of supplies. Even that old German standby, the 'goulash cannon' or mobile field kitchen, usually horse-drawn, was absent; for these young men going into their first action, there would not even be the customary sausage and thick pea soup — 'fart soup' as it was known to Stern's 'old hares'. What they lacked in equipment, however, they made up for in spirit. By this stage of the war they were no longer all volunteers, nor for that matter were they all German either. Among their ranks were young men from half a dozen European countries, attracted to the SS because they believed in Germany's 'holy mission' or simply because they sought adventure. Others were 'booty Germans', as their comrades sneered at them behind their backs: ethnic Germans from the lands to the east, who were proving themselves by joining the Armed SS. Yet whatever their motive for joining, they had by now been imbued by the spirit of the 'black guards'.

While all around them the morale of Model's soldiers was crumbling, these keen fit young men still believed that Germany was worth fighting for — and dying for, too. Now as Stern set them off marching in three columns to meet the Americans, there were none of the malingerers or deserters who would have been found in the ranks of Model's other units this March. Stern's men went to do battle willingly, even enthusiastically, and with them they took another group of volunteers, eager to die for 'Folk, Fatherland and Führer': a score or more of fourteen-year old boys from the Hitler Youth. On the morrow, Richardson's men would find themselves fighting — and killing — undersized kids, bearing rifles bigger than themselves and still wearing short pants.

While Model's staff, accustomed to dealing with whole divisions of tanks and hundreds of thousands of men, now struggled to organize a mere 3,000, their chief was still waiting to hear from Kesselring. What had Hitler decided? For Model knew that Kesselring could not make a move without Hitler's permission. As von Rundstedt, Kesslering's predecessor, had once complained, the only real power he had was to change the sentries standing outside the portals of his headquarters. The Führer had the final say in all matters, political and military.

Model knew that the morale of his men was low. Transportation, fuel and ammunition were scarce. Even if he were prepared to fight it out in the Ruhr, he had sufficient supplies only for three weeks at most. He could defend the Ruhr all right, for those three weeks; he could turn the area into a giant Stalingrad, fighting from city to city and house to house while the ten million citizens watched their homeland disintegrating in the smouldering ruins demanded by Hitler's 'scorched earth' policy. But sooner or later his supplies would run out. And, unlike at Stalingrad, he would not even have the support of Goering's Luftwaffe. He would be forced to surrender what was left of his Army Group.

It was an anxious time for Model as he waited that evening, with a mixture of impatience and dread, for Kesselring's response to his signal. Would permission be forthcoming for Bayerlein's counter-attack and his own break-out to the east?

At last Kesselring's answer came through. The counter-attack by Bayerlein was approved; but under no circumstances was Model to follow up any success with a break-out to the east. He was to remain in place and tie down as many troops as he could. The Ruhr could well become a running sore for the *Amis*. In the meantime, Kesselring continued, the 80,000-strong Eleventh Germany Army under General Lucht was assembling in the east, in the rugged hilly area of the Harz, and preparing to link up with Model's forces in the Kassel area.

But Lucht's Army had been badly hit by the Russians and had lost most of its transport and armoured vehicles; it would take two weeks to replace them. Until then Model would simply have to hold out.

Model must have known that his fate was now sealed. He was committed to defending the Ruhr, whether Bayerlein's counter-attack was successful or not. By the time General Lucht was ready, Model's supplies would be exhausted. There would be nothing left for a break-out, for a continuation of the war to the east. Army Group B, or what was left of it, was doomed to go down fighting in the Ruhr.

Model went to bed soon after midnight. It was Good Friday, 1945.

FIVE

'Nothing but a geographical location'

While Richardson's men slumped in exhausted sleep just south of Paderborn and Bayerlein's formed up for the counter-attack, General Simpson's flying columns were hurrying to meet the First Army on the other flank.

In the lead was General White's 'Hell on Wheels' — the 2nd US Armored Division, one of the largest armoured formations in the Allied army. With its tanks, SPs (self propelled guns), armoured cars, half-tracks, trucks and looted German vehicles — including bulldozers — it formed a column seventy-two miles long. Broken down into three commands for easier handling, the Division still took nearly twelve hours to pass a given spot. And, although moving at a mere two miles an hour, it was running ahead of every other unit of Simpson's Ninth Army, just as it had been ever since it was ordered out of the Rhine bridgehead to link up with Hodges' First Army.

At the head of the column was the 82nd Reconnaissance Battalion, commanded by Lieutenant-Colonel Wheeler Merriam. It was their job to find the easiest route for the rest of the Division — a job now complicated by the widespread confusion of a country facing defeat. At one stage Merriam's light tanks were approaching a railway line when there was the hoot of a train whistle; Merriam called them to a halt. Moments later the train rumbled past — a troop train, packed with German soldiers and armoured vehicles. Merriam was so close that he could see 'the individual hairs on men's faces where they hadn't shaved'. As the train headed west, he stared after it open-mouthed, gaping like a village idiot. His men had not fired a single shot!

He grabbed the radio telephone. A few miles to the west, General White heard Merriam's shout of warning in the same instant that the train came in to sight. But he had no time to react. While he stood there mesmerized, one of his MPs directing traffic at the railway crossing held up his hand smartly and stopped the flow of 2nd Division vehicles. The train rumbled past completely unharmed.

On the 29th, however, the Division thought it was in for a fight. To their immediate front lay the medium-sized town of Ahlen, and General White knew from aerial reconnaissance that there were at least twelve German tanks in the place, plus a lot of enemy infantry. Up front Combat Command B, under the leadership of Brigadier-General Hinds, prepared for a fight. But the Americans had not reckoned with the war-weariness of the average German.

That afternoon there were two schools of thought in Ahlen. The local Party officials insisted that the town should be defended. The other party led by Dr Rosenbaum, a middle-aged military doctor, maintained the contrary. Finally Dr Rosenbaum took the initiative, though he knew he was risking his life; if the Party officials got hold of him they could lynch him with impunity. Together with some wounded soldiers from his own hospital, he had the streets cleared of retreating German infantry, persuading them to leave the town, to take the fight elsewhere. He was joined by local civilians who spread through the town, pleading and threatening, forcing the soldiers to head north, taking with them a column of horse-drawn anti-aircraft guns — which, used in a ground role, could have inflicted heavy casualties on the Americans, now poised just outside Ahlen. Then, having dealt with the Party officials, most of them ashen with suppressed rage and fear, Dr Rosenbaum set out to meet the Americans, his car flying a huge Red Cross flag. Behind him, Ahlen's streets were empty; white flags hung from every roof. A tense, heavy silence descended on the town, as the citizens waited anxiously behind locked doors, wondering what would happen next.

Brigadier-General Hinds met Rosenbaum personally. He eyed the decorations on the MO's chest and knew he was dealing with a man who had seen as much of war as he had. For forty-five minutes they talked. Once their discussions were rudely disturbed by a burst of German artillery fire, which forced them into a nearby ditch. But within the hour, Hinds was convinced. Together the two enemies of the day before drove into the now crowded market place, the Americans being cheered as liberators.

Happy that the town had been taken without difficulty, Hinds and his staff repaired to the local *Gasthaus* to eat while his weary soldiers enjoyed a well-earned rest; and it was during the meal that someone suggested they should 'make reservations' at the next town along their route of march, Beckum. Hinds agreed. This kind of fighting suited him and his men just fine.

His communications officer called the local telephone exchange and asked to speak to the town commandant of Beckum. He was duly put through, and told the unknown German officer to surrender; common humanity, he said, demanded that there be no further loss of blood. Behind him at the dinner table the staff officers roared with laughter, thinking this was some kind of vaudeville act for their evening's entertainment. But at first the German refused — until hearing that the 2nd Division's tanks would be on the outskirts of Beckum at midnight, and if one single shot was fired at them Beckum would be levelled to the ground. In due course, Beckum surrendered.

The triumphant tankers of the 'Hell on Wheels' Division were finding it all too easy. What they didn't know, however, was that the confused, demoralized German soldiers who had attempted to bar their progress so ineffectually up to now had been replaced. All too soon, the two US armoured divisions racing to link up at Paderborn would meet the 'first team' — those young men, eager for some glory, of *Obersturmbannführer* Stern's SS Brigade Westfalen.

Task Force Richardson moved out at first light on the morning of Good Friday. The weather had turned cold, dull and cloudy. Richardson told himself that air support would be missing again, at least until the weather improved; the 'flyboys', as the Army called its air force colleagues, would be safely back at their bases stuffing their faces with bacon and eggs. He dismissed the thought and concentrated on his mission.

To his immediate front was the village of Kirchborchen, six miles south of Paderborn, their objective. The village lay on the right flank of the divisional advance and it had to be secured in order to protect that flank. The approach roads were narrow and winding, running through densely wooded hills; it wasn't exactly tank country. But in spite of the terrain Richardson was optimistic. Besides, Rose was breathing down his neck again. General Collins wanted Paderborn this day!

'*Roll 'em! Load your doughs! ... OK, men, let's move out!*' The familiar old cries echoed the length of the column. Men crushed out their cigarettes or ran to the ditches to take a quick piss. The drivers gunned their engines. Abruptly all was noise, movement, hustle. The armoured column, broken up into sections, started to move forward. Task Force Richardson of the 3rd Armored Division was about to begin the last leg of the race for Paderborn. But some of the men would not live long enough to see the old German cathedral town.

They ran into trouble almost at once. The SS were waiting for them at Kirchborchen. The lead Shermans ran straight into the guns of the waiting Panthers. There was a whoosh, the flat crack of a 75mm firing, the ball of dazzling incandescent white as solid, armour-piercing shot hissed flatly across the ground, the smack of steel striking steel. Instantly the first Sherman reared back like a wild horse being put to saddle for the first time, a gleaming silver hole skewered in its side, and erupted in flames. The German Panther fired again. A second Sherman rolled to a halt, its track smashed and rolling out behind it like a severed limb. The fight was on.

It was midday before the first infantry — G Company, of the 36th Armored Infantry Regiment — had reached the houses on the out-skirts of Kirchborchen, lying in what the locals called the *Jammertal* ('Valley of the Wailing'). Then the house-to-house fighting broke out. For the village was defended by some 200 young SS men and boys from the Hitler Youth, well equipped with the fearsome German Bazooka, the *panzerfaust*, plus a number of quadruple 20mm flak guns which threw up a wall of whirling white death. Against this kind of fire, G Company could not progress further than the first few houses. The best they could do was dig in amid the smoking brick rubble, as the rockets from the *panzerfausts* slammed against the walls of the cottages, showering them with shards of burning metal and masonry.

Shocked by this sudden evidence of the enemy's renewed determination to resist, the 3rd's commanders decided to throw in Captain John Libby's relatively fresh I Company; the armoured infantrymen would rush the place and clear the remaining houses in a bold *coup de main*. But it didn't happen like that. The SS and the Hitler Youth were expecting them. The Americans moved out into a veritable hail of sudden death. Blindly they stumbled forward, leaving their dead and dying behind them, and finally sought refuge from this awesome fire in a quarry. Here Captain Libby changed his plan a little. Beyond the open ground to his front there was a spot which afforded better cover. He ordered his men to their feet and, grabbing his carbine, yelled above the vicious snap and crackle of the fire fight: 'OK men, let's go!'

With no hesitation his men left their cover. The enemy machine guns burst into action. It seemed the Americans were running straight into a blazing wall of bullets. Men went down everywhere along the line, writhing on the ground in agony or simply sitting down, as if suddenly surprised, a look of bewilderment on their young faces.

Libby knew it was no use. He ordered what was left of the company to retreat to shelter in the quarry. Behind them as they scrambled frantically for safety, they left the dead — and fifteen determined men under Sergeants King and Miller. For the next ten hours, this small team would brave the full fury of the young fanatics' attack. Time and time again the SS men launched their suicidal attacks. The casualty toll rose ever higher, while the buildings all around crumbled and burned. Somewhere, caught perhaps in a blazing sty, pigs were squealing with terror. Truly, the *Jammertal* was living up to its name.

While Task Force Richardson was being stalled at Kirchborchen, their comrades of Task Force Lovelady were doing little better to their right. After the latter's successful capture of Marburg, they had set off on two parallel course to Paderborn. But Captain John Haldeman, who had led his reconnaissance company right through France, Belgium and the Rhineland without a scratch, soon found his way blocked. At the small town of Colbe his reconnaissance men ran into what the Task Force history calls 'a hornet's nest of small arms, *panzerfausts* and mortars. They were trapped with nothing but soft-skinned vehicles'. The Americans didn't know it at the time, but they had bumped into the Germans' 'Volunteer Cripple Battalion', led by a one-armed lieutenant. But, cripple or not, they knew how to fight. Haldeman himself was wounded. The tanks he urgently summoned, the thinly armoured Honeys, were soon knocked out. For this day at least, one column of Task Force Lovelady was going no further.

At first the other column had fared rather better. They had knocked out five German trucks and captured two monstrous German railway guns, plus 170 artillerymen. For a while their main problem was DPs who, on seeing the American tanks, decided to walk out on their German taskmasters, usually giving them a severe beating before they did so. Thousands of them poured from their farms and factories to greet their liberators. As the Task Force history records: 'A constant stream of these happy folk lined the road as they immediately started towards home: French and

Belgians walking in the opposite direction from us, on one side of the road; Russians, Poles and Slavs following us, on the other side, all trekking hopefully toward their respective homelands.'

All too soon, however, Colonel Lovelady's second column was brought to an abrupt halt. Just outside the village of Wrexen, B Company ran into a roadblock. The German gunners were hiding in dugouts on either side of the road. They launched their rockets at the packed American tanks.

'*Panzerfaust!*' someone shrieked in warning.

Too late. The first tank was hit. A ball of fire exploded against its side, in the same instant that a second tank was struck and set ablaze, followed a moment later by a third. Frantic crews struggled to get out before they were burned alive. But the young SS men showed no mercy. They opened up with their concealed machine guns, cruelly mowing down the escaping tankers. A few seconds later, the merciless slaughter complete, they turned their guns on the infantry packing the decks of the armoured vehicles, showering them with a hail of lead.

Hastily the surviving tanks 'buttoned up' and started to pull back, while fresh troops were called for. Just like Task Force Richardson, its running mate Task Force Lovelady had been stopped dead by Stern's teenage black guards.

To their rear, hopping from one task force to another by means of his light plane, General 'Lightning Joe' Collins, the VII Corps Commander, was a worried man. For this Catholic at least, Good Friday of 1945 was not a day to be spent in quiet spiritual reflection. There was too much to do.

Only yesterday things had seemed to be going so well. Sam Hogan and the 3rd Division had made tremendous progress, covering almost ninety miles over twisting country roads. The link-up at Paderborn with the 8th, 4th Cavalry and 1st Infantry Divisions had looked well within his grasp. But now it seemed the Krauts were fighting back, instead of collapsing as his staff had confidently predicted. Maurice Rose had just reported that his advance was being held up by at least sixty Tiger tanks armed with a formidable new gun.

That afternoon Collins landed in his plane in a pasture just south of Korbach. He spotted one of Rose's columns and flagged it down. It was all too obvious that the men had just run in to an ambush. Even the commanding officer's aide was wounded. Collins spent the rest of the afternoon with the column, now halted in the cover of a sunken road. He agreed with Colonel Boudinot, commanding the column, that the tanks should go no further that night; after dark they would be easy meat for the Germans to pick off with their *panzerfausts*.

Collins was watching the medics vainly tending one young German who had suffered a mortal wound when there was the sudden heavy crump of a shell exploding. It seemed the Krauts were bringing up artillery as well. Colonel Boudinot and he scrambled up the embankment to see what was going on.

Clearly outlined against the darkening sky, the two men saw a stalled German train. One of the 3rd's other columns had ambushed it and set it afire. Now the ammunition it contained was exploding, shells zigzagging into the lowering clouds in crazy profusion. Much relieved, Collins and Boudinot slid back down the embankment to the road.

The German teenager had died. Collins's gloom returned, compounded by the news now crackling over the radio. Some forty miles to his rear, reported General Terry Allen of the 104th Infantry Division, the Germans had launched a major counter-attack; the 104th had already identified the elements of no less than three enemy divisions.

Like most experienced battle commanders — and 'Lightning Joe' had won the Silver Star for bravery in combat in the Pacific — Collins carried a map of the battlefield and the dispositions of his outfits in his head. He realized that if the Germans broke through the 104th's lines, the whole of the 3rd Armored Division would be cut off — and himself with it. Not only that, but Bradley's entire new strategy might be in jeopardy. Everything now depended on General Allen and the 104th's ability to hold out until help could arrive.

That same afternoon Field-Marshal Model had paid a visit to Bayerlein at his CP in the village of Milchenbach. He wanted the Corps Commander to launch his great counter-attack immediately.

Bayerlein was not happy. He recognized the urgency of Model's situation, of course; once the pocket closed round him at Paderborn, Model would be trapped — whereas an attack by Bayerlein might give the Field-Marshal time to break out. But Bayerlein's problem was his shortage of effective troops, particularly infantry. Loyally, however, he started to revise his plans in the light of Model's demands.

Bayerlein's leading unit was a battle group of his own old division, the *Panzerlehr*, under the command of Major Helmut Ritgen. It was very weak, consisting only of three reinforced companies equipped with tanks and self-propelled guns. Assessing the unit, Bayerlein decided it could best be used only under the cover of darkness and along the rugged forest trails of the area. He called in the local foresters and ordered them to guide Ritgen's tanks through the woods; the battle group would attack as soon as night fell.

What Bayerlein was hoping was that the Americans still suffered from what he thought of as 'Tiger-phobia'. Back in Normandy, even the oldest and most obsolete Panzer Mark III had sent the *Amis* panicking and shrieking, 'The Tigers are coming!' In addition, he had learned from captured Americans that the 104th Infantry Division included in its ranks nearly sixty black infantry platoons, all of them volunteers, who helped to make up the lack of riflemen; these 'chocolate solders', as the prisoners referred to them, might well be even more susceptible to 'Tiger-phobia'. A sudden night attack by Ritgen and his tanks might demoralize and weaken the 104th Division's lines — then Bayerlein would send in the rest of his corps to finish them off.

Summoning Major Ritgen, Bayerlein explained his tactics. Led by the foresters, Ritgen would follow the wooded trails and use his tanks to attack the village of Küstelberg, where the *Volkssturm* had surrendered so tamely the day before, then cut the main road between Hallenberg and Medebach. From this road — westernmost of the three highways serving the US 3rd Armored Division, some forty miles to the north-east — Bayerlein would then continue with the rest of the corps to the lake at Ederstausee where he hoped to link up with a corps from von Zangen's Fifteenth Army.

At seven o'clock, satisfied that Major Ritgen's attack was well under way, Bayerlein returned to his main headquarters at Winterberg, where the 1936 Winter Olympics had been held at Hitler's command. Assembling his staff and commanders, he told them of his new plans and gave them their final orders. Then he sat down to a frugal supper of hard black Army bread and sausage, washed down with *Korn*, the fierce local version of schnapps.

He would launch his own attack at midnight. It was, he knew, the last full-scale corps attack that the Wehramacht would make in the Second World War. If it failed, Bayerlein knew what he would have to do.

To the north and west the battle still raged. Under pressure from Simpson's Ninth Army and Montgomery's Second, the German

Army Group H was falling apart. Communications between the various formations were non-existent, so two of the Group's corps appealed to Model for advice and instructions.

As harassed as he was, Model was pleased by their appeal for it meant that fresh troops and armour would be available to him. He ordered the two corps, under the command of General von Lüttwitz, to form a new line and stand fast. Von Lüttwitz was an experienced tankman. Back in the winter he had nearly captured the key town of Bastogne and had then held the line below it against all that Patton was able to throw at him. Now if he could hold this new line, based on the Rhein-Herne Canal and the Lippe River, his two corps would make an effective defence of the northern face of the Ruhr.

Model knew, of course, that Kesselring would explode when he heard that Army Group B had taken over two corps from another army group without authorization. But times were desperate and in the end 'Smiling Albert' would have to accept the *fait accompli*. The main thing was that the new defensive line would help to prevent an Allied link-up, trapping him in the Ruhr.

To the east, he believed this Friday night, events were turning in his favour. The SS brigade was effectively halting the *Amis'* armoured drive for Paderborn. One of the few senior Wehrmacht commanders who openly admired the bravery and fighting qualities of Himmler's Waffen SS, Model knew the black guards wouldn't let him down. With luck, Bayerlein would cut off that drive altogether. Maybe in the end, if he could only buy time, Hitler would change his mind and allow him to break out to the east and link up with what was left of the Wehrmacht, still prepared to fight in Central Germany.

Even now in this 'last hour before zero', as the Germans call the eleventh hour, Field-Marshal Model still retained some of his old optimism. Of course he must have known in his heart that all was really lost; there was no hope for Germany, whatever the outcome of his dispositions and the counter-attack of the morrow. But his troops were still fighting, and that counted for something with men like Model, who had experienced the breakdown of morale in 1918 when officers had been spat upon and kicked by their soldiers and had their medals and epaulettes ripped off. In any case, he was bound by his oath as a German officer to continue the struggle even when it seemed totally hopeless. In 1934 Field-Marshal von Hindenburg had written in *The Duties of the German Soldier*:

> *The highest soldierly virtue is martial courage. It demands hardiness and determination. Cowardice is disgraceful, hesitation*

*unsoldierly ... The soldier's honour is embodied in the uncondi-
tional surrender of his person for people and Fatherland, even to
the sacrifice of his life.*

It was compulsory for every German soldier to know this creed
by heart, and no doubt Model remembered it now. But above all,
perhaps, what still kept him going was sheer stubbornness. Illogical,
uncompromising, it was the mood of the Götterdämmerung: 'If you go
under, then damn it, I shall drag the whole world under with me!'

After the war, one of Model's Corps Commanders, General
Friedrich Kochling, would tell his interrogators:

*The continuation of resistance in the Ruhr pocket was a crime.
It was Model's duty to surrender the pocket, since he was an
independent commander, once his Army Group had been cut off.
Only the danger of reprisals against my family prevented me taking
this step myself. My staff listened eagerly for news of American
advances, and we congratulated each other when we learned the
Americans had occupied another town, where our families were
living. You see, the occupation of those towns made men, free
men, of us again.*

But Model was not like the commander of the 81st Corps.
His wife and three children mattered less to him now than the
Army. It was the only life he had ever known since joining up
as a puny eighteen-year-old, excused PT on account of his poor
physique. What future could there be for him if that Army were
finally defeated?

There is an old German saying, dating back to the eighteenth century, which states: *'Mitgegangen, mitgefangen, mitgehangen'* (roughly:
'Gone with, caught with, hanged with'). That seemed to sum up
Model's present position. He had gone with Hitler, now he was
caught with him. Model must have known there was no future.

All the previous day Eisenhower's temper had been rising. He
had expected trouble from Montgomery over the new role he
was assigning to him once the Ruhr had been encircled; he had
anticipated problems from the British because he had left Berlin out
of his strategy. What he had not expected was the rumours that his
signal to the Soviet dictator occasioned.

This Friday he began to reply to the various messages he had
received. First he sent Marshall a preliminary cable, insisting that

he had not changed his plans and that the British charges against him had 'no possible basis in fact'. Then he wrote to Churchill, reiterating his intention of 'driving eastward to join hands with Russians' and telling the British Primie Minister that,

Subject to Russian intentions, the axis Kassel—Leipzig [the central thrust under Bradley's command] is the best for the drive, as it will ensure the overrunning of that important industrial area . . . it will cut the German forces approximately in half and . . . destroy the major part of remaining enemy forces in West.

But he made no mention of the sore subject of Berlin.

That difficult task over, Eisenhower returned to the job of mollifying his own chief in Washington. He complained to Marshall that the British Chiefs of Staff objected to his plan because it would weaken their own preferred strategy (the attack on Berlin). He protested that 'from the very beginning, extending back before D-Day', it had been his intention to 'link up . . . and then make one great thrust to the eastward'. The Leipzig region, he stressed, was the home of 'the greatest part of the remaining German industrial capacity'. Why he was so determined to capture this area Eisenhower did not explain. Admittedly German industry might still be producing weapons; but in these last few weeks of the war there were ever decreasing numbers of German soldiers available and willing to use them.

And in the final paragraph of his second signal to Marshall, Eisenhower really showed his anger at the British. This was not the Ike so beloved by the media, the man with an infectious ear-to-ear grin. This was the stern Supreme Commander, feared by his staff for his sudden outbursts of temper. Churchill and the British Chiefs of Staff had repeatedly opposed his wishes and plans, he declared:

Now they apparently want me to turn aside on operations in which would be involved many thousands of troops before the German forces are fully defeated. I submit that these things are studied daily and hourly by me and my advisors and that we are animated by one single thought — which is the early winning of the war.

In Washington the US Combined Chiefs of Staff gave Eisenhower their unqualified support. The following day they would announce that 'the Commander in the Field is the best judge of the measures which offer the earliest prospect of destroying the German armies' and that, in their opinion, 'General Eisenhower should continue to be free to communicate with the Commander-in-Chief of the

Soviet Army'. This was precisely the response that Eisenhower had been counting on.

Meanwhile in Moscow the Soviet dictator was summoning his two commanders in Germany, Marshals Zhukov and Koniev, for an urgent weekend conference. Stalin did not trust Eisenhower, the man who fondly called him 'UJ'. He had received Eisenhower's message of 28 March, but simply could not believe the Americans would leave such a prestigious target to the Russians. He ordered Zhukov and Koniev to plan an immediate drive for Berlin before the Western Allies did the same.

But today, while Eisenhower waited for Washington's reaction, he drafted a signal to Montgomery, knowing full well that this would finally put paid to the detested British commander's hopes of leading a joint Anglo-American attack on the German capital. 'I must adhere to my decision about Ninth Army passing to Bradley's command,' he said, and firmly repeated his determination to concentrate on the Ruhr operation. As a last flourish he added:

You will note that in none of this do I mention Berlin. That place has become, as far as I am concerned, nothing but a geographical location.

Washington's confidence that the war in Germany was about to finish would not have been shared by the hard-pressed men of the 3rd Armored Division that Friday night.

At Kirchborchen Captain Libby's I Company was still taking repeated attacks by the SS men, supported by tanks. All around them the half-timbered houses burned fiercely. Masonry shivered like theatrical backdrops and bricks slithered to the ground in noisy avalanches as yet another enemy mortar bomb slammed down. Libby's men had twice managed to knock out a German tank with their inferior bazookas; but more and more tanks came rumbling down the heights towards the Americans. As a weary Captain Libby cracked to his men: 'Well, boys, maybe we'll be in the same camp together.'

His CO, Colonel Richardson, had no time even for gallows humour. His attack had come to an abrupt halt and he knew he couldn't proceed without air support. But the 'flyboys' were not prepared to fly in the heavy cloud. Desperately Richardson radioed for an air drop; he needed fan belts, ammunition and gas.

'No aircraft available,' was the laconic reply.

(above left) 'Field-Marshal Walter Model looked like the typical Hollywood stereotype of a Prussian officer'. He chose suicide rather than surrender.

(above right) Albert Speer became Hitler's Minister of Armaments in 1942 and in 1943 took charge of total war production. He survived the war to spend 20 years in prison. He is seen here at the Nuremburg trials.

(below left) Fritz Bayerlein was a Corps Commander in the Battle of the Ruhr Pocket and was taken prisoner in April, 1945.

(below right) Heinrich Himmler, described by Speer as 'half-schoolmaster, half crank', eluded his captors by committing suicide with a phial of cyanide.

5. *(above left)* General Lawton Collins, known since Guadalcanal as 'Lightning Joe'.
6. *(above right)* General Omar Bradley, in Patton's opinion 'a man of great mediocrity'.
7. *(below left)* General Eisenhower, the Supreme Commander, regarded Berlin as 'nothing but a geographical location'.
8. *(below right)* General Ridgway, said *Time* magazine, 'looks like a Roman senator and lives like a Spartan hoplite'.

9. Field-Marshal Montgomery with General 'Big Simp' Simpson, of whom Eisenhower wrote, 'If Simpson ever made a mistake as an army commander, it never came to my attention'.

10. Hitler on an aeroplane with von Papen, nearest the camera. Von Papen was the most senior Nazi to be captured in the Ruhr Pocket (p. 147).

11. Schloss Wewelsburg (p. 94).

12. Flight controllers and pilots of 'the dreaded *jabos*' – the Allied fighter-bombers (p. 21).

A few minutes later the first news arrived of the impending German attack forty miles to his rear. Not only was he running out of supplies, but now his rear was going to be cut off. Nothing would be able to reach him by truck either.

To Richardson's flank, Lovelady had finally withdrawn his two companies which had been pinned down by the SS at Wrexen. But Colonel Richardson, ambitious as he was, could not bring himself to do likewise. Instead he decided to dig in for the night and pray that the SS would not attack. Fortunately for him *Obersturmbannführer* Stern's tankers had another objective in mind: the splitting of Task Force Welborn, some five miles to the right. So, for the time being at least, a very worried Richardson was left at peace to dig in and wait for further developments.

But Richardson's problems were not yet over this Friday night. His infantry had barely started to dig their foxholes, while his Shermans 'buttoned up' against any surprise attack by fanatical SS teenagers with a *panzerfaust*, when his radioman alerted him to a visitor. 'Big Six' (General Rose) was coming up and he wanted someone to meet him and guide him to Richardson's CP.

Urgently Richardson radioed back that he didn't have a single spare jeep. 'Don't send Big Six this way!' he added before signing off abruptly. He didn't want to have to argue the matter out.

At the moment Rose and his small staff were with Colonel John Welborn. Welborn's task force had been cut in two by enemy tanks — seven Tigers in all — so that his column's tail was now separated from its head. At the point four more Tigers were clearly visible in the garish light of the burning American vehicles. Behind them were at least another seven, blasting away at the length of the stalled column, and SS infantry were already sneaking out of the woods like wolves, ready to deal with the survivors.

Rose realized that he and his party were effectively trapped. German machine-gun fire rattled down on the vehicles all around him like metal hailstones. Yet somehow he had to move out. He had no choice. It was either move or be killed.

The scene was like something from Dante's *Inferno*, thought Rose's artillery commander Colonel Frederic Brown as he eyed the skyline. Everywhere the flames of fire and slashes of shells cut the darkness. Flares hissed into the sky. Bright white tracer spat back and forth. Howling mortar bombs came raining down, slamming into the ground and making everything tremble as if in an earthquake.

The Colonel advised Rose to make a run for it while there was still time. He suggested a route through the woods to their left; despite the sporadic bursts of enemy machine-gun fire, that seemed the safest way to skirt round the German tanks blocking the rear. But Rose ignored the advice. To their immediate front, he pointed out, the four Tigers appeared to have withdrawn, and that was the route he was going to take to link up with the rest of Welborn's column. It was typical of Rose, bold, decisive and forthright. Brown objected no more.

Hastily the drivers of the little party — two jeeps, an armoured car and a soldier on a motor-cycle — moved out, braving the small-arms fire coming from both sides, dodging in and out of Welborn's blazing vehicles. About a mile up the road, they came to a small junction. Rose peered through the darkness and thought he could make up the distant silhouette of one of his own Shermans, standing a little way up the side road. He snapped an order to his driver. They turned in that direction, heading for Task Force Richardson's last reported position.

With a feeling of relief they approached the Sherman. But their relief was short-lived. The Sherman had been hit and abandoned. Where was Task Force Richardson? Suddenly there was a burst of firing from the woods to the right. That decided them. Hurriedly they reversed down the side road to the main junction, followed by the glowing morse of tracer.

They began to climb up a winding rise, crowned by a fir wood. Brown spotted a dark shape to their front. 'There's one of Jack's new tanks,' he told himself, knowing the Welborn task force had several of the new Pershings. The drivers quickened their speed to catch up. But as they approached the big tank with its massive overhanging cannon, one of Brown's companions, Colonel George Garton, gasped. The Pershing had only one exhaust. This tank had two.

'*Tiger!*' he yelled in alarm. 'Get off the road!'

Brown gunned his engine and the jeep shot forward. Two more Tigers loomed alarmingly out of the gloom. Desperately Brown looked for a place to turn off the road. Any moment now they'd be spotted for sure.

As yet the SS men had not seen them. But now a fourth tank appeared. It started to cut in front of Brown, its massive tracks built for the snows of Russia sending up little fiery sparks. Brown acted instinctively. He hit the brakes, changed down in a flash and just managed to squeeze the jeep between the Tiger and a tree. Behind him he heard a ripping sound: the Tiger had torn off his gas can. He flung a glance behind him. Was the General going to get through? But in that same instant a fifth Tiger appeared. Brown hit the gas. He shot forward, raced over a ditch and came to a halt in a slither of mud and grass in the middle of a field, shocked but unharmed. Hastily, as German flares started to sail into the night sky, bathing the scene in their lurid, unreal light, Brown and his fellows dived for cover.

Behind them Rose's jeep skidded to a stop, all progress blocked by an enormous Tiger. Hesitantly they got out, followed by the Tiger's gun as if it were a monster just waiting to gobble them up. A moment later a head poked out of its turret and snapped something in German.

'I think they want our guns,' Rose said.

Miserably the driver, T/5 Shaunce, and Rose's aide, Major Bellinger, started to unbuckle their shoulder holsters. Rose, who stood between them feeling trapped and helpless, kept his .45 in a holster at his belt; his movement was thus different from those of the other two.

The nervous German gunner misunderstood it. There was the sudden chatter of a machine gun. Rose yelled with pain and crumpled to the road, dead before he reached it.

Shaunce leapt behind the tank, out of the line of fire, and Bellinger flipped backwards into a ditch. Pursued by bursts of tracer, the Major started to run. Somehow he managed to reach cover, and waited till the Tiger grew impatient and trundled off. Then, venturing back to the road, he discovered that Shaunce had broken a leg. And, of course, General Maurice Rose was dead, the eleventh American general to be killed in action in the Second World War.

Not that Rose would have objected to such a death, if he had known it was coming. For Rose was cut in the same mould as Patton, who had once been his boss, and who desired to be killed 'by the last bullet of the last battle' rather than die in bed, old and senile. When the veteran war correspondent Hal Boyle, who had known the General since North Africa, heard the news of his death he wrote: 'Rose lived and died as a professional in a career he loved and followed since he was a boy of seventeen. He would be the last to regret that he had a soldier's ending.'

'Lightning Joe' Collins, who had unwittingly sent him to his death, remembered how Rose had always been up front when the battle was fiercest; as Rose had personally told him: 'General, there is only one way I know to lead this division, and that's at the head of it.' And that is how he died, thought Collins sadly when he heard the news.

Somewhere nearby, sprawled out on a debris-littered road beside a wrecked jeep, the body of General Rose started to grow cold and stiffen, the secret he had kept hidden these nearly thirty years about to be revealed at last.

SIX

'Bradley has feelings too'

In the pre-dawn darkness of this Saturday morning, the last day of March, 1945, two lone American sergeants were creeping towards the site of General Rose's ambush, with orders to find his body if possible and bring it back. General Collins had decided that Rose's body should not fall into enemy hands, and the officers of the 3rd Division agreed.

The two sergeants, Bryant Owen and Arthur Hauschild, had themselves been caught in an ambush that night, but in the confusion had managed to flee, ripping off their 'souvenirs' — German watches, Luger pistols and the like — while enemy tracer chased them across the fields. No one wanted to be taken prisoner by the SS with loot in his possession. But Owen and Hauschild were two of the lucky ones; they managed to make it back to their own lines within hours. Others, such as the dead General's aide, Major Bellinger, would take four days to return; some took weeks, and a few never returned at all. Not only did the two sergeants survive, they arrived back at their lines bearing an astonishing gift: one hundred Germans who had greeted them with hands in the air and surrendered eagerly.

'Je-sus Christ!' exclaimed the first American sentry they had encountered, on seeing the company-strength bunch of prisoners. Later Owen recalled that at that moment he could have kissed the bug-eyed, unshaven GI.

Now he and Hauschild were back out in the dark, looking for the spot where their dead commander lay. Apprehensive of lurking SS men, particularly as daylight was fast approaching, they moved cautiously from cover to cover. And within the hour they had found Rose, crumpled on the road where he had fallen, his body damp with dew.

Nervously the two sergeants searched the area. The General's jeep still stood nearby, and the armoured car, and neither appeared to have been touched by the Germans. Now they turned to the body. Rose's .45 pistol was still in its holster. Owen drew it out and put it in his own belt; one day he would return it to Rose's family. Even the General's maps had not been taken, all marked with information that would have been invaluable to German Intelligence. The two sergeants realized that the Krauts had not known whom they had killed.

Rummaging through the vehicles they found a brown GI blanket and wrapped it round the General's body, placing his helmet on his chest as befitting a dead warrior. Then they began to make the long return journey with their sad burden.

It had been a hard night. Both men were utterly exhausted, drained of all energy. They had seen their comrades dying like flies around them; some of their buddies still lay out in the dawn dew. They arrived back at their own lines with stumbling steps, dragging the corpse behind them, longing only for sleep.

This time their welcome was very different. They were met by a new second-lieutenant — a 'sixty-day wonder' as his kind was called by the veterans, because it took only sixty days to train a lieutenant of infantry. The baby-faced officer took one look at the corpse and exploded with anger. Why were they dragging Rose down the road like that? Couldn't they show any respect for their dead commander?

Owen's temper snapped. He had been through too much. Fiercely he gave the young officer a piece of his mind. The result was predictable. He was arrested and had to face a court-martial on a charge of insubordination.

General Rose was buried with full military honours. Six officers carried the coffin, draped with 'Old Glory', to the provisional cemetery at Ittenbach where Chaplain Maurer of the 3rd Division performed the last rites as it was lowered into the ground. The cemetery was already filling up. Long lines of simple wooden crosses, laid out with military precision, indicated the graves of so many young Americans who were paying the price of this drive into the Ruhr. And young Germans too, though the nearest German grave was fifty yards away from the American ones, separated from each other even in death.

By this time Rose's secret had begun to emerge. The General had been Jewish. The news spread through the 3rd's lines like wildfire, then reached the men of other divisions. The US Army newspaper, *Stars and Stripes*, reported the information in its columns and soon it appeared in the press back in the States.

In Berlin, Josef Goebbels received the news with glee. This was exactly the sort of fact that the 'Poison Dwarf' could build on, layer upon layer, turning it into propaganda to feed to the German people. Within hours he was reshaping the story of the Jewish general's death, both to strengthen the morale of his own side and to intimidate the enemy. The Werewolves were everywhere, he boasted; why, these brave undercover patriots had even been able to strike down an American general! A day later, one of his newspapers reported:

As this Jewish General appeared in Paderborn, he was surrounded by a group of German civilians and ordered to put his hands up. The Jew followed the command. Then one of the civilians drew a pistol and shot him down with five shots . . .

Another newspaper referred to *Fememord*, the medieval German custom of secretly condemning someone to death and then carrying out the sentence by murder; Rose's death, it declared, was just such a 'Werewolf-revenge murder'.

For a while the US Army Judge Advocates's Branch would take Goebbels' propaganda seriously. Under the file number 'Case 12-407' they would start a murder hunt for the alleged Werewolves who had slain the Jewish General. But in the end they gave up, concluding that Rose had been killed in combat through a genuine misunderstanding. By that time, however, many young SS prisoners had paid for his supposed murder with their lives. That lonely village cemetery at Ittenbach still contains the mouldering bones of some who died in 1945 simply because they wore the silver SS insignia of the black guards, the back of their heads smashed in by a single shot fired at close range.

That same dawn on which the two sergeants dragged in their dead General wrapped in an army blanket, the men of A Company of the 104th Division's 410th Infantry were just beginning to wake up in the tiny village of Medelon.

One of them, Staff Sergeant Chris Cullen, was just rubbing the sleep from his eyes — the previous day had been hell for the 104th — when he saw some newly liberated Polish slave labourers running down the cobbled street towards their house in panic-stricken terror. '*Panzer . . . panzer!*' they seemed to be crying.

'Damn crazy Polacks,' he cursed, telling himself they were drunk or something. Suddenly there was the unmistakeable high-pitched hiss of a Spandau machine gun. Grabbing his combat boots, he was just pulling them on when one of his men rushed into the room. What was going on, Cullen asked.

'Plenty!' the other man gasped. 'There's a Kraut tank coming down the street!'

Cullen wasn't particularly alarmed. He was a veteran; he told himself that people always exaggerate when they get excited. Still, he would go and see for himself. To his horror he found the man was right. About forty yards away there was a German self-propelled gun with a cannon in its turret that 'looked as large as a telephone pole', he remembered later.

Cullen did some quick thinking. His group consisted of sixteen infantrymen, two disabled tanks and their crews, all under the command of Lieutenant Howard Doyle — perhaps thirty men in all, and now there seemed to be Germans everywhere. But already the little bunch of trapped men were reacting. Sergeant 'Hub' Turley rushed to his broken-down Pershing tank and struggled single-handed to get the gun into action. Another brave NCO, Sergeant Luna, pelted out under fire towards another tank to fetch extra bazooka ammunition, going all out, arms working like pistons. As Sergeant Cullen said admiringly afterwards, 'That little guy could sure move fast when the spit (and he didn't say '*spit*' to the reporter) was flying.'

Now the battle began as a crazy wild group of SS men came running down the street, 'yelling and hollering as loud as they could,' as if they were high on drugs or drink, or both. A German officer popped his head out of his turret in the same instant that his gunner slammed a shell at close range into one of the helpless, stalled US tanks. '*Heil Hitler!*' he yelled in triumph. His gunner fired another shell. It screeched in white fury towards the next American tank. Again the commander popped up his head. This time it was 'just once too often' for one of Cullen's men named Shorty. He 'nailed him'.

But there were plenty more of them to nail as Americans and Germans slugged it out in the twisting, narrow streets of the medieval village and the buildings shook and trembled under the impact of exploding shells, with plaster and bricks raining down on the confused mêlée below.

Gradually the Americans got the upper hand. The German SP backed out of the village. Cheered by this sight, Cullen's men stepped up the pressure, and soon captured one of the feared German Spandaus which could fire a tremendous 1,000 rounds per minute. They turned it against its former owners. Now the SS began to give ground, while the Americans cheered each other on. They forced the SS to retreat along the road which led up the heights towards Winterberg — until finally the Germans' spirit broke and they fled in a headlong scramble for safety from the lethal fire of their own Spandau.

It was time for the handful of defenders to tally the score. There were dead and dying Germans lying everywhere. The little group of American infantrymen had been attacked by a company-strength SS unit supported by four tanks; but had sent them flying, with fifteen killed and twenty-six captured — at the price of one casualty: Pfc McBride, who had suffered a slight wound in the leg.

It had not been a very promising start for Bayerlein's counter-attack. In fact, all along the line he found the Americans were reinforcing. He hit two battalions of their 1st Infantry Division in Büren; but now their 8th and 9th Divisions were rushing in to help.

The men of the US 9th Infantry Division were veterans; they had been fighting the Germans for three years now, ever since North Africa. Both they and their comrades of the 8th had fought in the Hürtgen forest and they were eager to pay off those old scores, to avenge the deaths that Model had inflicted on them in that 'Green Hell'. The 'Old Reliables', as the men of the 9th called themselves, had suffered nearly fifty per cent casualties in the Hürtgen — indeed, in one of their regiments, the 60th Infantry, the turnover of fighting troops had exceeded one hundred per cent. They had good reason to hold a grudge against the Germans.

Now the Americans faced their enemy with renewed determination, undeterred even by a freak snowstorm in the hills. But their doggedness was matched by the fanaticism of the young SS men. Fierce battles broke out in villages, in country lanes, in the resort hotels of the area, wherever the two sides encountered each other. In one village the 'Old Reliables' found themselves fighting 'gangster style' as their Divisional History records, with the SS men trapped in a hotel lobby, 'shooting it out from behind sofas and chairs'; and

when they ran out of ammunition they bombarded the Americans
with champagne bottles.

The 8th Division, too, was meeting ferocious resistance from
the SS. On one day alone the men of the 'Golden Arrow'
Division, as they called the 8th, suffered no fewer than seventeen
counter-attacks. It was during one of these that Private Wenzel
became the recipient of the fifth Congressional Medal of Honor to
be awarded in the battle of the Ruhr. He and his comrades were
caught in a cottage, battling it out with the *Volksgrenadiers*, when
a stick grenade was lobbed through the window. Yelling a warning
to his fellows, Wenzel threw himself on the grenade, giving them a
moment's respite in which to seek shelter. The grenade exploded
beneath him. He died within minutes from the terrible wounds he
received — never knowing that his comrades successfully fought off
the German attack, or that he had won the posthumous award of
America's highest honour.

Still the Americans were attacking and Bayerlein's men counter-
attacking. Pushing ever onwards, Task Force Lovelady of the 3rd
Armored eventually reached the outskirts of Paderborn — unaware
that the Corps Commander, 'Lightning Joe' Collins, had changed
his plans and Paderborn would no longer have any significance.
And it was here that they avenged what they thought to be the
cold-blooded murder of General Rose.

The German General Lippert had been quietly working in his
garden when informed of the approaching *Amis*. He hurried into
his house and changed into dress uniform, complete with medals,
before attempting to escape through the nearby woods. He was
too late. Some men from the 3rd had spotted him. According to
the Task Force history, the Americans ordered him to halt, but he
refused, so they shot him with 'a few well-placed bursts from a
Tommy gun'. Well, that is the official story.

The fact is that the Americans at the point, from both the
3rd and the 2nd Armored Divisions, were in no mood to play
games with the Germans. If an enemy soldier failed to surrender
immediately — especially if he wore the tell-tale insignia of the SS
— he was brutally shot down. Not only soldiers; German civilians
too were killed if the Americans suspected them of treachery or of
harbouring the enemy. In one village just south of Paderborn where
the 3rd was still slogging it out, an American ambulance was fired
upon. The men of the 3rd promptly turned on the locals, dragging
them out of the nearest houses. While the houses were set on fire,

at least two young German boys were shot in revenge. As even the official US history of the war, Charles MacDonald's *The Last Offensive*, admits:

The more serious crimes — desertion, misbehaviour before the enemy, murder, rape, and assault with intent to commit rape — sharply increased in March and would continue to do so through the rapid drive across Germany . . . . In great measure it could be attributed to the larger number of troops in Germany, to lessened control and supervision by officers in mobile warfare, and possibly to the soldier's knowledge that he would be moving on rapidly and thus was less likely to be apprehended for the crime.

To this day, local historians and old people in the villages along the Americans' route still tell horror stories of the time when the *Amis* arrived. '*Vae victis — wehe dem Besiegten!*' (woe to the conquered) is the universal phrase on their lips. They talk of looting, rape, wanton destruction and murder. In the village of Etteln, the locals still point to a hedge behind which they found eighteen young SS that Saturday, all killed by a shot at the base of the skull. In the cemetery at Friedental-Boddeken they point to the graves of young men, telling of one who had just been called up for the Wehrmacht and was still wearing his civilian suit beneath his army coat when he died.

Yet these same locals, decent retired farmworkers, housewives, schoolmasters and the like, deny any knowledge of the greater horrors that for years had been perpetrated under their very noses: in the mysterious seventeenth-century castle at nearby Wewelsburg, soon to be blown off the face of the earth by SS commandos, taking its grisly secrets with it.

Wewelsburg and its castle, Schloss Wewelsburg, lay in a valley to the south of Paderborn, not far from the small town of Büren. The Schloss had first attracted the attention of *Reichsführer SS* Himmler in 1933, the year that Hitler came to power. One year later the 'half-schoolmaster, half-crank', as Speer once called Himmler, rented the derelict, turreted castle from the Büren authorities for a token payment of one Reichsmark. Thereafter the Schloss and its surroundings became a restricted area for all but senior SS personnel.

A sallow-faced man, who, with his prissy air, pince-nez and paunch, really did look like some provincial schoolteacher, Himmler was obsessed with pseudo-Germanic mythology. He had heard the old legend that Schloss Wewelsburg would survive alone when the pagan hordes attacked from the east; he knew its predecessor, on the same site, had withstood the attacks of Attila the Hun back in the fifth century. Now he intended to turn the castle into a kind of SS Valhalla. He set up a vast circular table in the castle's banqueting hall and surrounded it with chairs each bearing the name of an important SS general on a silver plate. Down below in the crypt, with its walls five feet thick, he had his holy of holies: whenever an SS general died, his body would be brought here and burnt ceremonially and an urn containing the ashes would be placed on one of the stone pedestals standing around the walls.

For all his crack-pot theories, however, Himmler was eminently practical. The reconstruction of Schloss Wewelsburg demanded labour, cheap labour; and Himmler knew where to look. Unlike many of the other Nazi leaders, such as 'Fat Hermann' Goering, Himmler had never tried to enrich himself by confiscating the possessions of others, by requisitioning whatever he took a fancy to or even by downright theft. On the contrary, he was exceedingly careful to account for all public monies in his charge; he even took out an official Party mortgage to pay for a home for his mistress. Now he turned to the teeming concentration camps for his source of labour. It was too costly and inconvenient to collect his slaves from camps all over Germany, so in 1938 he set up the smallest self-supporting concentration camp in the whole of the Nazi empire, specially to work on his castle. Here, at Camp Niederhagen, a total of 3,500 prisoners were set to work reconstructing Schloss Wewelsburg.

Between 1938 and 1943, at least 1,285 of the camp's inmates died. In 1943 most of the survivors were transferred to Buchenwald, where their fate was not recorded. For in that year the castle's reconstruction was halted; Himmler's dream project now had to be shelved while the Schloss took on a new role — that of a training centre for the young men and women who had volunteered to join the top-secret Werewolves.

A few hundred prisoners were kept behind to serve these fanatical young volunteers, but thousands of others had died. Of course the local people must have known what was going on — the same people who later complained so bitterly of the 'war crimes' committed by the Americans during the Battle of the Ruhr. Prisoners had to be brought in by public transport and bodies had to be disposed of (there were no ovens at Niederhagen). Local

German skilled labour — architects, surveyors and the like — had to enter the camp and castle to assess who was available and what had to be done. Local doctors had to issue death certificates when the inmates died.*

But now the Schloss was in an uproar. The *Amis* had almost taken Büren, where 'they even defecated in the Burgomaster's office' as one female clerk complained over forty years later; soon they would turn their attentions to the Schloss and the camp. Something had to be done to hide what had been going on there all those years since 1938.

The Werewolves were ordered to blow up their ammunition dump and leave the castle, to filter through American lines and make for Bavaria if possible. Meanwhile, the last surviving inmates of the camp — forty-two men and women in all — were 'liquidated' just hours before the Americans could reach them. And, on orders from Himmler himself, now in Berlin, Schloss Wewelsburg was destroyed in a series of vast explosions.

The evidence of Himmler's evil-doing at the Wewelsburg was thus blown to the winds. Elsewhere, however, there were other dark secrets that the retreating Germans had been unable to hide.

Although the SS still held the Americans below Paderborn and Bayerlein's counter-attack was having some success, cutting the 3rd's main supply route in two places and forcing the 104th Infantry Division to attack to the rear, Model was a worried man. In fact, his nerve was beginning to crack. Time was running out fast if he wanted to escape the trap the *Amis* had planned for him; and Berlin was sitting on its hands doing nothing! Indeed, ever since the *Ami* attack had started, Model repeatedly complained to his Chief-of-Staff, General Wagener, not one single senior officer of the Wehrmacht's General Staff had come to visit him on the 'Remagen Front' to see what was really going on.

But on this Saturday Model's HQ did receive a message from Berlin: 'I need Colonel Reichhelm for a task which will be decisive for the fate of Army Group B,' it began. And it was signed 'Adolf Hitler'. Wagener handed the message to the officer concerned, one of Model's senior staff, with a blunt suggestion as to what he should do with it.

*It is from these death certificates that we know the approximate number of those who died at Camp Niederhagen. *Reichsführer SS* Himmler was very pedantic in his book-keeping.

The task Hitler had in mind for Reichhelm was to join a new army being formed on the other side of the Elbe by General Wenck, one of Germany's most capable generals. But Reichhelm did not want to go. Not that he had much desire to stay here where the Field-Marshal treated him little better than a dog. Day after day he had brought Model only bad news and Model always expected a staff officer to have three different solutions ready at hand whenever he reported bad tidings. But this March there had been no possible solutions he could offer. As a result he had repeatedly taken the brunt of the Field-Marshal's fury.

Reichhelm greatly admired his Chief but one day he had been unable to stand it any longer. He had grabbed a bundle of papers and thrown them at Model's feet before storming out of the room, fists clenched in impotent anger. And yet, despite Model's constant bad temper and insults, he was loyal; he didn't want to leave him. But no one dared to disobey an order that came directly from the Führer. So Reichhelm prepared to leave. Before going, however, he went to see his Chief one last time. Model suddenly rounded on him, accusing him of cowardice, of seeking to save his own skin by escaping from the *Ami* trap. Reichhelm left, burning with rage.

That same day Berlin asked for another of Model's senior officers to take over a unit in Wenck's new army: the tall, blond General Gerhard Engel, commander of the 12th People's Grenadier Division. Formerly Hitler's Wehrmacht adjutant, up till 1943 when he asked for frontline duty in Russia, Engel had served under Model's command in the west since September, 1944. Now as Engel came to his headquarters to take his leave of Model, the latter had a request.

Engel found Model to be 'very earnest' and wondered what was coming. The Field-Marshal told him he thought the situation very serious, though Engel had the impression that Model had made no decisions about his personal future. In the end the Field-Marshal asked Engel, if he chanced to speak to the Führer, to explain to him just how serious the situation in the Ruhr was; it might only be a matter of weeks, perhaps days, before it was all over. It was Model's opinion that this was Germany's last opportunity to make peace with the Anglo-Americans. Engel promised he would pass on the Field-Marshal's views to the Führer if he saw him in Berlin, then left. He would never the see the Field-Marshal again.

Many years later, however, just before his death (and Gerhard Engel would die in bed an old man, unlike the Field-Marshal), he maintained:

I think, despite everything, Model still felt there was a chance. Of course, most of us were blinded by Goebbels's propaganda at the time, believing that the Western Allies and Russia would go for each other in the end and that Germany might find a place fighting against the Russians in the Allied camp. But Model didn't cling to that kind of vain hope, I feel. Somehow I think on that Saturday he believed we could just stop the war, in the west at least, and walk away from it — to let somebody else pick up the pieces. You know, like those gallant officers in those romantic nineteenth-century paintings of the battlefields. All heroics and bleeding hearts. In essence, he was just sticking his head in the sand.

Model was not the only senior soldier sticking his head in the sand that day. Field-Marshal Bernard Montgomery still believed that he, his friends in the British Army, and Churchill could change Eisenhower's mind and reverse the minor flank role that apparently would soon be allotted to his Second British Army.

Churchill was indeed trying. That Saturday, 31 March, 1945, he wrote to Eisenhower to restate his own preferred course of action.

I do not consider myself that Berlin has yet lost its military and certainly not its political significance. The fall of Berlin would have a profound psychological effect on German resistance in every part of the Reich. While Berlin holds out, great masses of Germans will feel it their duty to go down fighting .... Therefore I should greatly prefer persistence in the plan on which we crossed the Rhine, namely that the Ninth US Army should march with the Twenty-First Army Group to the Elbe and beyond Berlin. This would not be in any way inconsistent with the great central thrust which you are now so rightly developing as the result of the brilliant operations of your armies south of the Ruhr. It only shifts the weight of one army to the northern flank and this avoids the relegation of His Majesty's forces to an unexpected restricted sphere.

But Brooke, the dour Ulsterman, did not feel that Churchill's flowery compliments would work. 'Brilliant operations' indeed! In Brooke's opinion, Eisenhower's unilateral change of strategy and the whole matter of Simpson's Ninth Army being transferred to Bradley could all be ascribed to 'national aspirations', as he put it, 'to ensure that the US effort will not be lost under British command'.

And Brooke was right, of course, though Eisenhower's loyal supporters didn't think so.

Eisenhower and Kay Summersby spent the 31st at Bradley's HQ in Luxembourg, where Bradley had thrown a party for them, and he did not receive Churchill's plea until the following day. As Mrs Summersby noted in her diary:

Message from the PM. He does not agree with E's directive. He wants Monty to retain command of the Ninth Army and march to Berlin. The PM points out the importance of the latter plan, he also emphasizes that the fall of Berlin would have a profound psychological effect and political effect on the Germans. He almost accuses E of belittling the British forces. The PM's message upset E quite a bit. He is the only person in this whole campaign, irrespective of nationality, who is utterly selfless! *

But perhaps the most revealing comment on the in-fighting of that Saturday is the interchange between 'Simbo' Simpson, Montgomery's partisan at the British War Office, and 'Jock' Whiteley (Eisenhower's British Chief-of-Operations), a partisan of the Supreme Commander. 'Simbo' said to 'Jock': 'Can you not imagine Monty's feelings when he finds that his most promising plan has been whittled down?'

Jock replied: 'Oh Simbo, do try and be fair. Bradley has feelings, too. He must be allowed to have the Ninth Army for a bit.'

Despite all their efforts, the British failed to make Eisenhower change his mind. The die was cast. Montgomery was out of the running and Bradley was in sole charge now. A few days later the Ninth Army would come under Bradley's command, and he would become the first American general ever to command four US armies in the field — just under one and a half million US soldiers.

Bradley's wishes were now paramount. How else can one explain what happened as dusk fell on this Saturday?

Collins was worried. Although he seemed to have stopped Bayerlein's counter-attack, his Corps was strung out over 175 miles from Remagen to the outskirts of Paderborn. Admittedly he

---

*It is interesting and significant that Mrs. Summersby records virtually the same points made by Churchill. It would appear, therefore, that she was privy to the most secret messages passed between heads of state and the Supreme Commander.

now had five infantry divisions — the 78th, 8th, 9th, 104th and 1st — plus the 4th Cavalry Group defending this line; but they were thinly spread out, boxing in a whole German army group. Besides, there was an escape route open to the Germans: west of Paderborn, on the north face of the Ruhr. This was on the Ninth Army's front 'which as far as I then knew was still under Montgomery's control', Collins recalled long after the war. So he now took a step which was eloquent testimony to the toughness of the SS resistance south of Paderborn — and also to the fact that he realized Montgomery's power was on the wane.

Bradley wanted his 'bag- — the encirclement of the Ruhr — and Collins was determined he would get it. As he later admitted himself, he now 'went outside normal command channels'. Just as Eisenhower had caused a rumpus in the British camp on 28 March by addressing Stalin, the head of another state, without reference to his political masters in Washington, Collins now approached the head of another army, the US Ninth, without approaching Montgomery through channels first.

Collins and General William Simpson, the head of the US Ninth Army, knew each other well, of course. Their fathers had both fought in the Civil War, albeit on opposite sides. In the cutbacks of the early '20s, both men had languished for years as humble captains, then both had been appointed instructors at the US Army's War College. Finally they had both come to Europe as divisional staff officers. 'Big Simp', an immensely tall man with a shaven skull and huge beak of a nose, would understand his problems, Collins thought this Saturday evening, and decided to call him on the telephone.

Simpson did indeed listen sympathetically as Collins explained his position. He had run into an 'SS hornets' nest' that might sting for days, Collins said. Meanwhile, prisoners were telling their interrogators that the German High Command was planning another major breakout of the Ruhr further south. The whole Ruhr 'sack' was in jeopardy.

'For God's sake, Bill,' Collins said plaintively, 'get Monty to let you release the 2nd Armored for a drive on Paderborn! I'll send a combat command of the 3rd Armored across to meet the 2nd at Lippstadt. We'll then have the Ruhr wrapped up.'

In other words, Collins wanted to shorten the distance between the two armies by linking up at Lippstadt, twenty-two miles east of Paderborn. Thus he would avoid having to wait for that 'hornets' nest' to be cleared before the link-up was achieved.

Simpson agreed to do what 'Lightning Joe' requested. He'd switch the 2nd Armored from the Beckum area and direct it to Lippstadt. And that was that. Collins had made an unprecedented move (channels of communication were as strict in the American Army as they were in the British), and now Simpson did something equally significant: he ordered General White, commander of the 2nd Armored Division, to attack towards Lippstadt — *without consulting Monty.*

As Churchill was to comment ruefully, when he realized that the future in Germany lay now in American hands: 'There is only one thing worse than fighting with allies and that is fighting without them.'

Back on 28 March, the same day that Eisenhower made his fateful decision in Rheims, they were still digging out the bodies from the ruins of what had been Hughes Mansions in Stepney. On Tuesday, the day before, a V-2 rocket had landed directly on the estate of five-storey flats in Vallance Road in London's Stepney. It had killed 134 humble cockneys and seriously injured many others — some of them still trapped. One eye-witness from Whitechapel Fire Station later recalled the horror and confusion as distraught relatives sought each other amid the crowds of onlookers: 'I remember one chap covered in blood, running down the road, carrying what had once been a whole, live baby, calling his wife and some people grabbing him and leading him away.'

That had been Rocket No 1114. Rocket No 1115 landed even as the wreckage at Hughes Mansions was still being cleared. It struck home at Staveley Road, Chiswick, injuring about seventy. But that was the last rocket. The terrible V-2 campaign launched by the Reich against Britain the previous summer was over. The rockets had killed 2,754 and injured a further 6,523. Morale in south-east England, the main target of the V-2, had sunk to a low ebb; although the Germans didn't know it, their scientists had created a war-winning weapon, but one that had come too late. As Hitler told General Dornberger, head of the V-2 project, in 1943, 'If we had had this rocket in 1939, we would never have had this war.' And undoubtedly Hitler was right. With a weapon against which there was no defence, he could have blackmailed any nation into surrender without a fight.

On that same Wednesday, just as the V-2s had stopped falling on the British capital, far away at the remote village of

Bromskirchen in the Ruhr a goods train pulled into the Station, each wagon laden with a long cylindrical object hidden by a tarpaulin. According to Willi Wind, the station master, the engine driver of the first locomotive then drove off hurriedly in the direction of Winterberg, while the driver of the second engine started to fill the boiler of his steam engine with the water he would need to continue his journey. As Herr Wind later recalled: 'Suddenly a tank appeared on the country road to our left. Immediately the tank — an American one — opened fire. The steam engine took a shell in the boiler which opened up a fifteen-centimetre hole. At once the train personnel took off, followed a minute later by the military guard.'

At first the American tankers, from one of the many marauding groups of the 3rd Armored, didn't know what to make of this strange goods train. As Herr Wind said, 'They could identify the flak guns mounted on the wagons of course. But the long goods wagons with the objects covered in tarpaulin puzzled them. Finally they figured out that the train was carrying some of Hitler's "wonder weapons" — the V-2.'

Thereafter things happened fast. Technicians hurried up, swarming over the train. As the Americans apparently feared that there might be some sort of counter-attack to recapture the V-2s, or perhaps that their own air force might attack the train, the damaged locomotive was speedily uncoupled. A tank crawled onto the lines facing the train. In low gear, its engines racing mightily, with the other American tankers cheering its sweating driver on, the Sherman began to push the wagons into a nearby tunnel, where it could more easily be protected.

The officer who would now take over that train and its all-important cargo was a young American of Irish-American descent, James Hamill. He had arrived at Supreme Headquarters in Paris a couple of months before, to help in the task of collecting prime-quality German weapons for testing back in the States — Tiger tanks, electric mortars and the like.

When news of the discovery of the first intact V-weapons reached Hamill's boss, Colonel Holgar Toftoy, Head of US Ordnance Intelligence in Europe, he urged Hamill to take very particular care of the train's top-secret cargo for 'our people back in the States' wanted to examine the rockets in every minute detail. And then, looking oddly embarrassed, Colonel Toftoy had added a warning: 'If anyone discovers you trying to get these things, remember you have no authority and I know nothing of the matter.' Hamill knew what his boss meant. The first eight V-2s were to be smuggled out of Germany, if possible, without the knowledge of America's erstwhile ally — *Britain*!

This ran quite contrary to Eisenhower's own edict which stated that all military secrets of this nature should be shared with the British. However, Captain James Hamill obediently set off for Bromskirchen to collect the rockets and ship them back across the Atlantic. Within days he had found several score more; they too were sent to the States under conditions of strictest secrecy. Soon they would be followed by the very German scientists who had built them and who now would play such a crucial role in turning America into a superpower.

For Hitler's scientists had just escaped in time from the trap being sprung in the Ruhr on this last day of March. Heading south to Bavaria, they reached the haven of a mountain village, seemingly unaffected by the war. As one of them — Dornberger himself, leader of the V-2 programme — later wrote:

We lay on the terrace of our quarters and let the sun beat down on us. We gave ourselves to our thoughts, argued about our more important projects and slowly achieved detachment from the march of events. Above us towered the snow-covered Allgäu Mountains, their peaks glittering in the sunlight under a clear blue sky. Far below it was already spring. The hill pastures were a bright green. Even on our high mountain pass, the first flowers were thrusting buds through the melting snow. It was so infinitely peaceful here!

Far from the pastoral scene, in the grimy working-class boroughs of London — Stepney, Finsbury, Deptford and the like — there was no joy in the new spring, only mourning for the dead and a weary resignation as they tried to resume some semblance of a normal life among the ruins. While the German scientists settled down in their cosy Alpine retreats, enjoying esoteric discussions about the cosmos as they awaited the arrival of their new employers, the *Amis*, the mutilated survivors of their handiwork prepared for a lifetime of illness, disablement, blindness.

Thus March, 1945, came to an end. It had been a tremendous month for American arms and American generals. The Germans were virtually defeated, and the US Army had played the major part in that defeat. The British had been put firmly in their place by the 'Johnnies-come-lately'. American generals were making all the decisions now. With no regret, even with a sense of vindictive satisfaction, they overruled that old man in London, much given to whisky and brandy. As for his holier-than-thou senior commander in Europe, Montgomery, he was where he deserved to be — well and truly out in the cold!

Now, for better or worse, *they*, the American generals, would shape the face of Central Europe for the future. And, to cap it all, they had just come into possession of a new and terrible weapon which, together with the atom bomb they were already manufacturing, could make them the masters of the world if they so wished. The American Age was already beginning to dawn. The future was *American*.

That day a skinny little boy with a strange purple birthmark edging from beneath his hairline like trickling blood went to his lessons in a school in the far-off Russian Caucasus. On the other side of the world, in California, a handsome Hollywood actor in his thirties went about his business, masquerading as an officer in the US Army Air Corps. Neither of them knew of the events of 31 March, 1945: the decision that would change the shape of Central Europe; or the capture of that German weapon which, coupled with the atom bomb, would create the most formidable instrument of destruction of our time. But nearly half a century later, as General Secretary of the Soviet Union and President of the United States, they would still be trying to solve the problems created that March, while the rest of the world held its breath and hoped.

SEVEN

'A Soviet Target'

Now the great race was on. It was Sunday, 1 April, 1945 — April Fool's Day. Early this morning General Hinds, commander of the 'Hells on Wheels', ordered his Combat Command B to start rolling towards Lippstadt to link up with the First Army. Up front at the head of the leading American column was Lieutenant William Dooley of the 67th Armored Regiment. The young officer had no idea of the importance of his mission. All he knew was that he had been ordered to advance with all speed towards Lippstadt — so he did.

Somewhere to the east of his column, another American task force was heading for the medieval town of some 20,000 souls. It was Task Force Kane of the 3rd Armored Division, under the command of Lieutenant-Colonel Matthew Kane. It included a battalion of tanks, carrying the 'doughs' of the 104th's 414th Infantry who had ridden with the 3rd ever since the break-out from the Remagen bridgehead one week before.

Neither column met serious resistance. It was mainly small-arms fire, with here and there some lonely German youth armed with a *panzerfaust*, intent on the sudden destruction of a Sherman. Now and then the leading tanks ran into opposition from 88 mm anti-aircraft guns used in the ground role. For this had once been 'flak alley', where the massed ranks of German anti-aircraft guns defending the Ruhr had turned the approach run for RAF and USAAF planes into a bloody nightmare. But after a few rounds the dispirited German gunners, some of them young women, many of them boys of just sixteen, either fled or surrendered.

The Americans' progress was slow, however, hampered by thousands of refugees streaming south-west and by smaller groups of sullen men in field-grey looking for someone to surrender to. In the van, the battalion commander of the 3rd Armored Infantry asked for reinforcements to speed up progress. But General Hinds didn't want to delay while reinforcements were brought forward. He told the battalion commander, Colonel Arthur Anderson, that *he* was the reinforcements.

At least Hinds managed to divest himself of one unnecessary hindrance. General Raymond S. McLain, the heavy-set corps commander of the US XIX Corps to which the 2nd Armored belonged, had come up front to see how the great drive was going. Simpson was breathing down his neck and he knew Collins was desperate to achieve the link-up this Sunday. But Hinds didn't want McLain breathing down *his* neck. Persuading McLain that he was in danger so far up front, Hinds generously offered him his 'reserve' — his own personal tank and an armored car — to escort the Corps Commander to safety five miles to the rear. Fortunately McLain obliged and Hinds was able to get on with the business of winning the war without interference from the Top Brass.

Now it was dawn. The morning was bright and warm. The tanks and half-tracks rattled up the dead-straight roads, past orchards that were full of peach and cherry trees heavy with premature blossom, a bright pink and white; through little villages that had been untouched by war; past churches where the bells were pealing, calling the faithful Catholics to mass. It was Easter, after all. But here and there the local people, dressed in Sunday best, were met by groups of grim-faced Party officials who turned them back. God, this fine Easter Sunday morning, would have to wait until the imminent battle was over.

In Lippstadt itself, as the thunder of artillery grew ever louder, with black mushrooms of smoke ascending to the blue sky to the south, the authorities prepared for the action to come. Since 1936 this had been a German garrison town, but most of the garrison had now fled. The defence of Lippstadt would be in the hands of the local *Volkssturm* battalion under the command of a reserve infantry captain, Wilhelm Oberwinter. The battalion, made up of boys and old men, some older than sixty, was poorly armed. It was equipped with several antiquated machine guns and rifles, many of them Czech. Most of the men had no uniform either, but wore civilian clothes; the only thing that marked them out as soldiers was the armband each man wore bearing the legend 'Volkssturm'.

Hauptmann der Reserve Oberwinter was a realist. He knew that this collection of 'old buffers and callow youths' couldn't do much to stop the *Amis*. If he attempted to defend Lippstadt, the

Americans would promptly shell the town and his birthplace would be senselessly destroyed. But Oberwinter's views were not shared by everyone in Lippstadt. The local Party boss, Lücke, was adamant that the town should be defended — he personally would see that it was — and he found an ally in a wounded engineer officer, Friedrich Gerke, currently recovering in the local military hospital. The two of them decided that, come what may, they would destroy the two key bridges across the River Lippe, from which the town took its name, and thus halt the Americans' advance. But where would they get the necessary explosive? Captain Gerke had an idea. He knew that a number of V-1s, the celebrated 'doodle-bug', were stored in Lippstadt, each one containing a ton of high explosive. Volatile and dangerous as the explosive was, he felt he could manage to extract it from the bombs. That would give them enough to destroy at least two bridges.

Calmly Gerke went to work, apparently ignoring the fact that his actions might well result in the destruction of the whole town. Lücke meanwhile sent his bully boys into the streets, rounding up anyone who looked fit enough to help them erect barricades of earth, trainlines, furniture, anything to block the streets. The bully boys had lost some of their former swagger, but they were still armed and dangerous. Thus, while long columns of beaten German soldiers retreated through the town, some of them dragging their pathetic possessions in prams and carts, the Party members prepared to make a fight for it. As Oberwinter later remarked of Lücke's decision, 'Not only was it ludicrous, it was criminal as well.'

While the 3rd and 2nd Armored Divisions drove for the link-up at Lippstadt, the 104th and 9th Infantry Divisions of Collins's VII Corps were still struggling to keep Bayerlein's 53rd Corps from breaking through the ring that now almost encircled the Ruhr. In the wooded hills around Winterberg, armour was of little use. Neither was the Allied air force, for there was too much danger of the fighter-bombers hitting their own troops in the close battles below.

Now it was man-to-man fighting, with the American 'dough' slogging it out against the German 'stubble-hopper' — though the latter was supported by self-propelled guns. For the Germans had learned how to use armoured vehicles in poor terrain in Russia and were well in advance of their opposite numbers in tactics of this kind.

The Americans considered the terrain worse than the enemy. The Germans were up on the hilltops, some of which reached 2,500 feet or more, and it was a hard slog up the steep forested slopes, where every firebreak might conceal a German machine-gun firing along fixed lines of fire. Here the gasping, sweat-lathered GIs, laden down with fifty or sixty pounds of kit and weapons, were expected to make a last bold rush at the enemy with legs that felt as if they were made of soft pliable rubber.

Then there were the mines. The Germans were past masters in the art of sewing these evil devices; even at this eleventh hour they were still laying both anti-tank and anti-personnel mines — under the trails, the verges, even the ditches. Not only the forest, but any form of human habitation was always mined, down to that tempting bottle of wine or 'abandoned' camera; they were always booby-trapped.

And the mines came in all sizes, shapes and forms, with some being linked to others by fiendishly constructed 'matchbox detonators' — clip-like spring devices. When the first mine was found by an infantryman prodding at the ground with his bayonet, if he was not careful enough the matchbox detonator would set off a second and even a third mine, linked by wires to the first. There were wooden mines, plastic mines, even glass mines — none of which could be found by the conventional US Army mine detector but which, when they exploded, would leave another unfortunate 'dough' blinded or slumped on the floor, the blood jetting in a bright arc from a wounded leg or severed foot.

Prisoners when they were taken were still truculent and tough, as if these were the great days of 1940 when the Greater German Wehrmacht was at the height of its power and triumph, instead of 1945, with the German Army on the run and defeated, at the end of its tether.

One twenty-year-old lieutenant of the 751st *Jäger Regiment* (Light Infantry), captured that day by the men of the 104th Infantry Division, held forth to his captors without fear:

The Allies may succeed in occupying all of Germany north of Wurttemberg, Bavaria and Moravia. The Russians and the Anglo-Americans may join at the Elbe River. We shall then entrench ourselves in the impenetrable mountains and forests of southern Germany and Austria. But whatever stretches of land you may occupy in Germany you will never conquer or defeat the German nation. . . . A master race born to govern cannot be held down eternally.

The young officer, a product of nearly twelve years of National Socialist indoctrination, ranted on and on, lecturing his listeners on the true face of the Reich:

Do not underestimate us Germans. We have learned to hate a world of nations that is denying us living space. Great deeds inspired by this immortal and sacred hatred have been performed in the past. New war ruses will be born and new methods of fighting. . . . We Germans shall not rest until we fulfil Germany's mission. This mission is closely linked with the fate of National Socialism and if you want to destroy National Socialism, you must exterminate the German people first. We shall never capitulate!

It was a frightening, even awe-inspiring, torrent of defiance from someone whose life hung on a thread. It would take just one trigger-happy GI — and after the supposed murder of General Rose, there were many trigger-happy GIs now — and the young *Jägerleutnant* would be dead, there on the spot.

Fortunately, however, there were not many such fanatics left in the German Army, save in the paratroopers and the SS; and, slowly but surely, the men of the 9th, 1st and 104th Divisions succeeded in containing Bayerlein's thrust.

Bayerlein himself, although personally exhausted after nearly six years of constant combat, urged his men to greater efforts. At half a dozen points that day he exerted pressure in a desperate attempt to break through the American ring. When one failed, he thrust home another attack, and yet another.

As one disgusted, weary GI expressed it at the time, 'We wondered where the SOBs were coming from. We'd plug up one escape route out of the hills and the Heinies'd start coming outa another one. There were hundreds of the creeps!'

It was on this first day of April that the 'chocolate soldiers' of Hodges' First Army got their first taste of action.

Back in December, 1944, when the shortage of riflemen in the American Army in Europe was becoming acute, it was decided right at the top to break with segregation in the US Army, which had been strictly observed since the turn of the century. All-black combat outfits seemed to the Top Brass to have been failures,* so

---

*In Italy the all-black 92nd Infantry Division proved a total failure, breaking before the enemy. There were, however, all-black Army Air Corps units and two all-black tank outfits in Italy and north-west Europe which fought well.

in that month an appeal was launched, asking for volunteers from black service units to come forward and 'enjoy the privilege' of serving at the front with white infantrymen. Surprisingly enough there had been several thousand volunteers, despite the fact that the black was treated as a third-class citizen in his own country, totally ignored by the whites — 'the invisible man', as he called himself cynically. Whole units volunteered, many senior noncoms sacrificed their stripes in order to be accepted, and in the end some 2,500 black rearline troops were trained in a short conversion course as infantrymen. By now there were some fifty platoons of them scattered throughout Hodges' Corps.

In the case of the 104th Division, an all-Negro platoon — soon to be dubbed the 'Dusky Devastators' by *Stars and Stripes* — first went into action to clear two hills held by Bayerlein's men inside the Hardahausen Forest. Led by Staff Sergeant Harvey Moseley and Sergeant Howard Williams, a former boxer who had come to Germany in 1936 to box in the Olympics, the 'Dusky Devastators' advanced up the first hill. 'We had been told there were SS men in the woods,' one of them related afterwards. 'We didn't know exactly where they were — but we found out mighty quick!'

Moving forward in an extended line, tense and nervous, they had almost reached the edge of a clearing when an enemy machine gun opened up. The men hit the damp grass fast, but two or three had been wounded. One man called 'Big Slim' hearing the moans of his wounded comrades, decided to try and help the nearest of them. Ignoring the slugs cutting the air all around him, he got to his feet and darted forward. A German shell exploded, sending him flying again. Meanwhile his injured comrade, despite the fact that he had been wounded in arm and back, sat up and started firing wildly; under this covering fire 'Big Slim' at last managed to reach the wounded man and drag him to the safety of a ditch.

For a while the intense German fire kept them pinned down, but eventually the platoon began to advance again and cleared the two hills that were their objectives, in the process killing or capturing forty SS men. It was quite a credible effort for the 'invisible men' — or 'coons', according to some of their white comrades, who ate peanuts because they'd 'just come out of the trees' and still had their 'monkey tails' hidden beneath their pants (at least, that was the rumour the 'rednecks' spread among the wide-eyed German civilians who were seeing black men for the first time in their life).

That same day another black man in the 9th Division's 60th Infantry, Pfc Jack Thomas, went one further. Thomas was leading his squad to knock out a German tank which was covering a road block, holding up the advance of his company, when they came under intense fire. Undaunted, Thomas deployed his men and went on alone. He lobbed a couple of grenades at the Germans defending the barricade. Several reeled back wounded. But the two-man bazooka team that Thomas was relying on to deal with the tank once he had cleared the barricade, had by now been knocked out. He ran for the bazooka himself, despite the lead flying everywhere, and launched two rockets in rapid succession at the tank. Thereupon, the danger removed, he picked up the nearest wounded man and carried him back to safety under what the citation called 'intense fire'. For Jack Thomas had earned America's second highest decoration for valour, the Distinguished Service Cross, and he was the first black serving in the whole of the US Army in North-West Europe to do so.

But the price of proving themselves equal to their white comrades was high. Before the war ended, these black rifle platoons had suffered some twenty per cent casualties.

By now Bayerlein realized his attempt to break out around Winterberg had failed. His weakened three divisions, little more than battle groups, were no match for the American defenders; and from prisoners he knew that the *Amis* were hurriedly rushing more and more troops into the line to hold his attack. It was criminal to continue attacking and throwing away the lives of brave young men to no purpose. But what could he do?

Of course to his rear he did have the ski resort of Winterberg itself, an ideal place for a defensive stand. From there he could dominate the area around for many kilometres. But there was a catch. Winterberg was filled with German wounded. If he attempted to defend it, the helpless wounded, grouped in makeshift hospitals all over the resort, would suffer. The *Amis* wouldn't hesitate to throw the whole weight of their artillery and aerial bombardment at Winterberg. These days their *jabos* no longer respected the Red Cross flag. Even individual peasants working in their fields were shot up by the enemy pilots. Again, young men would die unnecessarily for a cause which was already lost.

Bayerlein decided that his only hope now would be if Model's promised attack, launched into the pocket from outside, caught the *Amis* off guard. But where was the 56th Corps and when was it going to attack?

The same question was bothering not only Model that April Fool's Day but his Supreme Commander, Field-Marshal Kesselring, too. Model was already worried by the three-pronged attack being launched on Paderborn by the 3rd Armored Division. The Americans were driving everything before them, attacking with tremendous élan, and it could be only a matter of hours before Paderborn fell. Now he signalled 56th Corps, 'Report your attack position . . . . Please report hour of attack.'

But no answer came. In despair he sent off a staff officer to contact the commander of the 56th Corps. After an adventurous trip, the young staff officer managed to reach the Corps and duly reported the situation of Army Group B, stressing the urgent need for an attack. If Paderborn fell, which Model thought likely, the whole Army Group would be trapped. But the harassed commander of the 56th Corps had bad news for the weary, dirty staff officer. His Corps and Stern's *SS Brigade Westfalen*, which had withdrawn from the Paderborn area after the Rose ambush, were virtually surrounded themselves. There were *Amis* on three sides already. There would be no relief attack by the 56th Corps this day — or any other day for that matter.

As yet, of course, Kesselring had not heard the grim news. But he was already in a filthy temper. All day long, at his HQ in the village of Reinhardsbrunn, deep in the heart of the Thuringian Forest, he had raged at what he considered to be Model's mistake. He thought Model had ordered Bayerlein to attack in the wrong spot. Still, he hoped, an attack by the 56th Corps might even now bring success.

Kesselring was in for a shock. His Chief-of-Staff, General Westphal, now informed him that whether the 56th Corps attacked or not was immaterial. Bayerlein's own attack, in addition, had been for nothing. The Führer had just ordered that all further attempts to break out should be abandoned. The Ruhr was to be defended as a fortress.

Kesselring was dumbfounded. Hitler apparently 'thought that by defending the Ruhr, Model could pin down considerable numbers of enemy troops', as Kesselring himself recorded; enough troops in fact 'to prejudice a strong eastward drive' by the Americans. But as Kesselring knew, 'There was only enough food in the Ruhr to feed the troops of both Army Group and population for at most two or three weeks.' The Führer's orders were crazy. Kesselring admitted to himself now that the only hope lay not in defence but aggression, which — 'judging by what I had seen' — was no longer on the cards.

Model's reaction, however, is not recorded. We do know that upon receipt of the news he discussed surrender with his Chief-of-Staff. But both of them rejected it. Their comrades were still fighting elsewhere in Germany, and in the east against the hated Russians; both men felt they couldn't let those comrades down.

It is also known, from family letters and contacts, that Walter Model had still not lost all hope, although the situation in which he and his men now found themselves was desperate. Five days before, he had visited his eldest daughter, Hella, who found her father 'as active as ever' and animated by a 'certain degree of optimism'. Two days later Model wrote to his wife — on the occasion of Easter, for Model was still a believer and a church-goer — 'All fear comes from the Devil. Courage and joy come from the Lord.' However, there had been a slight note of pessimism, even fatalism, in the letter, which went on to state that 'we all must die at some time or other' and that one should be prepared to 'die happy'. In further letters, though, he insisted to his wife that soldiers and their wives must remain loyal and 'try twice as hard to do their duty'.

Now, as he learned that there would be no escape for him or his men from the Ruhr, Model set about tackling the new situation with his usual energy, as if there were still hope. He ordered von Lüttwitz, the gross-looking, bemonocled head of what was left of three divisions, now grouped together under his name as *Gruppe von Lüttwitz*, to send out Hitler Youths armed with *panzerfausts* to destroy Allied tanks and supply trucks.

Von Lüttwitz's Chief-of-Staff refused point-blank to accept the suggestion. He would not risk the lives of twelve- and thirteen-year-old boys in such a crazy fashion.

Model flew into one of his usual rages. He visited the Chief-of-Staff and threatened him with a court-martial. That would mean the death sentence for having refused a superior's direct order. But the Chief-of-Staff stood his ground. Model left, flushed with anger and bellowing at his driver and aides, shouting that he'd be back on the following day; if the Chief-of-Staff hadn't carried out his order by then, he'd be arrested. The Chief-of-Staff told himself he hadn't long to live. Model already had a reputation for summary executions of deserters, cowards, defeatists and the like. But he need not have worried. Model did not appear the following day. The juvenile fanatics in their short pants were not sent on their 'Ascension Day Commando', as the Germans called it — meaning a mission with a one-way ticket.

The episode was typical of Model. Even now he still believed that he could solve the overwhelming problem with these crazy stopgap measures, as he had often done in the past. Perhaps, too, he still had that illogical faith in the Führer possessed by many otherwise sane Germans: the belief that their leader still had something up his sleeve. But the Führer had no more aces. By the time that dusk came this April Fool's Day, the Americans would have linked up at Lippstadt and the fate of Model's Army Group B would be irrevocably sealed.

That Sunday Eisenhower received an answer to his communication of 28 March from 'Uncle Joe' himself. Stalin made four points: first, he stated that Eisenhower's plan to cut the German forces by linking up with the Russians at Leipzig 'entirely coincides with the plan of the Soviet High Command'; second, he thought the main Russian thrust should be in that same direction; third, he agreed 'Berlin has lost its former strategic importance'; fourth, only secondary Red Army forces would be allotted to the Berlin front. In short, Stalin was in complete agreement with Eisenhower's strategy. Berlin was only a name.

For years after the war, Eisenhower's supporters claimed that the Supreme Commander had been very naive about the Russians and that Stalin's answer, with reference to the lack of importance of Berlin, showed just how easily he was hoodwinked by them. He believed that Russia, like America, was 'free from the stigma of colonial empire building by force', as he wrote in 1948 in *Crusade in Europe*, and that the ordinary 'Russian man-in-the-street' was not much different from his American counterpart. Surely, therefore, America and Russia could 'work and live together' in a world at peace, couldn't they?

Naive Eisenhower may have been about the Russians, but that April he did know quite a deal about their real intentions. For one factor that all of Eisenhower's supporters left out of their calculations in the 1940s, '50s and '60s was that war-winning secret — Ultra. Through the decodes coming from Bletchley Park he knew virtually everything that was going on east of the German capital. For those tweed-jacketed, professorial gentlemen who ran that rusty Nissen hut were reading not only the Germans' top signals, but very probably the Russian ones, too!*

Why else would the Anglo-Americans go to such great lengths for decades after the war to keep the secret of the wartime Ultra? Why else would a top American general — 'Dutch' Cota, the hero of Omaha Beach — be threatened with a court-martial after a couple of his men lost 'a coding machine' while they were enjoying themselves in a brothel? What was so important about that machine? Why did neither Bradley nor Eisenhower explain in their memoirs that they had *known* the Germans were going to counter-attack at Mortain in 1944, when the US Army was waiting for them? Why did that uninhibited Anglophobe Ralph Ingersoll, with his constant distrust of British intentions, never elaborate on his statement made in 1946† that 'the British circulated documents amongst themselves labelled with a code-word known only to them'?

Why, when the war was over and the Germans indisputably beaten, did no senior Allied commander ever mention Ultra? The British were sworn to secrecy under the Official Secrets Act, but the Americans weren't. So why did they keep silent about Ultra? What value could it have had after May 1945?

There can be only one explanation. Ultra was being used against the Russians, too. David Eisenhower, the Supreme Commander's grandson, seems to think that in April, 1945 his grandfather was fully aware of the scale of the Russian build-up outside the German capital:

The estimated 750,000 troops that remained opposite Berlin would comprise the largest concentration of combat troops and supporting artillery of any battle in world history . . . . Berlin was a Soviet target, and a target of more than secondary importance — a point that required no elaboration.

So that April Sunday when he received Stalin's communication, Eisenhower must have known the Soviet leader was lying. Berlin *was* important to the Russians.

Yet still Eisenhower stood by his decision. For him, the German capital was 'nothing but a geographical location'. For him, the only important thing now was to win the final battle in Germany; it mattered not a whit where that battle was fought, only that the US

---

*It is known that, under the code-name of 'Bride', the Americans were reading the Russian diplomatic code traffic in the late 1940s.

†In his book *Top Secret*, Ingersoll, a one-time newspaperman, had also been a staff officer in Bradley's inner circle.

American medics with casualty on the west bank of the Rhine.

Foreign workers freed by the Allies after the advance into the Ruhr Pocket.

15. Germans looting an abandoned military goods train after the retreat of the *Wehrmacht*

16. German civilians show the white flag – but the troops fight on.

7. Essen, home of the Krupp steel works, after the Allied raids.

8. The Russians enter Berlin – 'nothing but a geographical location' – 28 April, 1945. The shattered Reichstag building bears witness to the extent of the devastation.

19. The last resource – children of the Hitler Youth taken prisoner in the [Pocket.

20. The *Wehrmacht* goes home.

Army should win it — and be seen to have won it by the folks back home. American prestige was at stake. What did it matter to him if some European city were seized by the Soviet Army? The postwar future of Europe was not his business. He could leave those problems to Churchill, de Gaulle and all the other Allied statesmen who'd been such a pain in the neck to him since 1942.

As President Truman acidly remarked a few years later, 'Eisenhower had to be led every step of the war'; as Supreme Commander he 'presided over meetings' and 'approved strategy that had been drawn up by other people, but he never did originate anything.' Well, now Eisenhower had approved Bradley's strategy. The US Army was going to win the final battle of Germany — in the Ruhr.

Meanwhile, in Moscow that first day of April, Stalin and his marshals were putting the final touches to their preparations for an all-out assault on Berlin.

By eight o'clock that morning, the Party Boss of Lippstadt had had his way. The two key bridges had been blown up with Gerke's explosives — and not a moment too soon. Already the Americans had reached the nearby village of Cappel and the first enemy tanks were heading for Lippstadt. The rumble of gunfire was approaching. Some of the town's church services were interrupted as parishioners were urged to take cover before the artillery bombardment began. Now the very air was heavy with suspense.

It was about this time that *Hauptmann der Reserve* Wilhelm Oberwinter of the *Volkssturm* decided that Lippstadt's only chance of survival lay in his hands. His plan was simple:

Pretending that it was necessary militarily speaking to do so, I was going to withdraw my battalion — without handing out the panzerfausts allotted to us — to the woods and beyond the canal. As soon as the men I left behind signalled that the Americans were entering the outskirts of Lippstadt, I would dissolve my battalion and send the men home as harmless civilians .... My hope was that if we didn't fight, the city would be spared by the Americans.

Even as Oberwinter began to put his plan into operation, Colonel Matthew Kane's column of the 3rd Armored was entering Lippstadt from the east. But the column soon ran into trouble. Advancing in single file, the men of the 3rd were led by a tank company, with the battalion headquarters half-track just behind the tanks; and in the half-track, standing bolt upright, was Captain Foster

Flegeal manning a .50 calibre machine gun. Suddenly the tanks rumbled to a stop, halted by a German roadblock, and ten enemy armoured vehicles came barrelling down a side-road. Their intention was obvious: they were going to cut right through the 3rd's line. But they hadn't reckoned with Captain Flegeal's quick thinking. He hit the button of the machine gun. A burst of tracer zipped towards the German vehicles, bouncing off their steel sides like glowing golf balls.

That first burst seemed to act as a signal for the rest of the US gunners. Everywhere they opened up with a will — and at that range they could hardly miss. Armour-piercing shells slammed into the enemy tanks, which erupted in a sudden fireball. Mushrooms of black, oily smoke, tinged with yellow flame, ascended to the morning sky. One by one the German vehicles shuddered to a halt, wrecked and burning. Screaming survivors stumbled black-faced towards the Americans, their arms raised in surrender.

Captain Flegeal halted for a while to detach a group of US medics to take care of the German wounded, and then he moved on again. The link-up, he knew, was vital; it had to take place this day.

Meanwhile, the leading column of the 'Hell on Wheels' was also approaching Lippstadt. A lone German tank attempted to bar the way, but didn't last long; soon it was a flaming wreck. Next a primitive barricade stopped them for a few minutes. Relentlessly the Americans pressed on, increasingly aware of the sound of firing to the east — though whether it was their own guns or the enemy's they did not know.

It was now that Sergeant Werner Osthelmer took up the point in his Sherman tank. He had only been with the 67th Armored since February and in spite of his rank was a relative new boy. But Sergeant Osthelmer, right out in front of the whole column, had an advantage that even the oldest veteran would have envied in his present situation, the most dangerous position of all in an advance. For Sergeant Osthelmer knew these roads as well as he knew the back of his own hand — he was returning to the place where he had been born!

Eight years before, Werner Osthelmer had left Lippstadt as a trained butcher to emigrate to Detroit where he had soon started his own shop. Now, after all those years, he was returning to his native Germany courtesy of the US Army. Later no one could state with any certainty whether it was pure chance that Osthelmer was at point that Easter Sunday, or whether it was by intention. One thing was for certain. If anyone was going to find his way into Lippstadt, bridges destroyed or not, it would be the ex-butcher.

Captain Gerke, the engineer officer who had blown the two bridges over the River Lippe at Lücke's orders, was watching from an upstairs window of a house in Wiedenbrucker Strasse when the first US Sherman rumbled into town. It stopped in front of the half-destroyed bridge near North Station. Gerke tensed himself, expecting the blast of a *panzerfaust*. But nothing happened. He cursed; where the hell was the *Volkssturm*? Even those old cripples should have seen this was the perfect target.

Calmly, as if this was peacetime, one of the *Amis* clambered out of the tank and walked to the bridge, examined the damage, then proceeded to jump up and down as if testing its strength. Still not a single shot was fired; the hidden engineer captain cursed again. He strained his ears to catch what the man was calling back to his fellows in the tank, and heard 'Okay', the only English word he knew. Slowly the Sherman started to move. Gerke tensed again. Surely the bridge wouldn't hold? But it did. With a growing sense of hopelessness he watched the Sherman cross the bridge, followed at a snail's pace by the other tanks.

Suddenly, as if from nowhere, a group of French ex-POWs sprang forward, cheering the Americans as they crossed the river into Lippstadt. Still standing upright in the lead tank's turret, Sergeant Osthelmer — who had been born less than a mile from here — acknowledged their cheers with due dignity.

Soon the town was swarming with American armoured infantrymen. Crowds of displaced persons and former POWs joined them in plundering the stores, throwing rocks through windows and grabbing what they could, breaking into the great warehouses and dragging out fifty-litre carboys of the powerful local schnapps. The Americans entered the Catholic Hospital and found a few of their own comrades being attended by the nuns, having been wounded and captured a few days earlier. Then, moving on to the central square, they burst into the bank, *die Landeszentralbank*, where they grabbed handfuls of banknotes, lighting their cigarettes with hundred-mark notes and using the thousand-mark notes for more basic purposes; latrine paper was in perennially short supply.

They approached the townhall a little cautiously. If the Krauts were planning a last-ditch effort anywhere it would be here. But Burgomaster Fuhrmann had ordered the policemen to leave. Now as a first burst of machine-gun fire hissed towards the building,

Fuhrmann went out to meet the *Amis*, frantically waving a makeshift white flag. The American infantry relaxed.

By half past twelve that glorious day, the Americans of the 'Hell on Wheels' had penetrated well into Lippstadt's suburbs. In charge of one group, Second-Lieutenant Donald Jacobsen was ordered to check out a rumour that some men were cut off in a hospital and needed help. He rounded up his men, still busily engaged in looting, and they pushed forward, suddenly anxious and tense again.

They need not have worried. In the German camp all was chaos, panic and confusion. *Hauptmann* Wilhelm Oberwinter had been watching their advance from his position near the Main Post Office. Now he sent a runner to his *Volkssturm* Battalion, with orders that all companies were to withdraw immediately. Once they were safely clear, they were to dump their arms and go home. They needed no urging. Swiftly they got rid of their weapons and armbands and demobilized themselves. Then they hurried off to their families, some returning from the big war by cycle!

While the Lippstadt Home Guard thus ended its brief inglorious career, the local population set about plundering the barracks they had just abandoned. One eye-witness remembers people staggering away with 'mountains of uniforms, underwear, feather beds, wool, boots and shoes. If the situation had not been so serious, one could have laughed at the sight.' Another eye-witness of that breakdown of order in Lippstadt was more inclined to weep. He was Major Dunker, the former commandant of Beckum — the very man who had taken the telephone call from that inn at Ahlen. The American staff officer had ordered him to surrender, and he had at length agreed to do so. Fleeing to Lippstadt, he was one of those who saw the American tanks arriving. It was a bad moment for him. 'I felt a cold shiver go down my spine,' he later confessed. 'Because I had given up Beckum without a fight, I now knew I had contributed to the closing of the Ruhr Pocket.'

But it was too late for such thoughts now. Already the survivors of the beaten *Wehrmacht*, those who had stayed behind in Lippstadt, were being rounded up. And not always just soldiers. Tramdrivers, postmen, railway men, anyone in a uniform was seized by the angry GIs and forced to march towards the rear, hands in the air.

Private Fritz Moos was with two companions when the dreaded moment arrived. To their astonishment, the GIs politely asked if they were soldiers. Amazed at such courtesy by frontline troops, they said they were and could they gather their few possessions before being taken away? Affably the GIs said they could. But once outside: 'We got a mighty kick in the arse so that we nearly fell to the ground, our possessions flying everywhere.' Fritz Moos and many hundreds more would spend the next few days crowded into a wet field with no food. Thereafter the Americans would 'sell' him to the French, who gave him one year's hard labour in France as the price of defeat.

Lieutenant Jacobsen and his men had completed their earlier mission; the hospital rumour had been false. Now they rejoined their comrades of the 'Hell on Wheels' on the eastern edge of the town. The battle for Lippstadt was nearly over. Just then someone spotted a distant trail of dust rising along one of the country roads. Jacobsen ordered his tanks to stop. He had heard nervous talk about the German 116th Panzer Division attempting to break out in this area. Were they Krauts?

The same thought went through Kane's mind, up front of the 3rd Armored's column. Those tanks he could see on the edge of town — they were not Honeys like his own. For it was Colonel Matthew Kane and his Honeys that Jacobsen had seen; and it was Jacobsen's new Pershings with their unfamiliar silhouettes that had worried Kane.

After a few minutes' stand-off while the two groups eyed each other apprehensively, one man detached himself from Jacobsen's group: Sergeant Snodgrass, from the 2nd Division, who drove cautiously forward in a lone Staghound armoured car. The link-up had been achieved!

For a while there was the usual backslapping, corny jokes and group photographs against the background of armoured vehicles; then it was over. It was just another job done. Or so they thought, those young men posing for the photographers. What they didn't realize was that, by completing the link up, they had just sealed the fate of over 300,000 men of Model's Army Group B. The Germans were trapped. The Ruhr Pocket — or 'Rose Pocket', as it was now being called in honour of the dead General — had been sewn up.

As Lieutenant Jacobsen later said, commenting on his own lack of concern about this historic moment: 'It's amazing how ignorant the fellows who really fight the war are.'

And on that Sunday, the Supreme Commander wrote a letter of condolence to the widow of that dead General:

Dear Mrs Rose

Although I have not been privileged to meet you personally, my admiration, respect and affection for your late husband were so profound that I felt impelled to send you some word of sympathy in your tragic loss. He was not only one of our bravest and best, but was a leader who inspired his men to speedy accomplishment of tasks that to a lesser man would have appeared almost impossible. He was out in front of his division, leading it in one of its many famous actions when he met his death. I hope that your realization of the extraordinary worth of his services to his country will help you in some small way to bear your burden of grief. The thoughts and prayers of his legion of warm friends in this theater are with you.

Maurice Rose was dead. So were hundreds of young men who had contributed their lives to the battle for the Ruhr Pocket. They, just as much as he, had died for an objective that soon proved to have been pointless, an objective that may even be said to have delayed the end of the war in Europe. They would soon be forgotten.

PART II

A Trap is Sprung

'Somebody ought to smack him down.'
Eisenhower (about Montgomery)
to General Marshall, February, 1945

ONE

'We're not going to Berlin'

On Monday 2 April, 1945, *Time* magazine featured on its front cover the US general who it proclaimed was 'the world's No.1 active airborne commander'. In its 'pony-size edition', reduced to the size of a pocket book and carrying no advertising, which was circulated to the men in Europe, it stated that the general in question 'looks like a Roman senator and lives like a Spartan hoplite'.* *Time* described him as 'ruggedly built' and 'husky, aggressive, driving'; his deeply tanned face was 'austere' and 'crinkled with lines natural to an outdoorsman'. The lead article stressed the general's love of sports and the great outdoors — he hunted, played tennis and rode — and maintained that his favourite leisure activities were playing cribbage and reading the British author Kipling. He was 'no hater of change and challenge' and he had welcomed his assignment from conventional infantry duty to the command of an active airborne unit.

The general the magazine honoured that day was the head of Bradley's XVIII Airborne Corps, Matthew Ridgway, and he certainly lived up to most of *Time*'s rhetoric. He had dropped with the 82nd US Airborne Division in Sicily back in 1943 and had been in the thick of combat ever since. Only the week before the article appeared he had been in action with his Airborne Corps on the Rhine, where he was involved in a fierce firefight with a German patrol. He killed one German personally before a grenade was flung at him. Fortunately for Ridgway the grenade merely wrecked his jeep; 'by the grace of God', as he wrote later, 'the wheel was between me and the blast and all I got was one small chunk that hit me in the shoulder'.

---

*Heavily armed foot-soldier in ancient Greece.

For that episode he was awarded the Purple Heart and received a letter from no less a person than the Supreme Commander himself: 'Someone told me you were slightly wounded. Thank God it wasn't serious!'

Ridgway was naturally very pleased by the *Time* write-up. As he wrote to the correspondent who had interviewed him:

I find my feelings hard to explain. Boyish pleasure, gratitude, and the sober determination to 'meet with triumph and disaster and to treat those imposters just the same' are mingled. My deepest pleasure will come from that which my wife will feel.

After all, a mere five years previously he had been an obscure middle-aged major; now, thanks to the magazine, he was known to the whole world.

But Ridgway was not so pleased by his new assignment this Monday. He had lost his airborne troops and it looked as if he would not command them in action again in Europe. The four American airborne divisions in Europe — the 13th, 17th, 82nd, his own old division, and the 101st — were now being used either as ordinary infantry or as reserves, waiting for their next combat jump which would probably be over Japan. As a result, the Airborne General had been given command of what was an ordinary infantry corps. Despite the fact that it would still bear the designation XVIII Corps, his new command was made up of footsloggers, pure and simple. Ridgway was back where he started, albeit much elevated in rank. He was back with the 'poor bloody infantry'.

Two of the divisions he had been allotted for his new assignment — General 'Count' Melasky's 86th and General Halsey's 97th — were completely new to combat. Both divisions were led by West Point classmates of his, but neither had heard a single shot fired in action. The other two did have some experience: General Parker's 78th Infantry Division and General Moore's 8th Infantry Division. But Ridgway was not impressed with either. The latter in particular, the 'Golden Arrow' Division, had had many ups and downs since first going into action in France in the summer of 1944. McMahon, the first commander, had been removed as incompetent after endangering the 82nd Airborne, then being led by Ridgway himself. Two further commanders had come and gone, and in the Hürtgen Forest the Division had been badly mauled. Indeed, in February, 1945, Ridgway had specifically asked General Hodges of the First Army *not* to assign the 8th Division to his command. Now led by their fourth divisional commander in nine months, General Byrant Moore, the 'Golden Arrow' men were an unknown quantity for Ridgway.

He was also dubious about Parker's 78th Division, the 'Lightning Division', as it was known from its divisional patch. The men of the 78th had first gone into action on the German frontier the previous winter, and they too had suffered badly in the Hürtgen. But Parker's leadership had been found wanting and his operations were in effect planned for him by General Craig, commander of the veteran 9th Infantry.

Now, with these four divisions, Ridgway was going to embark on a new mission. Earlier this day he had been summoned at short notice from his HQ at Epernay to meet Hodges somewhere on the Rhine. For hours on end he had driven up and down in a borrowed jeep, together with his aide Don Faith, looking for the elusive Army Commander. There was a heavy, murky fog and as Ridgway remarked afterwards, 'my driver had not been taking his carrot juice as he should have been'. Time and time again, groping through foggy woods, the hapless driver narrowly missed running off the road or into trees. In the end Ridgway ordered the driver to move over and he took the wheel himself. Now and again they saw MPs, whom they stopped to ask where Hodges was; but the MPs apologized, saying they had no idea. As Ridgway commented tartly, 'I thought the people who should be apologetic were the members of the staff back at First Army rear. It is a serious thing to lose your own advanced CP — especially when the Army Commander is in it!'

But finally Ridgway had found Hodges who then briefed him on his new operation. While both the First and Ninth Armies would head on to the Elbe, Hodges informed the Airborne Commander, some eighteen divisions would remain to watch the Ruhr Pocket. In the First Army sector, General van Fleet's III Corps and his own XVIII Airborne Corps would take over this task. Ridgway's task was to hold a line sixty-seven miles long, anchored on Bonn on the Rhine in the west and Siegen on the River Sieg in the east, where the XVIII Airborne Corps joined with General van Fleet's III Corps.

Ridgway's reaction was not enthusiastic, but he promptly responded with a characteristic question. Would his men just be sitting on their thumbs, or would there be any prospect of action?

It was a question that many senior Allied commanders, both American and British, had been asking themselves over the last twenty-four hours, ever since the two armies had linked up at Lippstadt. Was Bradley, the Twelfth Army Group Commander, just going to seal off the Ruhr and let Model starve himself into surrender

— the course which sensible commanders thought the most realistic — or was he going to launch an attack into the Pocket?

Hodges now revealed to the attentive Airborne Commander a secret which Eisenhower would not share with General Marshall for another five days. As the Supreme Commander then wrote:

I regard the substantial elimination of the enemy forces in the Ruhr as a military necessity. At the very least we must compress his remaining elements into a relatively small area where they may be contained with a few divisions.

Bradley's influence was paramount. He was going to use *eighteen* divisions, some 300,000 men, to attack into the Ruhr. It was against all military logic, but Bradley was determined to capture that 'bag' about which he had been dreaming and rhapsodizing for the last two weeks.

Ridgway was disgusted. In his opinion, the operation would be 'a real meat-grinder'.

Another airborne general that day was feeling displeased with his lot. General 'Gentleman Jim' Gavin, the youngest major-general in the US Army, who had enlisted as a private soldier twenty years before, considered that he too had been given an assignment unworthy of an airborne commander.

Like Ridgway, the thirty-eight-year-old commander of the 82nd Airborne Division, which had been raised by no less a person than Bradley himself, had seen much of battle these last two and a half years. He had fought in North Africa, Sicily, Italy, France, Holland and Germany. Now it seemed to him as if his 82nd and its running mate, the 'Screaming Eagles' of the 101st Airborne, which had won immortality for its defence of Bastogne the previous December, had been relegated to the role of occupation troops.

The 101st had been deployed along the west bank of the Rhine facing the Ruhr Pocket at Düsseldorf, while his own 82nd had been similarly deployed from Worringen, near Cologne, to Bonn on the River Rhine. Here Gavin found his main problem was disciplining the 10,000 former Russian POWs. They raped and looted in the Cologne area as it pleased them, for they were mostly armed — and they were a headache. Could one shoot an ally for stealing a sack of German potatoes? Another problem was his own paratroops, who found the 'frowleins' of the area decidedly attractive. Eisenhower, however, threatened anyone who fraternized with a German, whatever their sex, with a prison sentence or a fine. But the men reasoned that 'as long as they kept on their airborne caps and their jump boots, as tokens of their patriotism, they should be allowed to do anything — or almost anything,' as Gavin put it.

That day he met his new corps commander, the gravel-voiced, barrel-chested General 'Ernie' Harmon, and protested that his men 'didn't want to sit and do nothing'. As he explained: 'If the Germans were on the other side [of the Rhine], we wanted to attack them.'

Harmon was a noted combat commander himself, who had once refused promotion in order to stay with a fighting unit. He sympathized, but stood firm. He wanted Gavin 'to incur no casualties in the 82nd, since there was still an airborne assault envisioned' for the division. This was welcome news to Gavin: 'The words "airborne assault" had a particular meaning to me. They could mean only the airborne capture of Berlin.' He was momentarily appeased. 'If that was to be my next mission, I wanted to have available every man I could get my hands on.'

So General Gavin returned to his boring job of policing the Russians and ensuring that his randy airborne troopers didn't break the non-fraternization edict too openly. As General Patton, who believed that 'a man who won't fuck, won't fight', would put it to him a little later: 'So long as my men keep their knees off the ground, it ain't fraternization, it's fornication!'

However, while the two airborne commanders champed at the bit, the one not pleased with his new assignment, the other appeased only because he believed he would soon be taking part in the greatest airborne operation of all — a paradrop on Berlin — to left and right of the new Pocket, other commanders were directing their troops in fresh operations.

General Simpson's men of the Ninth, those who were not allotted to guarding the Pocket, were moving on in grand style. 'My people were keyed up,' he recalled much later. 'We'd been the first to the Rhine, and now we were going to be the first to Berlin. All along we thought of just one thing — capturing Berlin, going through and meeting the Russians on the other side.' It was to be a vain hope, but neither Simpson nor his excited eager men knew it at the time.

Now the rivalry between General Macon's 83rd Infantry Division and General White's 'Hell on Wheels' reached a peak as these two leading divisions of the Ninth Army raced for the Elbe. In theory the armoured division should have had the running. In practice the infantrymen paced them mile for mile, using a weird and wondrous collection of captured and looted German vehicles. Indeed this 'Rag-Tag Circus', as it became known, often confused Allied pilots, who thought at first sight they were over a German column. But if it confused the flyers, it confused the Germans even more. On this day a German staff car, full of high-ranking officers, began to weave its way in and out of the column, which it took to be German, the driver honking his horn as he did so.

Finally the startled doughboys reacted. A rapid burst from a Tommy-gun brought the staff car to an abrupt halt. The surprised German staff officers were hustled off to the rear, while someone gave the staff car a swift paint job, with the US star slapped on its side. The 83rd had acquired another German vehicle: a high performance Mercedes.

Opposition was light. A small show of strength or a light artillery bombardment usually sufficed to quell it, and the Americans would be streaming through empty streets hung with white flags. Here and there they were hampered by barricades or local military commanders attempting to make a stand. But the locals themselves usually dealt with these obstacles, pulling down the barricades and disarming the soldiers, who had no heart for a fight either. The civilians were war-weary; they wanted to surrender and get it over with.

But as the two divisions, plus the US 5th Armored Division, began to reach the 'Gate to Westphalia', the pass which led through the rugged Teutoburger Wald — where, legend had it, the heathen Germans had once trapped and slaughtered Varus's Romans back in the first century AD — their commanders started to worry. These wooded heights made an ideal defensive position and Intelligence knew that the area was dotted with Wehrmacht barracks and training camps. Here there would still be a reservoir of trained, battle-experienced officers and noncoms, who might well put up a fight before they surrendered.

Intelligence was right. Under the command of Major-General Becher, the area *was* prepared for defence. Becher had divided his force into three groups: one on the autobahn running through the pass itself; and one on each side of the great motorway. His resources were limited, however. They were a motley, mixed company including two 'ear battalions' — made up of men who suffered from ear trouble — as well as *Volkssturm* and young recruits from a nearby SS training battalion. It was the latter, led by the more experienced men of an officers' training battalion, who would form the keystone of Becher's defence.

On the morning of 2 April, while six American divisions were groping their way through the foothills that led up to the pass, Becher was in the nearest big town, Bielefeld, pleading with the local Party bosses in their concrete bunker for more men. Couldn't they release fresh *Volkssturm* units to him? The brown-shirted Party leaders — who were drunk already, and would remain that way until they surrendered two days later — told Becher he was a traitor, a defeatist. They threatened to have the General 'strung up' there and then for making such demands. A little later the local *Volkssturm* commander came into the bunker to report he had little ammunition. Wasn't five rounds per man enough, the Party bosses demanded. 'That means five dead *Amis*. Fight to the last man!' And that was the end of the Party's contribution to the battle soon to come. Becher and the *Volkssturm* commander both departed empty-handed.

The Americans attacked that afternoon. First the massed fighter planes came winging their way in at tree-top level, machine guns and cannons blazing. They swamped the German defences, blasting them with light bombs, spraying them with the dreaded napalm — hitherto reserved for use against non-whites, such as the Japanese. Then, while the ground still rocked and flames and smoke rose everywhere, the American ground attack went in. North of the autobahn, dazed and panicked by the bombing, the German defence soon crumbled. As the Chief-of-Staff of the 5th Armored Division, Colonel Farrand commented: 'The advance was really nothing more than cracking rear guard actions.' All the same, his own half-track, which he was using as a mobile divisional headquarters, was hit and stopped by an enemy shell.

Here in the northern forests the Germans had resorted to guerrilla warfare, with isolated American outfits being ambushed or shot up from behind by small groups of SS men and Hitler Youth. Wherever they found themselves trapped, they fought their positions to the last man — in some cases to the last child; for in several instances these last-ditch fanatics turned out to be mere children. Colonel Roland Kolb of the 84th Division found himself fighting against boys of twelve that day, and he was not the only one.

But on the autobahn itself and to the south, the German resistance was stiffer. Here the SS recruits and officer-cadets fought for every inch of ground, making up for their lack of heavy weapons by using the wooded terrain to best advantage and turning even the least likely site into a defensive position. At one stage that day, the American infantrymen discovered a group of young fanatics entrenched at the base of one of Germany's holiest national monuments, the massive metal statue of *das Hermanndenkmal*. Here, on a dominant height crowned by the giant figure of a helmeted Hermann the German, who supposedly defeated the Romans in the year AD 9 at this spot, a handful of German youths tried to emulate the feats of their pagan forefathers — but without success. The modern invaders were too strong for them. After a kind of cowboy-and-Indian battle and shoot-out around the statue, the few surviving defenders surrendered.

But at nearby Oerlinghausen, the defenders stopped the American attackers dead. In the little town itself and at the pass beyond it, the two forces engaged in a furious hand-to-hand battle. The young SS recruits, most of whom had only been in the Wehrmacht a couple of months, fought bravely and boldly. Their arms were limited — rifles, machine guns and *panzerfausts*. But they made good use of them, including knocking out one of their own Tiger tanks by mistake; whereupon the unfortunate culprit was shot by his enraged comrades. By darkness the Germans had gone over to the counter-attack and now it was the Americans' turn to dig in and beat the teenage German infantry off the best they could.

Unknown to the men of Simpson's Ninth Army trying to break through the passes and race for the Elbe, there was an urgent need to reach the river and finally seal off the Ruhr Pocket from Central Germany. For American Intelligence knew — again thanks to Ultra — that there was still a danger the Germans might counter-attack into the Pocket.

In the Harz Mountains to the east of the Pocket there were still 80,000 soldiers of the German Eleventh Army; and on the other side of the River Elbe, one of Germany's most celebrated younger generals was busy setting up another army, 200,000 strong, which would include some of the best young soldiers still available to the Reich. He was General Wenck. Still strapped in a steel corset after a recent car accident and assisted by only a handful of trained staff officers, Wenck knew that Hitler had earmarked his new army for an attack into the Pocket.

Wenck personally thought the idea crazy. How was his new Twelfth Army supposed to cut a 200-mile corridor through the American lines into the heart of the Pocket? Wenck's feelings were shared by his new Chief-of-Staff, Colonel Gunther Reichhelm. But

Reichhelm himself had been present when Hitler had announced his plan: 'The Twelfth Army must drive a wedge between the English and American troops and reach Army Group B. They must go all the way to the Rhine.' Reichhelm, who had just arrived from the battlefield, felt that Hitler was mad. There was no hope of relieving the Pocket. But Hitler even had a suggestion on how the Twelfth Army was going to do it. Wenck should borrow a trick from the Red Army, he said: 'They filter in through our lines in the night with little ammunition and no baggage.' He told Reichhelm to assemble 200 Volkswagen jeeps and do the same, infiltrating the *Amis*' lines by night and causing such confusion in the enemy's rear that the Twelfth Army could then make a complete breakthrough.

But while Reichhelm thought Hitler's proposal was totally unworkable, if not downright crazy, General Sibert, Bradley's Chief-of-Intelligence, had already considered this as a possibility and took the threat seriously enough. He urged that the Elbe line should be captured as quickly as possible. For he knew, too, that within the Pocket Model still possessed Colonel-General Harpe's Fifth Panzer Army, a battle-hardened force which had not seen any serious fighting since the Allies had crossed the Rhine. In Sibert's opinion, it could still cause trouble for Simpson's Ninth Army, especially as the Fifth Panzer would be defending the complex of ruined cities around Essen, Dortmund and Duisburg, where the Germans could well hold the Americans up for weeks in a long and bloody siege.

The same thought had occurred to Model. He knew from his talks with Harpe's Chief-of-Staff, von Mellenthin, that the Fifth still functioned efficiently. As the latter told him, 'Despite the breakdown of the normal system of transport and supply, the various headquarters and staffs continued to function with the same coolness and efficiency which distinguished the Wehrmacht in its greatest days.' Why, the Fifth had even managed to push several patrols across the Rhine to test the *Amis*' strength!

And so, at Model's suggestion, the Fifth had regrouped. In that first week of April, the Fifth's 12th SS Corps was ordered to hold the Rhine from Duisburg to Siegburg, while the 58th Panzer Corps took up the defence of the Sieg River Line with the elements of seven divisions: a formidable force still. Indeed, the first American attempt to cross the Sieg at Betzdorf would soon be thrown back with great loss, including several hundred prisoners from panicked American battalions who fell tamely into the hands of the 12th People's Grenadier Division.

Dedicated National Socialist that he was, General Harpe, and the men of his Fifth Panzer Army would give a good account of themselves. Sibert knew this, and he wanted the Pocket to be completely sealed off at the Elbe as soon as possible. Meanwhile Sibert's superior, General Bradley, was waiting impatiently for Simpson's Ninth Army to come under his control — on 4 April — so that he could set about attacking into the Pocket. For his mind was still set on that enormous 'bag' of prisoners he anticipated taking there. Nothing, but nothing, could be allowed to interfere with that.

Thus, while the generals dreamed and schemed, the ordinary GI slogged away at the defenders of the Teutoburger Wald. On the morning of 3 April the Americans renewed their onslaught. The pressure on the Germans was mounting. Desperately General Becher tried to bolster up his cracking line, but Oerlinghausen was taken at last. Now the men of the 'Hell on Wheels' pushed on to the next town, the medieval city of Detmold. One battalion passed through with hardly any trouble; indeed, there was a formal surrender of one German unit, complete with salutes, handshakes and all the rest. But, only a few hours later, the next American unit to pass through Detmold, General Macon's 83rd Infantry, was fighting for its life. For the 83rd discovered that SS troops had filtered back into the empty city and were now sniping at the infantry on all sides. As General Macon recalled after the war, 'I walked quite safely through the front entrance of my headquarters, but when I tried to leave by the back door, I almost had to *fight* my way out!'

Some Germans, it now transpired, were still imbued with the *Zivilcourage* that Model lacked. Sickened by the senseless destruction when it was obvious that Germany had lost the war, they had the sense to try to stop it. The burgomaster of Lemgo, for instance, Herr Wilhelm Graefer, surrendered his town to the men of the 'Hell on Wheels'. But his action was ill rewarded the following day when, after a summary court-martial ordered by General Paul Goerbig, Graefer was shot.

Other German civilians were threatened or tricked into surrendering their towns by the advancing Americans. Fluent German-speaker Captain Francis Schommer of the 83rd Division used his linguistic gifts — and a drawn .45 calibre Colt — to convince several burgomasters that it would be advisable not to make a fight for the place. As Schommer would say: 'If he wants the place to remain standing, he'd better get the people to hang sheets from the windows — *or else!*' And the panic-stricken official would usually comply, telling the next burgomaster in the American line of advance that the *Amis* in his town had thousands of tanks and artillery pieces just itching to raze it to the ground. Time and time again, the same ruse worked.

But still the fight for the passes through the Teutoburger Wald continued and with it all the horror of war. Approaching one of the wooded ridges, Major James Hollingworth of the 'Hell on Wheels', 67th Armored Regiment, suddenly found himself surrounded by what appeared to be German tanks. Fortunately for him, the tanks were without engines and immobilized. They were, however, manned and the young German tank gunners knew how to use their dreaded 88 mm cannon.

One of Hollingworth's own gunners, Staff Sergeant Cooley, a veteran of North Africa, ducked as the white blur of an armour-piercing shell hissed towards his tank, then swung his own 75 mm cannon around. At the extreme range of 1,500 yards, he knocked out the first German tank. Desperately he swung his turret round again and aimed at another relic only seventy-five yards away. Then, as Hollingworth recalled afterwards, 'All hell broke loose!' But the Americans had all the superiority of movement and manoeuvre; gradually they gained the upper hand. One after another they knocked out the stationary German tanks. Then, just as they had finished off the last one, an enemy truck came rumbling down towards their positions.

Hollingworth ordered his crews to hold their fire until the truck was well within range. The unsuspecting German driver trundled on towards them. Then, when the big heavy truck was only a hundred yards away, the Major yelled '*Fire!*' The massed American machine guns burst into angry life. The truck's canvas cover was riddled like a sieve and it lurched to a halt, the driver slumped dead over the wheel. The next moment its gas tank exploded and it overturned, spilling its dead and dying occupants onto the trail.

It was only a few minutes later, when Major Hollingworth went across to inspect the result of his handiwork, that he discovered what he had really done. The occupants certainly wore the field-grey of the Wehrmacht — but from their peaked caps trailed long feminine tresses. The truck had been full of teenage, female auxiliaries who had served in an anti-aircraft outfit.

But the horror was lightened by more humorous moments. One task force of the 'Hell on Wheels' liberated a large winery and proceeded to get 'stinkin' drunk', together with a large group of DPs and Germans. A signals company joined in. Officers and men played a drunken tug-of-war, trying to snatch cases of some favourite tipple from one another. In the end the divisional military police were called in and sealed off the whole area. But as one sergeant later reported, 'Had there been an attack the first evening, we might well have lost the war.'

Sobered up a little, the men of Task Force A pushed on towards Hameln — or Hamelin as it is known to the British — of Pied Piper fame. En route, they encountered a black signal corps outfit commanded by a black lieutenant in a truck. The truck was flagged down and one of the combat troops asked the lieutenant if he knew where he was. Right at that moment a barrage of shells came raining down nearby. The officer exclaimed: 'Suh, I suah know now.' Then he turned to his men and announced: 'Men, at long last, you are now at the front!'

With that the scared driver whipped the truck round and they were off at top speed, back the way they had come, leaving the veterans chuckling.

A few hours later the men of the 'Hell on Wheels' and their running mates of the 30th Infantry Division had reached the outskirts of Hameln. Here a handful of SS men were preparing to fight to the last — but the Americans had other ideas. They whistled up their artillery and the heavy guns soon reduced the town to burning, blasted rubble. As one officer commented: 'This time we got the rats out with a slightly different kind of flute.'

By 4 April the Ninth Army was through the passes and setting off for the Elbe. It was on this same day that the Ninth finally came under the control of General Bradley. As yet 'Big Simp' (to distinguish him from another regular US Army officer named Simpson, who was known predictably as 'Little Simp', on account of his diminutive size) knew little of Bradley's plans for him. He still believed that once his divisions had crossed the Elbe they would race on to Berlin itself. Indeed, one of his divisions, the 2nd, already had a complete plan of advance worked out with code-names allotted for each phase of the drive for the German capital. But it was to be another *two weeks* before Bradley called Simpson to his new headquarters in Wiesbaden, telling the mystified Ninth Army Commander: 'I've got something very important to tell you and I don't want to say it over the phone.'

Only then did Simpson hear the news. 'You must stop on the Elbe,' Bradley told him. 'You are not to advance any further in the direction of Berlin. I'm sorry, Simp, but there it is.'

'Where in hell did you get this?' Simpson demanded.

Bradley looked at the stunned General coldly from behind his steel-rimmed GI spectacles. 'From Ike,' he answered simply.

Simpson was too numb to take in much of what Bradley said thereafter. As he later admitted, 'I was heartbroken and I got back on the plane in a kind of a daze.' As his plane flew over the war-torn countryside below, dotted here and there with ruined tanks and shattered artillery pieces, all he could think about was, 'How am I going to tell my staff, my corps commanders and my troops? Above all, how am I going to tell my troops?'

When he arrived back at his HQ Simpson would compose himself for a press conference with the correspondents attached to his Army, who had been alerted that something was afoot by his sudden disappearance. 'Well, gentleman,' he announced. 'Here's what's happened. I got orders to stop where we are. I cannot go to Berlin.'

There was a murmur of sympathy and surprise from the correspondents, who knew the new order meant that most of the Ninth's divisions would be condemned to sit out the war doing nothing. As one of them exclaimed, 'That's a hell of a shame, sir!'

To take his mind off his sore disappointment, Simpson decided to visit his frontline troops on the Elbe. The day before, his 'Hell on Wheels' had been able to throw three bridgeheads across the Elbe, though two of them had been forced to withdraw under German pressure. Now Simpson bumped into an exhausted Brigadier-General Sidney Hinds, of the 2nd Division, who had been in charge of the crossings. Hinds was slightly apprehensive that the Army Commander might feel it was his fault that progress on the road to Berlin was so slow. He said, 'I guess we're all right now, General. We had two good withdrawals. There was no excitement and no panic and our Barby crossings are going good.'

Simpson's sombre look wouldn't change. 'Fine,' he said without enthusiasm. 'Keep some of your men on the east bank if you want to.'

Hinds looked up at him puzzled.

Then the miserable Simpson explained. The break-out from the Rhine bridgehead, the fight through the Teutoburger Wald and on across the River Weser to the Elbe had been for nothing. General Bradley was concentrating solely on that 'bag' of his. The Ninth was ordered to halt on the Elbe. 'They're not going any further. This is as far as we're going.'

Hinds simply wouldn't believe him. It wasn't possible, now that Berlin was within grasping distance. 'No sir,' he said hotly. 'That's not right. We're going to Berlin.'

As Hinds recalled long afterwards, Simpson seemed to be struggling to control his emotions. When he spoke, his voice was flat and dead. 'No, Sid,' he said, 'we're not going to Berlin. This is the end of the war for us.'

TWO

'Drive . . . drive . . . drive!'

6 April, 1945. The morning was still black. The moon had vanished. To the east the horizon had still not begun to clear. There was an unseasonal nip in the air and in their foxholes the waiting GIs shivered.

The night before they had fried up great mounds of looted eggs and potatoes in addition to their usual canned rations, though the veterans had warned them that to be 'hit in the guts' with a sudden bellyful of food might be fatal. The younger GIs dismissed the warnings; come what may, they wanted full stomachs for a change. They had cleaned their equipment, too, checking the tracer in the machine guns, and studied the map overlays that had been distributed among the officers and senior noncoms. Some prayed. But not many. God in His mercy would have little to say in the violent events of the new day.

Most of the men of the First Army's eight combat divisions which were going into action this dawn were motivated either by fear or more often by a sense of anger. All of them were tired; all would have recognized this description by one of those among them:

He was just tired, tired of sleeping in a dirty wet cold foxhole, tired of dragging, pushing, forcing himself onward day after day through mud, briars and water, tired of being shot at and wondering whether his was to do or die — or both. He was determined to end all this; to finish the fighting; to be able to think freely of the things he loved most; to sleep; to relieve his tired body and mind of all that had been torturing it for such a long time.

But the time for rest had not come. This was still the time for hate and fear, and as the first streaks of the false dawn appeared on the horizon to the east the GIs waited for that first exultant scream, rising to a banshee-like howl, of the softening-up barrage which would plaster the German positions to their front. Let it wipe out the last trace of the Krauts on this earth. It was what they deserved.

On this day Hodges' First Army would be joining Simpson's Ninth in the first concerted squeeze on the Ruhr Pocket. Four of Simpsons's divisions — the 79th, 35th, 75th and the 17th Airborne — were to attack south from the River Lippe toward the great industrial cities of Dortmund and Essen. As for the First Army, they would be attacking in *two* different directions: to the east to reach the River Elbe and to the west to reduce the Pocket.

A two-corps attack, with 'Lightning Joe' Collins's VII naturally in the lead, spearheaded by the 3rd Armored Division yet again, would head for the Elbe to seal off the Pocket and the German Eleventh Army still in the Harz Mountains. At the same time, Ridgway's XVIII Airborne Corps and van Fleet's III Corps would carry the attack across the Sieg River and right into the Pocket; and Ridgway was not going to waste any time in an operation which he thought was not of the greatest significance. At this stage of the war, what did ground and prisoners matter?

As Ridgway had told his divisional commanders on the night of 5 April, 'The sooner we get this job done, the sooner we will get into the real final kill of striking into the very heart of Germany and getting into Berlin!' Just like Gavin, Simpson and all the rest of the subordinate American commanders, Ridgway had been misled by Bradley into believing that the US Army's main objective was still the German capital. Despite Bradley's 'GI General' image, the honest, down-to-earth American soldier, it seemed he could be as devious as the rest of the Top Brass when it suited his purpose.

Ridgway for his part pulled no punches with his commanders, especially as he was not too impressed by their divisions. '*Drive . . . drive . . . drive!*' was the message he hammered home that night before the attack. 'The minute a regiment is stopped for fatigue or battle losses,' he told his four divisional generals sternly, 'or for any other reason, the next one is to go through and keep it going night and day . . . There's no tactical genius required. It's *driving*, constant unrelenting pressure from the division commander down, that produces results.

And so, at dawn on 6 April, Moore's 8th Infantry Division and Parker's 78th kicked off the attack, both divisional commanders well aware that Ridgway's critical gaze was pinned on them, ready to seize upon the slightest fault. But the terrain favoured the defender and their progress through the rugged, well-wooded area was not as fast as Ridgway would have wished.

The 'Golden Arrow' men of the 8th Infantry were faced now by the German 3rd Parachute Division. The 3rd was only a shadow of its former self, for it had been shattered in Normandy and then again in the Ardennes; but even though the replacement troopers, culled from the Hitler Youth and the Luftwaffe, had never jumped out of an aeroplane in their lives, they were inspired by that same old para spirit. They gave the 8th a fight to remember, forcing the 121st Regiment to retreat in one spot and severely wounding its commander, Colonel Thomas Cross, who had to be evacuated. As had happened so often before, the 8th was unlucky yet again; even at this stage of the war, it was still losing regimental commanders!

Ridgway's 78th was more fortunate. Several times the men of the 'Lightning Division' caught the Germans by surprise, ambushing enemy platoons and knocking out their tanks in the thick wooded undergrowth. Even the 78th's black platoons, long derided as craven, proved their courage now. As Ridgway's Corps G-I commented after the first week of fighting, their 'morale and manner of performance' was 'excellent'. But the black volunteers paid the price — in their own blood. Of the 252 involved, some 43 had been killed, wounded or reported missing within the first forty-eight hours of the attack being launched.

Ridgway had no mercy with his soldiers, black or white. Thirty-six hours after the drive had started, he threw in his reserve to back up the 8th: General 'Count' Melasky's green 86th Division. Despite the fact that Melasky had been a classmate of his back at West Point, Ridgway refused to make allowances for him; after the 86th's first day of attacking he summoned Melasky to his CP and told him that his division's performance was 'thoroughly unsatisfactory', that 'results were not being obtained'. And when the unhappy divisional commander pointed out that he was meeting 'strong resistance', Ridgway laughed in his face. He produced Melasky's own casualty figures and described them as 'negligible'. His conclusion was, he snapped, that 'enemy resistance was not the cause of unsatisfactory progress'.

Privately Ridgway had concluded that Melasky was inadequate as a divisional commander. But now Melasky started to bluster; it wasn't his fault, he said, and tried to shift the blame to his assistant divisional commander, George van Wyck Pope. He demanded that Pope should be relieved of his command.

Ridgway despised Melasky for passing the buck; but he didn
think much of Pope anyway, so he agreed. Hodges concurred wit
his decision to relieve Pope but then Bradley stepped in. Pope, i
appeared, was an old friend of the Army Group Commander and ha
indeed served as his Chief-of-Staff back in 1942. Bradley expresse
the opinion that Pope had 'not been sufficiently tested in so brief
period of combat': so naturally Pope stayed on. No one was goin
to cross Bradley and get away with it.

Ridgway got on with the war, urging his green divisions an
equally inexperienced commanders to ever greater efforts. For th
time being, he had to be content with what he regarded as deficien
material. Perhaps, in the end, he consoled himself, he'd be allowe
to rid himself of the footsloggers and return to his beloved paras
they wouldn't keep letting him down.

While Ridgway fought the Top Brass, that other energetic para
trooper, General Gavin, was chafing at the bit only a few mile
away from the fighting on the other side of the Rhine. Gavin wante
to help Ridgway finish off the battle for the Ruhr, a fight which h
thought was secondary to the main task of capturing Berlin. It wa
only thirty-one years later that he would hear from his old corp
commander 'Ernie' Harmon that all along he, Harmon, had know
Gavin's next para-drop was not to be on Berlin but on Japan!

Then Gavin would conclude bitterly that Eisenhower and hi
staff had abandoned Montgomery's plan to drive and captur
Berlin because 'the American generals had the strength and the
intended to use it to win the war in the manner they considere
to be in the US interest'. Alone of all America's wartime generals i
Europe, James Gavin would be the one to point out that Berlin ha
been sacrificed to national and personal prestige and pride. But tha
would be later, much later.

Now, however, in this first week of April, Gavin burned t
get his 82nd involved in the Ruhr battle in support of his ol
commander Ridgway, despite Harmon's order to conserve his force
for the coming drop. His fellow airborne commander, Genera
Taylor, who led the 101st Airborne Division doing occupatio
duty further up the Rhine, felt the same. So it was that as the XVII
Airborne Corps went into action before dawn that morning, withi
gunshot distance, A Company of Gavin's 504th Parachute Regimen
started to cross the great river stealthily in their rubber assault boat
Their task, so Gavin had said, was to seize and hold the village o

Hitdorf, some miles north of Cologne. This village, Gavin reasoned, could be used as a bridgehead, not for offensive action deeper into enemy territory, but solely to draw further German troops into the area and away from Ridgway's advancing Corps. At least, that was the reason Gavin gave Harmon when the storm blew up.

The 140 men of A Company landed safely enough, but once ashore they ran into trouble immediately. All hell broke loose as the Germans turned their heavy artillery upon the lightly armed paras. They broke for cover, only to find themselves blundering about in the darkness inside a minefield. For a while confusion reigned. The company broke into two groups, both without contact with Company HQ further back.

But Gavin's paras had fought in Sicily, Holland and Belgium; they were used to this sort of confusion, with the enemy on both flanks. It was the customary airborne snafu: 'situation normal, all fucked up'. Independently the two groups advanced against heavy machine guns to their objective. By eight thirty that morning, while across the Rhine Ridgway was beginning to rage at the slowness of Melasky's 86th Division, the paras had captured Hitdorf in true airborne style and taken some eighty-six German prisoners.

Only fifteen minutes later, however, while Gavin's paras were still celebrating their small victory, the enemy counter-attacked Hitdorf in force. Before the paras had had time to dig themselves in, the Germans came streaming across the wet fields, yelling crazily and firing from the hip as they ran. Once again the little whitewashed Rhenish village changed hands as the paras were forced to retreat. Finally the steam went from the German attack and the Americans were able to bring them to a halt — but not for long. The paras were subjected to another heavy barrage; their observation post, secreted in the village church, was knocked out and all radio communication went dead. Smoke shells began to descend upon the American positions. And suddenly, in the distance, there was the rusty creak of tank tracks. Colonel-General Harpe's Fifth Panzer Army was reacting with all it had.

But the paras were not to be budged, even by tanks — not yet at least. The brave survivors signalled across the Rhine by hand. They called for their own short-range artillery to bring down protective fire just in front of their own positions. It was a dangerous thing to do, as they were unable to give co-ordinates. But it worked. American shells started to plough up the fields — even as the tanks responded in kind.

At his forward command post Gavin realized that what was left of A Company was going to be wiped out if he didn't do something to help, and swiftly. He alerted the same Regiment's I Company to prepare to rescue their comrades. Urgently the paras of I Company started paddling across the Rhine, while here and there random German shells threw up great spouts of whirling white water, rocking their frail craft alarmingly.

Almost immediately the newcomers were engaged in battle, facing 300 German infantry and a platoon of Mark IV tanks. Boldly one para stalked a German tank. Risking sudden death by the minute, he managed to clamp a gammon grenade to its side. After a muffled crump the tank was jerked to a halt, thick smoke pouring from its interior. No one got out.

The men of I Company pressed on, dodging the shells as they swept along the river bank to where their comrades were trapped. Now time was of the essence. The two companies, one badly depleted, knew they couldn't hold the Germans much longer. Hurriedly they started to pull back with their wounded across the Rhine, bodies tensed for the expected burst of enemy machine-gun fire; they would be sitting ducks in the middle of the broad river. But the Germans missed their chance. What was left of the two companies arrived back at their own side without any further casualties.

Whatever Gavin's true purpose was in launching his raid across the Rhine, it had undoubtedly been a failure. The equivalent of one whole company had been lost — 112 men, killed, wounded or taken prisoner. Harmon was furious. He called the crestfallen Gavin to his headquarters and gave him a scathing lecture. There would be no further raids across the Rhine by Gavin's paras of the 82nd Division.

The paras were much relieved. As their Divisional History put it: 'From the viewpoint of those GIs involved, the operation was a miniature "Dunkirk" with at most a hollow satisfaction. Fighting men don't believe in moral victories.'

Undaunted by the 82nd's lack of success in crossing the Rhine, another division — the 94th Infantry — put a small patrol across under Lieutenant Seeby a few days later. Seeby had orders to scout around near the village of Serm outside Krefeld, the great Ruhr manufacturing town. But the infantrymen soon ran into trouble just as Gavin's men had done.

Staff Sergeant Fatora, the patrol's senior noncom, describes what happened next: 'The Heinies brought 40 mmm AA fire to bear on the route we used. . . . Simultaneously other Krauts on the right and left, working with clockwork precision, were manoeuvring to outflank us, while keeping us hemmed in by fire.' It was time to withdraw.

Under Seeby's command the survivors managed to reach a solitary house, only to be surrounded once again as darkness fell. Now the Germans used the darkness to edge ever closer to the beleaguered Americans. 'Frequently during the night,' as Sergeant Fatora said later, 'we were asked to surrender only to reply with hot lead. Bazookas smashed the house and machine guns raked all the doors and windows. Early next morning after several attempts to escape had proved futile and the Heinies had battered the cellar entrance with *panzerfausts*, we gave up all hope of excape.'

At eight that morning the Germans rushed the house, its walls chipped and pocked by rifle fire like the symptoms of some loathsome skin disease, and at their head a young officer shouted melodramatically, 'Gentlemen, you have five minutes to surrender!'

Despite the tension Fatora was amused: 'All of a sudden he considered us *gentlemen*!'

Seeby tried to bluster it out. 'Surrender to *us*,' he called back.

'Sir', came the reply, 'I am a soldier and as such I have my orders which I must obey. You have *four* minutes.'

'But you are already caught in the centre of a huge pincers,' Seeby said, meaning the Ruhr Pocket.

'My men and I realize that but we have superiors over us to whom we must answer,' the German announced. 'And anyway,' he hesitated a few seconds, 'you will be prisoners of war only a few days before you are freed by your comrades. You have *two* minutes left.'

While the parley was going on, one of the trapped men, a Private White, had been frantically trying to repair their radio. Finally he succeeded: it crackled into life and he started to contact the battalion command post. But before he got through the radio went dead again.

The German officer said, 'Your time is up, gentlemen. Are you coming out?'

As Sergeant Fatora described it, 'Silence fell on the room as Lieutenant Seeby said, "Yeah, we're coming out."'

Seeby and his men were marched off and imprisoned with some Frenchmen who had been captured at Dunkirk back in 1940, when most of the Americans were still in high school. But as the German officer had predicted, they weren't prisoners for long. They were released within days by Ridgway's 13th Armoured Division, and fought alongside it as riflemen until the Pocket finally surrendered and they were returned to their own unit.

So far, all attempts to establish a permanent bridgehead of permanent patrols over the Rhine in the German Fifth Army's sector had failed. Colonel-General Harpe, the convinced Nazi, wasn't going to give up that easily.

But on the same day that Gavin launched his abortive attack, another US airborne general struck lucky. Since making its first combat jump across the Rhine under Montgomery's command, General Miley's US 17th Airborne had been fighting as infantry with the British 6th Guards Armoured Division. Together these two elite formations had captured Munster, with one of the airborne battalion commanders using the tank of a certain Lieutenant Runcie, MC, of the Scots Guards as his mobile command post.*

It was during the process of being transferred to the Ninth Army to join the drive into the Ruhr Pocket that one lieutenant and seven soldiers of the 194th Glider Combat Team made an interesting capture. They came across a man in his thirties, unshaven and wearing civilian clothes but undoubtedly a soldier, perhaps even an officer to judge by his somewhat haughty bearing and flawless English. Under interrogation by Lieutenant Thomas McKinley, the man finally admitted that he was in fact a captain in the Wehrmacht and that his name was von Papen.

That name rang a bell for McKinley. Wasn't it a von Papen who had been made chancellor of Germany back in 1932 and then handed the country to Adolf Hitler?† It was indeed, and this man was his son. Realizing that he had a potential coup on his hands, McKinley now pressed Captain von Papen to reveal his father's whereabouts. Eventually von Papen did. His father had been living in one of his several residences in the Saar area, but when he seemed threatened by the advancing Americans Hitler himself had ordered von Papen senior to move into the safety of the interior of the Reich; he knew too many dirty secrets for Hitler to let him fall

---

*Now Dr Runcie, the Archbishop of Canterbury.

†Fritz von Papen, the Catholic-conservative politician. After helping Hitler to power, he then became his special ambassador, first in Vienna and then in Ankara. In the latter city he was involved in one of the Germans' greatest espionage successes of the war, Operation Cicero, during which they discovered the secret of D-Day. Hitler, however, refused to act on the information.

into enemy hands. Travelling by night to dodge Allied planes, he had moved to a remote hunting lodge at Stockhausen, twenty-five miles south-east of the great industrial city of Hamm. Here, according to his son, he had surrounded himself with his grandchildren, plus his son and son-in-law, both recovering from war wounds, who helped to protect him from the attentions of looters such as the newly liberated prisoners-of-war.

Now McKinley asked Captain von Papen if his father was worried about the Gestapo, for it had been reported in the US Press that von Papen had fallen out with Hitler.

'Why should he?' the Captain answered. 'He has nothing to fear.'

The Captain's smug words infuriated McKinley. This man seemed indifferent to the fact that his father had delivered not only Germany into Hitler's hands but Austria too, using his own Catholicism to convince the Catholic Austrians of his good faith. It was the same attitude that von Papen senior would display in coming months following his capture and subsequent trial at Nuremberg.

The next morning, with General Miley's eager approval — for this was just the coup McKinley had supposed — the lieutenant set off with a patrol to capture the Nazi statesman. They arrived at the hunting lodge at noon. McKinley ordered his men to surround the house; then, accompanied by Sergeant Hugh Frederick, armed with a pistol, he burst in the door.

Von Papen was sitting at a table drinking soup. A man of routine, he always took his *Mittagessen* punctually at midday.

McKinley produced a photograph, taken before the war, and held it under von Papen's nose. He asked if von Papen was the person in the photograph.

'Yes,' von Papen admitted. 'But I can't imagine what you Americans want with an old man of sixty-five.' Then, after asking permission to finish his soup before packing a few things to take with him to prison, he remarked wearily: 'I wish this war were over.'

'So do eleven million other guys!' Sergeant Frederick snapped angrily.

Thereafter they took von Papen to Army Headquarters itself, driving him under a heavy escort. On the way they passed through Werl, the town where he had spent his youth and which had honoured him during the Nazi period by making him an honorary citizen and naming a street after him. But soon the honest burghers of Werl would prefer to forget that Franz von Papen had been born in their town; after the war they changed the street's name back again and resisted the von Papen family's protests.

Finally the little convoy reached the town of Haltern. Here von Papen was photographed standing next to General Anderson of the US XVI Corps and his army commander, Simpson, both grim-faced and sombre, while von Papen — wearing a well-cut tweed jacket, complete with handkerchief in the upper pocket — looked the very picture of injured innocence as if still wondering what he'd done wrong. Why, his expression seemed to say, was he being treated in such an ungentlemanly manner? He would soon learn why, when in two days' time the men of the US Ninth and First Armies started to uncover the true face of Nazism for the very first time. But for now he was transported out of the Reich to a camp in the little state of Luxembourg. The site was pretty and peaceful, just outside the small holiday town of Mondorf and beside the River Moselle.

The camp would soon hold all the surviving *Prominenz*: the ministers, field-marshals and state secretaries, strolling up and down behind the glass-windows of the verandah, in what would become after the war an old folks' home. As Speer remarked of his arrival here: 'It was a ghostly experience to find all those who at the end had scattered like chaff in the wind to reassemble here.'

The prisoners would call their camp *das Prominentlager*, 'the camp of the prominent people'. But the GIs who would guard them scoffed at such pretensions. These men who had run the Nazi Empire, who had decided the fates of nearly 200,000,000 men and women of a dozen different nationalities, were non-persons now. Nobodies. For the GIs into whose tender care von Papen was now delivered, the place was simply 'Camp Ashcan'.

THREE

'If the American public only knew'

The Ruhr had always been red. Despite the fact that most of the citizens of the great industrial area were Catholic by faith, the Ruhr had supported first the German Social Democratic Party and later various left-wing factions, such as the Communists. It had been the same ever since the nineteenth century. Hadn't Model himself fought the Left here back in 1919, that terrible year of anarchy?

Even through the twelve long years of National Socialist terror, there had been a few in the Ruhr who had stuck to the left-wing creed of their fathers and grandfathers, distributing anti-Nazi leaflets and writing seditious slogans on the walls. The three-year bombing campaign by the RAF and the US Army Air Corps had hardened the support of the local populace for Hitler. The effect was much the same in Britain during the blitz-year of 1940–41. But the bombs and the general destruction of the Ruhr's great cities — Hamm, Essen, Dortmund and the like — had also increased the number of subversive groups prepared to work against the Party.

In places like Lippstadt, Bochum and Herne, local left-wingers grouped together with French and Russian slave workers to form anti-Nazi cells, which by the end of 1944 had begun to alarm the Gestapo. This alarm was increased when the local Party boss of Cologne was assassinated by a Russian slave worker. Even the mass public hangings of some dozen German youths, suspected of subversion by the authorities, failed to stop the rot. It was a strange and motley collection of people who joined the resistance. Teenage boys, who lived off the black market, listened to 'decadent nigger jazz' and refused to join the Hitler Youth: 'The Edelweiss Pirates', they called themselves, somewhat obscurely. Then there were deserters from the Wehrmacht, who now opposed their former employers. There was even a liberal French–German theatre group, of all things, dedicated to overthrowing the Führer.

By February, 1945, the police and Gestapo were cracking down on the resistance everywhere in the Ruhr. On the night of 8/9 February the Gestapo rounded up 300 resistance workers in Dortmund. Two weeks later some thirty more were arrested in Herne. The theatre group followed, as did a group of Frenchmen who were interned at Iserlohn on charges of sabotage and spying. More and more were arrested as the Ruhr came under increasing pressure, until the Gestapo began to realize that these prisoners were an embarrassment; they knew too much of Gestapo methods. On 7 March the shootings began, and continued until 9 April. The prisoners' skinny corpses were then thrown into water-filled bomb craters, often followed by a couple of grenades to ensure that the bodies were ripped to shreds. Even on Good Friday, which was celebrated throughout the Ruhr despite the battle raging everywhere, the Gestapo continued their executions, shooting forty-two resistance workers in Dortmund's Romberg Park alone.

By the first week of April it had become clear that the Ruhr was cut off from the rest of Germany. Now the Nazi authorities turned their attention to the hundreds of thousands of foreign workers still trapped inside the Pocket. In charge of the operation was a certain Dr Hans Kammler, who, though he bore the rank of a general in the SS, had never fired a shot in anger in the whole of his life. Kammler was the typical German bureaucrat, who committed his atrocities from behind a desk: *ein Schreibtischtäter* ('a writing-desk criminal'), as the Germans called such men.

In fact Kammler was an engineer. He had contributed to the design of several concentration camps, and among his accomplishments he included the gas ovens at Auschwitz. In 1942 he had been put in charge of several minor sections of the German missile projects, the V-1 and V-2. At the time General Dornberger, who had been working on rockets for years, found Kammler 'obsessed by a morbid inferiority complex and a mimosa-like sensitivity'. But over the years Kammler's career progressed at a tremendous rate until finally he was supervising the whole of Germany's secret weapon programme, including the jet-fighters.

Of course, much of the hard labour in these projects was performed by the foreign workers. They were treated little better than slaves — indeed, as we shall see, many of them were drawn from the concentration camps. With the Americans drawing ever closer to the Harz Mountains, Kammler was getting nervous; for several of his key secret weapon factories were hidden in the region's caves and mines. He now gave out the order to reduce the number of foreign workers who could betray his secrets: 'They are threatening the very existence of our German population,' he proclaimed.

That command was clear enough for the Gestapo and the special SS units already roaming the area, shooting 'defeatists', stringing up officers and civilian officials who refused to fight and generally destroying 'Germanic cultural substance' that should not fall into the hands of the 'degenerate plutocratic-Jewish Yankees' (it was this group which finally blew up Himmler's SS castle at Wewelsburg on 2 April). They went to work with a will. They visited camps where the unfortunate foreign workers were housed, selecting their victims, then mowing them down mercilessly in the nearest woods. And it was not only the grown men they took, but women and even children. Some they tricked into going with them by offering to take them to a new camp with better food and accommodation. Many of the foreign workers were simple peasants, too credulous for their own good. In one case fourteen men and fifty-six women, plus one baby, were thus persuaded to leave the camp at Warstein. They were transported into a wood in the Langenbachtal valley where they were shot with machine pistols, the SS finishing off those who had not yet obliged them by dying with a shot to the base of the skull.

Weary of having to liquidate these third-rate citizens — 'the scum of the east', as Himmler had once called them — in small groups, the SS decided to get rid of thousands of them in one blow. As it happened, thousands of the foreign workers were crowded together in the enforced accommodation of the Sauerlandhalle, an enormous entertainment complex, famed before the war for the concerts and sports events that had been held there. This gave the SS men their idea. They would set fire to the building and destroy all the inmates at a single stroke.

The great central hall had been divided into two, with the French on one side and Russians on the other. One night in the second week of April, the hall burst into flames. There was rising panic as the fire took hold and the terrified inmates struggled to escape, only to find that the SS had barricaded the doors — and, on the Russian side, the windows too. But the French rallied to their allies. While some burst open the doors dividing their quarters, others used their bare hands to tear down the partitioning walls, making a hole in the wooden planking so that the Russians could scramble through. All but a few then managed to escape through the windows.

Kammler's nervousness increased. Most of his foreign workers were still alive, still capable of betraying his evil deeds to the ever-advancing *Amis*. Kammler made a run for it, escaping from the Ruhr Pocket just before it was sealed, and fled to the Czechoslovakian capital of Prague, then still firmly in German hands. But the Nazi Reich was dying, and Kammler died too; he committed suicide in Prague, biting into a cyanide capsule that he'd hidden in his teeth.

By that time Kammler's secrets had been discovered. The terrible weapons programme that he had supervised was already being transferred, to dominate the strategies of a new superpower.

The SS guards, the technicians, the scientists and all the other merchants of death had been expecting the *Amis* for nearly a week now. In the remote Harz mountains, seldom frequented by visitors except during the winter ski season, they had felt themselves safe for the last two years, ever since Kammler had established his first underground factory there. In all that time, while the rest of industrial Germany was being systematically bombed into ruins, the British and Americans had not visited them once. The reason was obvious. The enemy didn't even know of their existence.

By early 1945 this underground factory had become one of the two main production centres of the war-winning V-2 missiles. It was back in July, 1943, that Albert Sawatzki, Kammler's assistant, had arrived in these mountains with a huge entourage of technicians and experts to begin the enormous project. The slaves in striped pyjamas had toiled under the whips of their overseers to construct the largest underground factory in the world, with twenty-seven tunnels alone being allocated to the assembly of the V-2 rocket.

Speer himself had visited the site that year and was sickened by what he saw (or at least that is what he wrote after the war):

In enormous halls prisoners were busy setting up machinery. . . . Expressionlessly they looked right through me, mechanically removing their prisoners' caps of blue twill until our group had passed them. . . . As I learned from the overseers after the inspection was over, the sanitary conditions were inadequate, disease rampant; the prisoners were quartered right there in the camp caves and as a result the mortality among them was extraordinarily high.

That had been no concern of Kammler and his henchmen. All that had mattered to him was that the Allies should never find him here; for they had already discovered Peenemünde, the original home of German rocket research, and attempted to blow it off the map. With his foreign slave workers safely confined in these caves, he had been confident that this new location of his secret weapons plant would never be revealed.

But now it was April 1945 and the enemy forces were advancing through the mountains; at any moment they might discover the underground complex. Kammler had already fled, and now his henchmen prepared to do the same. First, however, they had to destroy what they could of the secrets they must leave behind, and send as much as possible of the rest to be hidden elsewhere. Altogether, fourteen tons of top-secret research material were loaded into trucks and driven off for disposal. Meanwhile, the 25,000 slave labourers were either herded off to the nearby concentration camp or shot out of hand.

By 10 April all work had stopped in the tunnels and most of the 4,500 German specialists — weapon experts, designers, engineers and technicians — had scattered to their homes or been transferred to Oberammergau, where General Dornberger was hiding out in the Bavarian Alps; they travelled in Kammler's own train, nicknamed 'the Vengeance Express'.

The vengeance was not theirs, however. The American armoured columns were already entering Nordhausen, just a few miles south of the Harz mountains.

Colonels Lovelady and Welborn had been warned by VII Corps Intelligence to 'expect something unusual in the Nordhausen area'. And as they were about to discover, the Intelligence staff had been right.

Task Force Lovelady and Task Force Welborn of Combat Command B, the US 3rd Armored Division, arrived at Nordhausen practically together, and thus, on 11 April, 1945, were the first US Army soldiers to liberate a German concentration camp. What they found here rocked even the most battle-hardened man to the core. As the Division's official history records:

Everywhere among the dead were the living — emaciated shapes whose fever-bright eyes wilted passively for the release of death. Over all the area clung the terrible odor of decomposition and, like a dirge of forlorn hope, the combined cries of these unfortunates rose and fell in weak undulations. It was a fabric of moans and whimpers, of delirium and outright madness. Here and there a single shape tottered about, walking slowly, like a man dreaming.

Most of the skeletal prisoners in their tattered, befouled pyjamas were suffering from dysentery. It seemed to the medical officer of Combat Command B, Major Sherman, that only half the camp's surviving inmates would last for another twenty-four hours, even though US Army medical teams were already being rushed in to Nordhausen. As he concluded sadly, 'A number who had not been starved had been shot to death by the SS guards. . . . They were in a way lucky.'

Horror built on horror as the Americans entered the camp, sickened by the stench of ordure, by the obscene sight of human beings tottering among the dead bodies like walking corpses, their bony shapes scarcely disguised by the ragged, flapping penitential uniforms. Soon they were hearing of the tortures inflicted on these suffering survivors, of the physical abuse they had endured, the beatings, the terror, the starvation diet of four ounces of black bread and two bowls of thin gruel per day. For these pathetic remnants of humanity had been among the slave workers at Kammler's underground factory.

Day after day, week after week, these people had been forced to work in the tunnels and caves of the weapons complex, watched over by the SS and guarded by German criminals wielding whips. Some had remained below ground for three months without ever seeing daylight, forcibly confined to their work benches; now they could barely even stand without aid. Terrorized by the *Kapos*, the strawbosses, they had been forced to witness the public hanging of some of their fellows; men, women and children were all obliged to watch while some unfortunate was dangled from a noose.

The 9th Infantry Division, which had followed the 3rd Armored into the camp, was assailed by similar sights and horrors. The 9th's Divisional History describes the prisoners as a 'death column' and notes one bizarre discovery in particular: 'The Nazis had placed a fountain of *Kewpie Dolls* near the gallows.' It was just one example of the strange German mentality, a mixture of brutality and cloying sentimentality, which in other camps — soon to be discovered elsewhere — had SS officers joining in the singing of Christmas carols with child prisoners before sending them to the ovens the next day.

For the ovens had been the ultimate fate of many who could no longer work. According to the 3rd's divisional history:

The bodies came in by the truckloads, stripped of all clothing, and were dumped on the ground. When crematoriums were full a pyre was constructed outside: first a tier of bodies, then a layer of dry wood, more bodies and kerosene. They burned well enough for the SS and it didn't matter to them if a few bones were left. In fact, the SS wasn't at all partial. When one of their own men died, he too was shovelled into the oven.

Now the American medics had reached the camp, just as appalled by what they found. Sergeant Ragene Farris, of the 104th Division's 329th Medical Battalion, later recorded his memories of that time:

For days and weeks, even months afterwards, the word Nordhausen brought us a mixture of emotions. We were battle-tired and combat-wise medics and we thought there was nothing left in the books that we didn't know. Blood and bandages and all kinds of hell was daily routine. . . . I, for one, in order to keep working efficiently and smoothly, had grown callous. Yet in a short period of two days, I and many others in the Division saw and lived a story we shall never forget.

The medical aid team carried their stretchers into the first building, unprepared for the further horror within:

It was the sharp sting of reality which met us at the first doorway. Rows upon rows of skin-covered skeletons met our eyes. Men lay as they had starved, discolored and lying in indescribable filth. . . . There were no living beings; only the distorted dead. We went to the stairs and under the casing were neatly piled about seventy-five bodies, a sight I could never erase from memories. Dying on the second floor were . . . about twenty-five men or half men. Some of these, lying on double-decked wooden bedsteads, were grotesquely yet tenaciously hanging on to a life's breath. They were still alive.

Elsewhere the Sergeant found that women had suffered just as much. One of those still alive was a seventeen-year-old French girl:

She lay there where she had fallen, gangrened and naked. In my own thoughts I choked up — couldn't quite understand how and why war could do these things.

Sergeant Farris's feelings were shared by many other American soldiers who had entered Nordhausen with him. Now they made for the underground weapons factory whose existence the camp's inmates had revealed. Two miles away they came upon the entrance to the huge complex — and found a few of Kammler's scientists still loitering on the scene. Some of the soldiers now expressed their pent-up horror and outrage in blind, unreasoning violence. Entering the tunnels and caves where so many thousands of slave workers had toiled under the *Kapos'* whips, they caught one German scientist and beat him up — then repeated the scene for the benefit of a Signals Corps photographer.

But there were other Americans who entered the underground plant with feelings of awe rather than fury. Penetrating ever deeper into the miles of subterranean corridors, so carefully designed with ventilation systems and artificial lighting, they found the V-bombs which Kammler's men had not had time to destroy. Some were half-assembled, with components lying all round them; others were complete. Here, with the stench of death and sadism in the air, where an estimated one hundred slave workers had been shot per day on suspicion of sabotage, where the rest of the wretched workers had laboured on under SS supervision, American Intelligence officers could hardly suppress their feelings of wonder.

To Major Castille, Intelligence Officer with the 3rd Armored, the secret factory was like 'a magician's cave'. As he stared around at one cave, taking in the orderly benches of precision-made tools and inspection machinery, he realized he had been granted a glimpse into the future. 'Everything was bright and shining,' he later recalled; but everything was an instrument of death. And the American Intelligence men were fascinated.

One of them, the young Irish-American Captain James Hamill, knew that what the bemused GIs were now viewing, wide-eyed like country yokels coming up to New York for the first time, was worth millions and millions of dollars in research alone. It was research that the US Army wanted, despite what it might have cost in terms of human misery. Hamill had been given the special mission of collecting as many of the V-2 missiles as he could. They, like the ones in the railway tunnel at Bromskirchen, would be transported out of Germany and shipped across to the States, to the White Sands Proving Ground in New Mexico. But the mission was to be completed as speedily as possible, within four days, and in conditions of utmost secrecy.

Hamill's chief, Colonel Holgar Toftoy, based in Paris, had made it clear to him that the missiles were to be removed 'without making it obvious that we had looted the place'. What Toftoy did not explain was the reason for the particular urgency of his mission. It was not just the British who should never learn of the Americans' haul, but the Russians too — and the Soviet Army was already approaching the Nordhausen area. Indeed, this region, according to the terms of the Yalta Agreement, would be incorporated in the Soviet Zone of Occupation. However sanguine the Supreme Commander might be about the future of US relations with Russia, his intelligence staff were determined that the Soviet Army should not get its hands on this secret weapon.

So Hamill set about his task. In all he collected 100 complete V-2 missiles and transported them by rail to Antwerp. Here he faced a potential problem. Antwerp was now under British control; yet somehow he had to transfer the missiles across the docks, from the train to the waiting American ships, without the British knowing. The Belgian port was piled high with equipment intended for the Front, but if the missiles were left there for any length of time they would surely be discovered. Ever resourceful, however, Hamill enlisted the aid of two Irish sea captains. While they helped him pull the wool over British eyes, the V-2s were smuggled through the docks and loaded onto the sixteen freighters, manned by American crews, for shipment to the States.

But someone in the port must have alerted the British. As the convoy set off across the North Sea, it was intercepted by vessels of the Royal Navy. The senior Navy captain, evidently well informed about the freighters' cargo, demanded that half the American ships should divert to British ports. At the same time the Foreign Office in London was making a formal diplomatic protest about the matter to the State Department in Washington. But by April, 1945, it was already clear that Britain's star was sinking; the Americans were making the decisions now, and in the end the V-2 missiles arrived safely in the States, docking at New Orleans.

Hamill's mission was complete. What he did not yet realize was that he had made one great mistake: before leaving the underground factory he had failed to destroy the weapons' remaining components.

Soon after Hamill's departure, the Americans moved on, leaving Nordhausen to the Soviet Army. Lieutenant-Colonel Vladimir Yurasov arrived here on a routine mission, in search of materials that could be seized and sent back to the USSR to help rebuild his shattered country. It was while investigating the local cement plant that he accidentally discovered the mountain tunnels and their secret.

He saw the weapons' parts still lying where Hamill had left them, and immediately recognized their value.

As Yurasov's driver Nikolai remarked: 'This was the most secret German weapon and the Americans left it to us! . . . Americans are not bad fellows, but somehow too trusting.'

Yurasov found a fellow colonel whose scientific background would help to identify this abandoned hoard of components, and laughed at his comrade's expression of disbelief as he exclaimed: 'The Americans gave us *this*? In five or ten years they will be weeping! . . . Imagine when *our* rockets fly across the ocean!'

But while ally betrayed and tricked ally, in a foretaste of what was to come in the postwar world when the two new superpowers began to flex their military muscles, the Battle for the Ruhr Pocket continued in its totally purposeless course. One day after the 3rd Armored liberated Nordhausen, one of its combat commands overran another German camp at Polleben, just outside the town of Eisleben. This was a POW camp and its inmates included 450 British soldiers and officers, some of whom had been in captivity since Dunkirk back in 1940. It was a great day for them and in the emotion of the moment traditional British reserve broke down.

'We knew you were coming,' one British airborne major told the liberators. 'But when that first Sherman tank rolled over the hill I was so happy I *cried*!'

After years behind barbed wire, cut off from all they had once known and loved, the British were astonished by the might and super-abundance of the 3rd's equipment. One British captain exclaimed, 'My God, you Yanks have enough material in this convoy to reach Berlin!'

The men of the 'Spearhead' division thought so too. Indeed, it was not only the British Top Brass, led by Montgomery, who felt that the Ruhr Pocket operation was a waste of time and human resources when a much more important target could be attacked; most of the US Army felt the same, right from the private soldier up to divisional and corps commanders such as Gavin and Ridgway and, in the final analysis, the Ninth Army Commander himself. As Simpson lamented, with his army now poised on the Elbe and Berlin so tantalizingly close:

The north Corps [of the Ninth Army] was about fifty-three miles from Berlin . . . . And this bridgehead was opposed by a kind of

crust of newly formed outfits that were putting up some opposition;
but with another pontoon bridge and another division or two across,
we could have broken through. I think we could have been in Berlin
in twenty-four hours.

But Bradley's orders were plain; Berlin was no longer a target, and
there was nothing that anyone — British or American — could do
to alter the fact. The Battle for the Ruhr Pocket must be continued,
to the greater glory of the US Army and its Supreme Commander.

'It really is frightful to think of all the lives being wasted to satisfy
American public opinion,' wrote 'Simbo' Simpson, Montgomery's
confidant in the British War Office. 'If the American public only
knew the truth!'

But they didn't; the US Army censors saw to that. Newspapers
back in the States would reveal only what Eisenhower and Bradley
saw fit for the American public to read. On 15 April the *Sunday*
Pictorial splashed its pages with optimistic headlines: *'End in a*
Few Days, US Told,' they ran. *'Paratroops Drop Near Berlin, Says*
Report.' 'How Long Now?'

The same question was on the lips of many an ordinary
combat soldier that week. What was he doing still battling
away in the Ruhr nearly a month after the big break-out from
the Remagen bridgehead? Why was he still fighting in this useless
industrial wasteland when most of the Army Group was just sitting
idly on the River Elbe, waiting for the Russians to fight their way
through to them?

But Ridgway, like the other American corps commanders involved,
kept urging his men to ever greater efforts, so the green 86th
Division fought on, its casualties mounting all the time. General
'Count' Melasky had got the message; he was to produce results
or his old West Point classmate would fire him without the
slightest hesitation.

All the 86th's senior commanders were up front now. They would
tolerate no vacillation from the 'Black Hawks', as the Division liked
to call itself. Fighting to capture the industrial town of Lüdenscheid
against strong enemy resistance, the assistant divisional commander
General Pope personally rallied some shaken rifle companies and led
them into action. Not far away that same day, another senior officer,
the divisional artillery commander General Ghelsteen was ambushed
by a German patrol right up front, miles ahead of his artillery, and
taken prisoner.

But by now Ridgway had command problems other than those
of the 86th. Since the start of his attack the previous week he had

been asking for an armoured division to spearhead the drive of his infantrymen. What he received from Bradley was the greenest armoured division in Europe: the 13th Armored under the command of yet another West Point classmate, John Wogan. The 'Old Boy Network', as it used to be called in Britain, obviously operated in the US Army too.

The 13th Armored, back in training, had thumbed its nose at that unlucky number — perhaps rashly as it turned out. For it had adopted as its divisional insignia a shoulder patch which incorporated a spilled salt cellar, an open umbrella, a broken mirror and a black cat. Unofficially the men of the division called themselves 'the Black Cats'. But, within the few short weeks of its combat career, the 'Black Cat' Division had already earned the reputation among other divisions of being 'the Unlucky 13th'. In fact, by the time it reached the front, after a 260-mile march, it had already lost one third of its troops and one of its three combat commands was missing half its tanks.

Nonetheless, an impatient Ridgway had ordered his old friend John Wogan to attack without delay; and Wogan did as he was ordered. But the haste of this sudden introduction to combat, after a lifetime of training and waiting for action, did not please him. Nor was he happy about Ridgway's order to 'destroy' German troops on the ground. That was not supposed to be the role of armour; an armoured division was intended for great thrusts, for breaking through the enemy's defences while the infantry followed behind to mop up.

Unfortunately for Wogan, whose fighting career was going to be of even shorter duration than that of his Division, he took the order literally. In brilliant weather, his Division attacked through that of General Halsey's, another West Point classmate, taking the autobahn north towards Cologne. All of Cologne on the west bank of the Rhine had been in Allied hands since the first week of March; the suburbs on the east bank, however, were still held by the Germans. Total chaos followed. All communications broke down. Tanks got lost or strayed away. The accompanying infantry got left behind. One combat team stopped to 'destroy' a small pocket of German infantry, a job that should have been carried out by a follow-up team. In short, the 'Unlucky 13th' had made a total mess of its first twenty-four hours in combat. And Ridgway was furious. As he later remarked: 'The men of the 13th just weren't moving . . . . The Germans were at a low ebb. The opposition wasn't heavy at all. In other words the progress of the Division was thoroughly unsatisfactory.'

By this time Ridgway had commanded eighteen different divisions during his six months' career as chief of the XVIII Airborne Corps. Some of them had not been of any great calibre; a few had been decidedly weak. None, he concluded, was 'as generally inefficient in combat as the 13th'. Its leadership was 'lamentable', with 'a complete lack of aggressiveness'.

For the time being, he gave Wogan a second chance. However, to make sure that the 13th Armored Division did better on the morrow, he sent his own Corps Artillery Commander, General Lemuel Mathewson, to help Wogan sort out his problems.

Mathewson was appalled by what he found at the 13th Armored's command post. He reported to Ridgway officially: 'As it stands today, I would say the Division is thoroughly ineffectual as a fighting machine and drastically in need of a major overhaul.' Furthermore, Wogan's HQ was 'poorly staffed' and his subordinate commanders generally 'incapable of providing forceful, aggressive leadership which the ordinary circumstances of combat require'.

Next day the chaos grew even worse. The whole divisional structure seemed to be falling apart, and it wasn't helped by the fact that the impatient Ridgway now began to sack the 13th's senior officers for incompetence. Bad blood occurred, too, when it appeared that the West Point 'Old Boy Network' was being used to replace non-West Pointers with officers from the Academy.

Fortunately for Wogan, he was now seriously wounded in the neck by enemy rifle fire. Thus he was evacuated from the battlefield just before Ridgway relieved him of his command. He was later recommended for the Distinguished Service Cross for his bravery in the action in which he was wounded — but Ridgway did not forward the citation. The stern unrelenting General was going to have no truck with that kind of whitewashing. Later he would state categorically that General John Wogan had 'failed' as a combat commander.

Hurriedly another general was whistled up to take Wogan's place. Again the choice of commander was hardly auspicious. He was John Millikin, an experienced general, but one who had only just been sacked from his post as III Corps Commander for failing to exploit the Remagen bridgehead. Ridgway had to accept him; after all, Millikin was senior to himself. But he did so reluctantly, putting in his own man, General Peter Hains, to ensure that Millikin didn't fall down on the job as Wogan had done.

Hains was just as critical as Mathewson when he went up front to the command post of the division's Combat Command B, led by a Colonel Holt; in Hains's opinion the situation there was typical of the whole 13th Armored Division:

I found him [Holt] and a number of his officers lounging around in chairs and chatting. I introduced myself and asked what was going on. He said they'd had a big battle and were reorganizing. I asked how many men had he lost. None. How many tanks knocked out. None. I commented sarcastically, 'It must have some battle!'

But Hains was not there just to criticize; he had brought an order from Ridgway's Chief-of-Staff, General Eaton. The Division was to push on for the Rhenish city of Düsseldorf straight away. And, Hains told Colonel Holt, 'If you don't have Düsseldorf by dark, your throat will be cut from ear to ear, as will every man's in the command, including me.'

As 'Simbo' Simpson had just sighed to Montgomery, '*If the American public only knew the truth!*'

By now the heart was going out of the German defenders. The daily count of prisoners surrendering to the victorious Americans had risen from 500 a day at the beginning of April to 2,000 — in one instance 5,000 — by the second week of that month. One proud GI of the 78th Division, for example, set off to the rear with 68 German prisoners-of-war. But by the time he reached the divisional cage, he found to his astonishment that the number of his prisoners had risen to the magnificent total of 1,200, including a score of officers!

It was clear that the German command structure was breaking up too. The 78th Division alone captured three generals in forty-eight hours; like their men they were only too eager to surrender to the once despised *Amis* — if, that is, they could find someone to accept their surrender.

But still there was the occasional German outfit determined to resist: paras, SS men and tankers from some of the formations which had once been the spearhead of German aggression, Bayerlein's *Panzerlehr* and General Siegfried von Waldenburg's 116th Panzer, 'the Greyhound Division', as its members called it. They knew, of course, that they could expect little mercy from the advancing Americans. If the artillery shells and aerial bombardments did not kill them, their captors would.

Seventeen-year-old Friedrich Schmidthausen, a member of the 116th, was captured with seven other members of his Division and a wounded captain, *Hauptmann* Gerling. They were lined up, as was customary, with their hands raised and their faces to the wall of a nearby house. Just at that instant firing broke out from the windows of houses opposite. Several Americans were hit and killed before the firing stopped. Now, as Schmidthausen recollected after the war,

We were taken inside the house under heavy guard with an American lying dead just underneath the window. After one of our number, a lieutenant, was interrogated, we were informed that we were going to be shot that evening at six thirty. Seven of the youngest were selected to be shot first, despite the lieutenant's protests.

At six we were led outside, carrying the wounded Captain Gerling on a door and escorted to the town of Budberg. Here an officer halted us and gave the order to fire.

Only three of us managed to make a run for it. I was wounded seven times and was only saved by a Russian worker and a German girl who managed to smuggle me into a nearby military hospital where my wounds were treated.

Four days later a similar atrocity took place at the tiny hamlet of Spitze, nestling in the hills of what the Germans called Bergischland. There the civilians had already hung their houses with white flags, including one on the church steeple, as the Americans began to approach from the direction of Biesfeld. A handful of armed stragglers from the beaten Wehrmacht decided to wait for the *Amis* and surrender to them when they arrived. What they did not know was that the crews of several flak batteries, fleeing through Spitze, had decided to stop there and make a stand.

A few hours earlier the Americans had sent over a spotter plane, which reported that Spitze was ready to surrender. So, taking no precautions because they expected no trouble, the American Shermans lumbered cheerfully into the village. At once the flak batteries opened up. Ignoring the villagers' pleas, the gunners — who were half drunk, having recently looted a nearby Army depot — intended to fight it out with the Americans.

The Americans' revenge was ferocious. All night long their artillery bombed the little village. At six the next morning they sent the infantry in to knock out the one surviving flak cannon. Then they stormed the houses, turfing out the civilians and soldiers at bayonet point from the cellars where they had cowered all night. There were just over a hundred of them, including a small party of Frenchmen who had worked in the village since 1940 at one task or another.

The Frenchmen's spokesman, Roger Vidal, told the angry Americans that nobody in the village had played any part in the events of the previous day. All of them had been prepared to surrender and none had borne a weapon during the fighting. Slightly appeased, the Americans told Vidal that the civilians could go back to their homes; but the soldiers were all taken prisoner — not just the crews of the flak batteries but also the stragglers who had been willing to surrender. Before moving on, they also seized a surprised middle-aged policeman who had been watching the proceedings, presumably because he, too, wore a uniform.

Two hours after the Americans had left, the villagers heard the chatter of a heavy machine gun from some fields nearby. Not daring to leave their homes to investigate because a strict curfew had been imposed, it was a few days before they discovered what had happened. The bodies of twenty-one soldiers and one policeman lay sprawled in the grass in a rough line, shot down where they had stood.*

Once again American troops had resorted to the kind of lynch justice that most of the 'folks back home' thought had died out in the nineteenth century. It was the sort of thing that nice American boys who dated nice girls and liked 'mom's' apple pie simply didn't do. Back in 1942 General Patton had sneered at his newly inducted draftees, calling them 'canteen commandos' — softies, callow young men who would have to be trained hard if they were ever going to fight. But the war had soon brutalized them. The lives of those young infantrymen who carried out the atrocities at Spitze, Budberg, and half-a-dozen other German villages that second week of April, were often short, harsh and brutish. They looted, raped and sometimes murdered as well. They had gone to war as nice American boys; they would go home — those who survived — as hardened bitter men. America wanted heroes, not horror stories.

*In 1952 a joint American–German team investigated this 'war crime'. But the mood of the time was against the Germans. The US Army effectively covered up for their troops, reporting that it was impossible to identify the units concerned (which was untrue). Nothing came of the investigation.

FOUR

'The senseless tragedy'

Now those great Ruhr industrial cities, which had been the workshop of German military might ever since Krupp had founded his first factory in Duisburg in 1811, started to fall to the victorious, if weary Americans. Here the weapons of war had been forged that had raised Germany from a collection of obscure provincial states, whose principal export had been their people, to a vast Nazi empire which had dominated Europe from the Urals to the Channel and from the Arctic Circle to the Mediterranean. Was it not in Essen, the heart of the great industrial complex, that Hitler had called upon Germany's youth to be 'as hard as Krupp steel, tough as leather and as swift as a weasel'?

Some surrendered tamely with hardly a fight; others such as Dortmund were fought over bitterly for days. But they all seemed to present the same picture of bombed-out buildings, blocked streets and twisted metal lampposts already red with rust. One GI later recalled the ruined street where one building had been totally destroyed save for a single drainpipe; it reached up to where the third storey had been, and there, in midair, it supported a bathtub with a long-handled loofah still dangling over the side. Others remembered the empty window frames on free-standing walls as looking like the eye sockets of human skulls. All noted the pathetic bits and pieces left behind by residents who had fled: the bright bit of junk in the grey rubble which turned out to be a kid's doll; the shattered kitchens with broken crockery littering the floor; the white enamel cooking stoves with pans still on the rings; the intimate glimpses of people's bedrooms now open for all to view.

Many were appalled by the characteristic stench, a composite of escaping sewer gas, faeces and urine — and human misery, too.

For beneath these ruins lay the bodies of hundreds of men, women and children who had been killed in the raids during these last terrible years and whose corpses had never been recovered. Their very existence might be forgotten save for a rough cross chalked on a wall with the legend '*Hier ruhen 20 Personen*' (here lie twenty people), and perhaps a jar of wilting flowers.

Some people were still alive, of course: strange nocturnal creatures living in the deep cellars of their derelict homes, who ventured out only under cover of darkness to forage for food and for wood with which to cook their meagre rations on makeshift stoves. Not only were they without water, electricity or gas, they were reduced to plundering abandoned houses for food or carving chunks off dead German Army horses — in one case, observed by some revolted GIs, off a horse that was still alive.

When the Americans finally brought them release, an end to the years of fear and suffering, they came out of their cellars, pale, haunted and emaciated, waving sheets, towels, bedspreads — anything to indicate surrender — and greeted their conquerors almost as if they were liberators.

Simpson, the Commander of the Ninth Army, was sick of this kind of fighting. To clear the industrial zone he had formed a special task force under General Harry Twaddle, consisting of the 95th Infantry Division, the 8th Armored Division, the 15th Cavalry Group and one regiment of the 17th Airborne. Task Force Twaddle cut right into the heart of the Ruhr. On 7 April it captured Gelsenkirchen, north of Essen. Next day it took Hamm, the largest rail centre in the world. Two days later, after a two-hour fight with von Waldenburg's 116th Panzer Division, the Task Force had won Unna. By 11 April, thanks to Ridgway's and Twaddle's urgent efforts, the Ruhr Pocket had been reduced to an average diameter of roughly sixteen miles.

It was the paras of the 17th Airborne who took Essen itself, the city which to most of them meant only Krupp and the German war machine. To their surprise they were met with 'welcome' signs, and the civilians coming to greet them as they crossed the Rhine–Herne Canal carried bottles of wine and gifts along with the usual white flags. Instead of the fight the paras had expected, they found themselves engaged in impromptu street parties, with signs plastered on the ruined walls reading '*THANK YOU*'.

Naturally the word went out: Capture Krupp! For the great-great-grandson of the founder of the dynasty had long been on the Allies' list of wanted war criminals. The infantry of the 79th Division, now also attached to Task Force Twaddle, went to search for him. First they checked the huge Krupp factory, or what was left of it; for six weeks before, on 1 March, the RAF had dealt it a massive blow which reportedly killed 2,000 workmen there and cut off all electricity. They were met by a 'tired-looking elderly clerk' who surrendered the place to them and said wearily, 'What a relief to know that all those awful nights and days of bombs have come to an end!' But his boss wasn't there, he told the Americans. He would be at his home, the Villa Hugel.

The clerk was right; his boss had not fled. Alfred Krupp, the head of one of the world's biggest industrial firms, which had produced armaments for dictators from Napoleon to Hitler and which had made $200,000,000 out of the First World War alone, had remained in Essen.

When the Americans reached the luxurious mansion, set in secluded grounds, it looked at first as if there might be trouble. The door was barred by several of Alfred Krupp's servants — big, beefy men. But Colonel Sagmoen, in charge of the party, drew his .45 Colt and the door cleared as if by magic. Now the industrialist himself appeared, looking nervous but trimly attired in a pin-striped business suit. Gruffly Sagmoen ordered him into the waiting jeep. As it started off down the long drive, a servant came running with a weekend bag for his master. But the Americans were not waiting this day for servants carrying weekend bags for war criminals.

Krupp was taken into the kitchen of the house which was now the Americans' command post. A month before, the assistant *Gauleiter* of Essen had proclaimed boldly, 'The enemy will be forced out with brutal hardness. We will not hesitate to use any and every means of defending our beloved Ruhr.' Now Krupp was asked why he had neither fought nor fled.

He shrugged his bony shoulders. 'I wanted to stay with my factory where I belong with my fellow workers.'

'Are you a Nazi?' he was asked then.

'I am a German,' was his reply.

'Are you a member of the Nazi Party?' the Americans persisted.

'Well, yes,' he conceded nervously, 'but most Germans are.'

'What is your present salary?' someone asked.

Krupp looked at Sagmoen in annoyance. 'Must I answer?' he demanded.

'Yes,' Sagmoen snapped back.

Krupp took his time. He took a cigarette from a silver case, lit it and took a nervous puff before saying: 'Four hundred thousand marks a year' (about £40,000). But this, he maintained, he had been forced to split between his family and the Nazi government.

'Do you think Germany will win the war?' he was then asked.

With ruin and utter destruction all around him, Krupp could still answer: 'I do not know. Politics is not business. My business is making steel.'

This response annoyed the Americans. The Krupp family, they considered, were merchants of death; over the last century and a half, their armaments had caused millions to die. But Alfred Krupp, whose 50,000 employees included 10,000 foreign slaves, seemed strangely blind to the weakness of his own position. When he was asked finally by his interrogators what his plans were for after the war, he pondered for a while before stating quite confidently: 'I hope to rebuild my factories and produce again.'*

Not all the great industrial cities of the Ruhr were captured as easily as Essen. Dortmund, which had had a pre-war population of 600,000 citizens, held up Simpson's men for days and involved the Ninth Army in a full-scale attack by the US 75th Infantry Division and Task Force Twaddle.

While the Gestapo brutally suppressed any kind of opposition to a fighting defence of the bomb-shattered city with their daily shootings of resistance workers in the public parks, the city itself was held by groups of fanatical young SS men. Outside, very determined groups of Wehrmacht soldiers and flak crews, using their anti-aircraft guns in a ground role, made progress for the 75th Division very difficult.

On one day alone, the 75th had to withstand *three* counter-attacks from determined groups of German paras, who penetrated to the rear of the Americans, cutting off several platoons as well as Divisional Provost Marshal, Major Charles LeCraw, and a handful of his MPs. LeCraw was wounded and his men were pinned down by the enemy. They were saved only by the coolness of Pfc Weiss, who changed into civilian clothes and — despite the risk of being shot out hand as a spy if he were caught — ran across some fields under fire to bring help. That day LeCraw and several of his men

---

*And he did. After the war he was sentenced to twelve years' imprisonment for having employed slave labour in his factories; but he never served the full term, being released prematurely by the Americans to a hero's welcome from the Germans. As he told a friend at the time: 'Now they have Korea on their hands, the Americans are a lot more friendly.' Then he went back to doing what he had said he would do in April, 1945: rebuilding his arms industry.

won the Silver Star for bravery in combat: an unusual event, for military policemen were more usually noted for their attention to spit-and-polish than displays of valour at the front.

Now the Americans called on the British, fighting on their left flank, for assistance in clearing the way into Dortmund. They arrived in the shape of men of the Fife and Forfar Yeomanry, who belonged to the 'Hobart Funnies' — or, to give the unit its real name, General Hobart's 79th Armoured Division.

Hobart, who was Montgomery's brother-in-law, had retired from the British Army and found a new role as a humble lance-corporal in the Home Guard, but suddenly he had been plucked from retirement to take over the 79th Division, a specialized armoured formation which was then being prepared for action on the beaches on D-Day. Among its weird and wonderful collection of armoured vehicles, many of them dreamed up by Churchill himself, the 79th had tanks that could lay bridges, tanks that could de-mine minefields and tanks that could knock out pillboxes with a kind of giant mortar; above all it had that most fearsome of tanks, the Crocodile.

Mounted in the chassis of a Churchill tank and towing a trailer of liquid death behind it, the squat cannon of the Crocodile could spurt out a searing blowtorch of flame for some seventy or eighty yards. It was a terrible weapon when used against houses or pillboxes. For it transformed the defenders, in an instant, into writing screaming human bonfires or shrivelled them up into charred pygmies.

By the spring of 1945 the British were using this terrible mobile flamethrower more and more often in built-up areas in Germany, to cut down casualties among their infantry. Now the Americans borrowed a whole regiment of Crocodiles. But even with their help — and once the Germans spotted the squat shapes with their familiar trailers behind them, they usually surrendered very hurriedly — the 75th Division could do little more than hold its divisional area and clean up a few remaining pockets of German resistance.

Simpson urged greater speed in Dortmund. He put pressure on General Twaddle's task force to link up with the 75th and form a ring of steel around the city. But the German defenders guessed the Americans' intention; they knew that a trap was being set for them, that somehow they would have to keep a way out open. They now launched one of the last counter-attacks experienced by American troops in Europe in the Second World War, driving at the positions of the US 8th Armored Division with several hundred infantry led by sixty-ton Tiger tanks.

The 8th Armored, however, stood their ground. Despite their

lack of combat experience they knocked out the Tigers one by one, and by evening the steam had gone out of this German attack at least; the ring had held. But elsewhere the frantic defenders fought on. At the local airfield small groups of SS fanatics attacked, counter-attacked and attacked again; according to some estimates the airfield changed hands seven times. By the time the Americans finally took it, the shattered hangars and plane-strewn runways were littered with silent figures of men in field-grey and khaki who would never rise again.

By 12 April the great pincer movement around the city was almost completed, while the Germans fought desperately to keep another escape route open at Witten to the south-west. From that direction the US 75th Division advanced against heavy opposition and difficult terrain; while from the north and north-eastern edges of Dortmund, the 95th Division entered the city itself.

Still the Germans refused to give up. There were snipers and young Hitler Youths everywhere, hiding in the ruins with their *panzerfausts*. Nor had the German engineers forgotten to lay the usual mines, and booby traps had been attached to anything that might look attractive to an unsuspecting GI — a doll, a bottle of wine, a German sausage.

Heinrich Bastian, a former manager of Dortmund's fashionable pre-war Café Corso, had been sheltering for weeks now in the cellar of his half-demolished house. With him was his pregnant wife and another couple, the wife of which insisted on her daily ablutions, taken openly in a tub on the floor of the cellar, much to the annoyance of Frau Bastian. Now as the snap-and-crackle of small arms fire came ever closer, Bastian — who had won the Iron Cross, First Class in the First World War for bravery as an artillery observer in France — decided he would risk having a peep at what was going on above. Against the protests of his wife and the other man's wife, who was sitting in her tub displaying her admirable breasts as usual, he crawled up through the rubble just in time to see a group of SS men setting a chain of home-made mini-mines in what was left of the road outside.

Many years later Bastian would find out that the *Ami* soldiers called these mini-mines 'deballockers'. For that was exactly what they did. When an unwary soldier stepped on one, the small charge exploded and fired a bullet right into his crotch, leaving him, as they said wryly, 'singing tenor' for the rest of his life.

Bastian watched in horror as the SS slunk back into the ruins, ready to snipe at the advancing *Amis*, while the first cautious figures in khaki, a colour he recognized from the Battle of the Argonne in 1918, advanced slowly on both sides, hugging what was left of the walls. What should he do? Should he grab a white flag and try to warn these unsuspecting young men? But if he did so, he risked being shot by the SS snipers. Besides, the *Amis* were technically still his enemies, though the future founding member of the postwar German liberal party, the FDP, had been longing for their arrival for weeks now. It was a terrible quandary.

In the end, the SS made up his mind for him. They started sniping the Americans just before they reached the line of mines. Instinctively most of them went to ground where they stood. One didn't. Perhaps he was brave, perhaps he just panicked. Bastian never found out. But in the same moment as he ducked back into his cellar, with a machine gun firing a vicious burst of tracer over his head, the young *Ami* stepped on one of the 'deballockers'. He collapsed with a hysterical screech, clutching at his groin, another victim of this fiendish device. Or, as Heinrich Bastian commented many years later: 'Another example of the senseless tragedy of still fighting on, at that hopeless, late stage of the war.'

Now the centre of Dortmund experienced the last throes of the senseless battle. Jeeps raced up and down, carrying out wounded GIs and bringing up fresh ammunition for the mortars and machine guns. Both sides still fired shells at each other, demolishing what was left of the ruins, endangering, in the case of the SS, their own soldiers and civilians. But the SS had been seized by a nihilistic sense of destruction. 'There will be no tomorrow for Germany,' they told any civilians who tried to reason with these half-crazy youngsters in their camouflage tunics. '*Nach uns die Sinflut*,'* they would cry, laughing cynically as they returned to their suicidal attacks.

Fighting continued from street to street, the GIs falling with sickening regularity as a hidden sniper's rifle cracked and another American soldier was hit. All the ruined houses, including doors to the cellars and what was left of the windows, were barricaded up. But the advancing infantry suspected snipers everywhere; there were enough crumpled, khaki-clad figures in the gutters to prove it. They didn't take chances. Barricades were blown apart by bazooka fire at close range. GIs followed, firing Tommy guns or flourishing fixed bayonets. Some of the more brutal thought the best way to deal with potential snipers was simply to toss a grenade or two into a suspect cellar; if it contained

---

*A literal translation of the French expression, '*Après nous le déluge*' (After us the deluge).

civilians, well that was tough shit! Wasn't the only good Kraut a dead Kraut?

Finally, however, on the evening of Friday 13 April, the battle for Dortmund was over. In one last burst of energy, the 75th and 95th Divisions had pushed forward and cleared the city, while the 95th's 379th Infantry Regiment drove on hurriedly and secured the high ground to the east, overlooking the Ruhr: the river that had given its name to the whole area. This move cut off all possibility of escape for any scattered groups of SS still lurking in the smoking ruins. Simpson's ring of steel was complete.

The battle had lasted nearly a week. As the sound of firing died away, dazed and dirty civilians started to emerge from their cellars to see what was left of their ruined city. The weary, unshaven GIs slung their weapons for the first time in days, wondering why things seemed so strange. It was the silence, the absence of artillery bombardment. The guns in the Dortmund area had stopped firing at last.

As Heinrich Bastian recalled many years later when he was a prosperous retired businessman:

We were shocked, dazed and hungry. We had nothing save the clothes we stood up in. My wife was pregnant and we didn't even have a drop of milk. Our flat was ruined and whatever savings we had in the bank would be, I knew, totally worthless. But we were happy, happy for the first time in years. There was no more Party, no more bombs, no more fighting. We were free!

The fall of Dortmund that unlucky Friday the Thirteenth seemed to take the heart out of many of Model's senior surviving generals. Bayerlein, commander of Model's 53rd Corps, had been considering his next move for days now. He knew there would be no freedom for *him* if he surrendered. It would be the cage for the senior tank commander who had fought for Hitler since 1939. He had no illusions on that score.

Three days before, Model had visited his command post and Bayerlein had raised the subject with him, suggesting that surrender was the only course left open to the Army Group. But Model refused to discuss the matter. Bayerlein had decided that the next time Model visited the 53rd Corps CP, he would arrest him and force him to surrender the whole Pocket. But there was no next time; Model made no further appearances at Bayerlein's command post. It was up to him now to do the awful deed: to commit high treason, a capital offence, and surrender his own Corps to the Americans. But how was he to do it?

Some of his officers, Bayerlein knew, were as ready to surrender as he was. They, too, thought any further resistance was senseless and could only bring more suffering on the war-weary German people. But other officers, like the Commanding General of his 180th Infantry Division, fiercely objected to his plans for mass surrender.

That afternoon a worried, haggard Bayerlein went to visit General von Waldenburg, Commander of the 116th Panzer — or what was left of it. The dashing, aristocratic commander was privy to Bayerlein's plans and was in full agreement with his Corps Commander on the matter of surrender. Hadn't his predecessor in command of the 116th, von Schwerin, risked death by refusing to defend Aachen the previous year, by refusing to turn it into a ruin? Then, the men of the 'Greyhound Division' had protected their Commander against the SS who arrived to arrest him. The 116th was a proud and independent formation and its Commander, like his men, was not afraid of taking risks.

Now Bayerlein and von Waldenburg set about preparing the way for something unprecedented on the Western Front — the surrender of a full, still active German corps.

In General von Waldenburg's case, the problem was complicated by the fact that within the divisional area there were 25,000 Allied prisoners-of-war, located in a camp to the east of the town of Hemer. Only a few hours earlier the camp had been hit by an American artillery bombardment and over seventy prisoners had been killed or wounded by their own shells. So Bayerlein now decided that his first move should be to contact the advancing Americans and let them know about the POW camp; it was obviously not marked on their situation maps. An American major, who had been captured only a few days before and was still in good shape, was selected from among the POWs and ordered to go under a flag of truce to make contact with the nearest US formation — the 99th Infantry Division. He was to tell them about Hemer and also mention that the 116th Panzer was prepared to enter into surrender talks.

In the event, the talks would not be with the 'Battle Babies', as the men of the 99th called themselves; they would have other surrenders to take care of. The first Americans to make contact with von Waldenburg would be the officers of the US 7th Armored Division, currently exerting pressure on what was left of the 116th Panzer, which had been in the thick of the fighting ever since Normandy.

Even Lieutenant-Colonel Guderian — son of the man who had first built up the German tank army, Heinz Guderian — who was now Chief-of-Staff to von Waldenburg, realized the game was up and further resistance was useless. 'Our losses in tanks and the lack of artillery shells made it virtually impossible to carry on the fight anyway,' he stated later, going on to add that in the Pocket as a whole 'our soldiers and vehicles were packed tightly together. There were the men, but we lacked weapons, fuel and room to move. . . . That is why we *had* to talk to the US 7th Armored.'

While the German generals were hesitantly planning their surrender, constantly watching out for the Gestapo and the young fanatics of the SS who might interrupt their plans, the ordinary soldiers had given up waiting for the brass. They were already surrendering by the hundred, by the thousand.

Outside Hemer, the Commanding General of the US 99th Infantry, General Lauer, received a frantic call from one of his battalion commanders on 13 April. He told his boss he needed help: 'The whole damned German Army is flowing right down the valley toward my position!' General Lauer came up in his jeep to see for himself. He had only just arrived on the scene and was observing the shabby flood of field-greys, one hand clutching their precious bits and pieces, the other raised in token of surrender, when a German prisoner wearing American uniform was shoved in front of him by a couple of GIs carrying Tommy guns.

A spy, Lauer wanted to know. No, the GIs growled. Some Kraut protesting he was, of all things, an American general.

It was just then that the prisoner spotted the Divisional Artillery Commander, General Frederick H. Black. 'Hey Freddie,' he yelled with relief, 'for Chrissake tell 'em who I am!'

Black laughed uproariously when he recognized the other man. It was General Ghelsteen, Artillery Commander of the unfortunate 86th Infantry Division of Ridgway's Corps, who had been captured days before. The captive was released immediately and, after being 'wined and dined', was hurried back to his old outfit. As General Lauer later commented: 'Thereafter the 86th Div, I am sure, cleaned up its flanks and rear areas as it advanced and no longer stormed headlong down main roads disregarding everything else, a procedure which in the past had caused the 99th considerable trouble along that flank.'

But this day Lauer was confronted not only by American generals with a problem, but also by German generals who wanted to talk with him urgently, eager to unburden themselves — General

Freiherr von Luttwitz, Bayerlein's neighbouring Corps Commander, for example. Von Luttwitz had told his guards that he had 'very important information to transmit at once to the high command of the American Army and desired to talk to a general officer of the American Army'.

General Lauer was intrigued. He had the gross, bemonocled German Corps Commander brought to him and asked what this information was. 'With tears in his eyes and a sob in his voice,' as Lauer wrote afterwards, 'his important message was to the effect that he was just a regular German soldier, a career officer, that he had never had anything to do with any atrocities. He wanted to say that he was not a Nazi at heart.' Lauer couldn't conceal his contempt. He told himself that von Luttwitz was 'pitiful, yet how typical. All he could think about was himself, not a thought about his men or the tactical situation.' He dismissed the babbling German Corps Commander without another word.

A year later von Luttwitz would be hard at work for the US Army's historical branch recording his part in the great siege of Bastogne, his immediate future secured, while most of his men still languished behind American barbed wire.

Lauer was similarly unimpressed by most of the other German generals his Division would capture in the next twenty-four hours, while only a couple of miles away Bayerlein was still nervously organizing the surrender of his full corps. There was General Ewart, commander of the 338th People's Grenadier Division, for example: 'a typical Prussian officer, extremely correct in his behaviour who bowed stiffly from the hips' — and who had brought his wife into the cage with him and expected Lauer to assign them both quarters. The wife was 'young and pretty', Lauer noted, but it was Ewart alone who 'found his quarters waiting for him in the north-west of an open field cage'. The only German Luftwaffe general officer to fall into Lauer's hands was another disappointment. Roemer, who had commanded the 22nd Flak Division, was not as correct as Ewart, but he too lived in a fantasy world. He had brought with him a massive amount of baggage which he now expected his captors to ship to his wife a hundred kilometres away. As Lauer commented, 'He *expected*' — and that was all.

Only one of his general officer captives seemed to show any sign of humour. He was General Denkert, an infantry commander, who admitted that he knew the war was lost. When asked what he thought of the situation in the Pocket, he grinned and nodded at the packed POW cage. 'Take a look at your cage, if you want to know,' he said and let himself be led inside, still grinning.

While two of his Corps Commanders, von Luttwitz and Kochling, had already surrendered and a third, Bayerlein, was contemplating doing the same, Model still seemed to feel there was a chance of escaping that fate.

By now he knew, of course, that it could be only a matter of hours before the Pocket was split in two by the First Army's advance from the south-east and the Ninth's from the west. Then his Army Group would have lost effective control of one half of the Pocket. He had already lost contact with Bayerlein, commanding his one remaining effective corps, and von Zangen, Commander of what was left of his Fifteenth Army, was on the run again. Only Colonel-General Harpe, that convinced National Socialist who led his Fifth Panzer Army, still seemed to be making some attempt to stop the *Amis*. What Model did not know was that even Harpe was planning to surrender.

That terrible Friday, Model sent a last message to Bayerlein. He signalled the 53rd Corps Commander (specifically against Hitler's own order that there should be no attempt to break out of the Pocket) to escape while he could with what was left of his Corps. Bayerlein, who now had other things on his mind, didn't even bother to acknowledge the message. Instead he went to say goodbye to what was left of his beloved *Panzerlehr*, the Wehrmacht's most formidable armoured division, the one he had raised and fought with all the way from Normandy. It was virtually his last military act in a career in the Army which had lasted thirty years.

Bayerlein thought that Model was clutching at straws. But the Army Group Commander had acted often enough as 'Hitler's Fire Brigade' in the past, seizing at the most unlikely opportunities and reversing situations which others had thought impossible; he had rescued the Wehrmacht in Russia four times, and had done the same in the West after the 1944 débâcle in France. Surely, Model seemed to think, there was still a chance that he could stem the tide, gain time for himself, for Hitler, for the German Army retreating before the Russians, for the great treks of civilians fleeing with them? Perhaps the Führer might pluck a last-minute political solution out of the bag? Perhaps, even now at the eleventh hour, the disparate alliance between East and West might break down? As a result, Germany might be needed by the Anglo-Americans as a valuable ally in a new confrontation with Soviet Russia. After all, just such a thing had happened back in the eighteenth century, during the Seven Years' War, when 'Old Fritz' — Frederick the Great of Prussia — was defeated by a similarly disparate coalition of his European enemies.

Besides, Model knew that General Wenck and his hastily assembled Twelfth Army was reacting fiercely to the American threat on the Elbe. Wenck's men might be green, but they were fresh and enthusiastic. Swiftly, mobile battle groups of the newly formed *Scharnhorst, Potsdam* and *Hutten* Divisions drove at the Americans with an elan that had been missing from the German Army for months.

While Bayerlein contemplated surrender, these young soldiers were overrunning the positions of the veteran 'Hell on Wheels' Division, which had closed the Pocket eleven days before, using American prisoners in some cases to shield their advancing tanks. By that evening the US 2nd Armored was withdrawing everywhere, having suffered its first defeat of the campaign in Germany at the cost of 304 men dead. All that remained of the American presence across the River Elbe was the bridgehead of the US 83rd Infantry Division at Barlby.

Thus it was that the doughty little Field-Marshal dug in his heels when all around him the talk was of defeat and surrender. Wenck might not be able to rescue him, Model reasoned, but there were at least some young German soldiers who, like those under Wenck's command, were still capable of fighting and beating the enemy. And so, that evening when his new Chief-of-Staff, General Wagener, suggested to Model that he should request permission from Berlin to surrender, the Field-Marshal flatly disagreed. Such a request, from a general of his reputation and calibre, might well convince Hitler and the German High Command that they should stop the war at once. If so, Model would have been instrumental in losing the war for his beloved Fatherland just as a glimmer of hope appeared on the horizon. No, he could not do that!

Later General Wagener maintained that Model had lost all contact with reality. He, Wagener, was resigned to his fate. There was no hope for what was left of the Army Group, just as there was no hope for Germany. Model, however, was as active as ever. He was constantly at the front, visiting whatever combat troops were left to him and trying to rally them.

Well, Model had never been a coward, Wagener knew that; the Field-Marshal had shed his blood in two wars for the Fatherland. But now the bloodshed had to stop. If Model wouldn't surrender,

Wagener would have to start looking after himself. Thus, while Model still hoped for the impossible, Wagener began to make his own plans for the future.

The air raid sirens in Berlin had just shrilled the 'All Clear' when Goebbels' Press Secretary received the tremendous news from the *Deutsches Nachrichtenburo*, the official German news agency. The man on the other end of the phone was almost incoherent with excitement but finally his news was clear: the American President had died.

Semmler, the Press Secretary, was disbelieving at first; but the man then read him the Reuters' message: '*Roosevelt died today at midday.*'

Semmler relayed the news to his cheering companions. One of them, a fervent Catholic, crossed himself and exclaimed, 'This is the miracle that Dr Goebbels has been promising us so long.' Goebbels thought so too. Pausing only to order a bottle of champagne, he promptly telephoned the Führer:

'*Mein Fuhrer*, I congratulate you! Roosevelt is dead. It is written in the stars that the second half of April will be the turning point for us. This is Friday, April the thirteenth. Fate has laid low your greatest enemy. God has not abandoned us. . . . Death . . . has now struck down our most dangerous enemy. *It is a miracle*!'

For Goebbels, who often believed his own propaganda, the death of 'the Jew Roosevelt', as he was habitually called in certain sections of the National Socialist press, did mean that Germany still had a chance. From their own agents, the German Top Brass knew that the Soviet–Anglo–American alliance was shaky. They knew, too, that Churchill had long been an enemy of Soviet Communism. Hadn't he attempted to have Lenin killed and ordered armed intervention in Russia right at the start of the revolution? Wasn't he even now engaged in a war against the communists in Greece?

Goebbels, and perhaps Hitler too, felt that with Roosevelt gone and Churchill clearly opposed to Soviet Communist ideals, there was now a chance of putting out peace feelers to the United States. As one of the longest-serving German cabinet ministers, Count Schwerin von Krosigk, wrote to Goebbels immediately upon hearing the great news:

I myself see in Roosevelt's death a divine judgment, but it is also a gift from God that we shall have to earn to order to possess. This death eliminates the block that has obstructed all roads leading to contacting America. . . . Considering the seriousness of the military situation we must not hesitate.*

The Germans — Goebbels and all the rest of the Top Brass — were living in cloud-cuckoo land. Churchill might conceivably have agreed to negotiate with Germany but he was no longer the dominant partner in the Alliance, even though the new President, Harry S. Truman, was a complete novice in foreign affairs. For all decisions in Europe were now being left to the military. Neither Germany nor Model, trapped in the Pocket, would be saved. Within the month Goebbels would be dead and Count Schwerin von Krosigk would be joining the rest of the surviving Nazi *Prominenz* at 'Camp Ashcan'.

Eisenhower had spent the evening drinking champagne with Patton and Bradley and four Red Cross girls — one of whom, Ruth Gordon, was Patton's cousin and mistress — at Patton's headquarters. Thereupon they had retired to bed when Patton heard the news of Roosevelt's death over his bedside radio. Dressed in his riding boots and elegant cavalry breeches he went first to Bradley's room. He wanted Bradley to go with him to tell Eisenhower. Now the three of them, who had virtually taken over military strategy of the 5,000,000-strong Allied armies in Europe during these last weeks, sat down and discussed the new situation caused by the death of the President.

Later it would be claimed that at this moment of tragedy for the American people, Eisenhower faltered, that once again a plan was broached for the whole might of the US Army to be flung into a drive for Berlin, using those divisions still investing the Ruhr Pocket so purposelessly. But Eisenhower knew he had the full support of Marshall, and in his turn Marshall was — by repute – venerated by the new President Truman.

In the event, Eisenhower would make no change. As Bradley's aide, Major Hansen, noted, 'Ike is waiting on an order, but until he gets one we have to make our [own] plans.' But no order would come.

*This is an allusion, hence the strange phraseology, to a quotation from Goethe: 'Was du ererbt von deinen Vatern hast, erwirb es zu besitzen' (what you inherited from your forefathers you must earn before possessing).

America, in its hour of victory, was leaderless; higher international politics and the shape of the future of Central Europe would be left in the hands of the US generals.

Mickey McKeogh, Eisenhower's long-time 'striker', who wrote a weekly letter to Mamie Eisenhower telling her how the 'boss' was getting on, realized that night before Eisenhower retired for a second time that his superior was shaken by the news. He chatted with the undersized private soldier, who had once been a New York bellhop, about his regret that Roosevelt had not lived to see the victorious end of the war in Europe. McKeogh then mentioned that he had not voted in the last election. Eisenhower frowned. 'Mickey,' he said, 'you are a civilian. The vote is the most precious right you possess. You should exercise it.'

McKeogh would long cherish the advice, though at the time he doubted whether the Supreme Commander himself had ever voted. In less than a decade, however, McKeogh would be voting for that same seemingly apolitical Eisenhower.

Meanwhile, Eisenhower and the other American Top Brass were running the war, not the politicians. The voice of the US State Department was particularly muted. Cordell Hull, the Secretary of State, later wrote, 'After Pearl Harbor, I did not sit in on meetings concerned with military matters'; and, he continued, 'The grand military movement to conquer Hitler was a subject never discussed with me by the President or any of his top military officials.' Stimson, the Secretary of State for War, told Cordell Hull that it was his duty merely 'to support, protect and defend his generals'. As for Marshall, the US Army's most senior soldier, Roosevelt was in such awe of him that he dared not even call him by his first name.

Politically untutored and poorly read, Eisenhower was now in sole charge in Europe, unconstrained by Allied or American politicians, but supported to the hilt by the most powerful man in Washington — Marshall. He could do just as he wanted. Patton might have sneered to his cronies of the Third Army, 'How can anyone expect any backbone in a man who is already running for President?' Now, however, future presidential candidate or not, Eisenhower would show backbone — some would say obstinacy. There would be no last-minute change of strategy, he decreed.

Model, Germany, Central Europe would be delivered to their ordained fate. There was no more hope for them.

FIVE

'The rational thing to do'

On the morning of Saturday, 14 April a battalion of General Moore's 8th Infantry Division reached Hattingen on the River Ruhr, the XVIII Airborne Corps' final objective. Across the river, the GIs of General Wyche's 79th Division greeted them with jeers; for one of their companies had already crossed and been withdrawn under pressure from higher headquarters. They had come back protesting angrily. But orders were orders. The official link-up between Hodges's First Army and Simpson's Ninth Army had to take place according to the rules laid down by the Top Brass.

The Ruhr Pocket had been split into two, leaving the bulk of Army Group B completely stranded in the western half around Düsseldorf and Wuppertal. As the History of the 79th Division commented, 'It was becoming more and more apparent that the war was drawing to a close and the opportunities for high deeds and heroic accomplishments were becoming fewer and fewer.' So the men of the two armies contented themselves with shouting a few tired insults across the river and then began to dig in. It was just another day at war. There was nothing heroic about it. The *Stars and Stripes* didn't even send a photographer to record the link-up; its staff were too busy covering the funeral of the dead President, noting that there had even been a note of condolence from the new Japanese Premier, Susuki, expressing his 'profound sympathy'. The men of the two divisions that had split the Pocket, after two weeks of slogging away through the rugged country and the ruins of the industrial area, crouched in their holes, enjoying the sudden calm and strange silence, and wondered if there would be 'hot chow' to celebrate the event. Their hopes were in vain.

Meanwhile Bayerlein had cleared the way for his own surrender;

he had solved the problem of Hemer, its camp now packed with Allied POWs, mostly Russian, and the town itself filled with several thousand German wounded. When he surrendered, he wanted no last-minute accusations of war crimes levelled at him.

The commander of the 116th Panzer Division's *panzergrenadier* regiment, Colonel Stephan, was delegated to hand over the camp to General Lauer's 99th Infantry. Stephan was scared of the Russian POWs, who lived like animals and behaved like them too. It wasn't surprising. The Russians had been systematically brutalized and beaten ever since they had been captured; all over the Reich 600,000 Russian POWs had volunteered to serve in the Wehrmacht (twice the number of men in Patton's Third Army) simply in order to escape from these virtual death camps. As a result Stephan feared that once the Russians were released they would set about the locals, raping, plundering, murdering and generally taking revenge for what they had suffered at German hands. He asked the American officers of the 99th to ensure that the Russians were kept under lock and key. According to Stephan, the Americans agreed to do so.

But Colonel Stephan and the good citizens of Hemer, who had long known of the horrific conditions under which the Russians were kept captive, were in for an unpleasant surprise when the 99th Division men took the camp over from the Germans. In their own first encounter with the Germans back on 16 December, 1944, during the Battle of the Bulge, the men of the 99th had lost many comrades to German POW camps. They did not intend to keep thousands of Allied soldiers locked up just because the Krauts were scared.

To their horror they had found 23,000 prisoners-of-war, including some Americans, crowded together in an area intended for a mere 1,000, a starving mass of humanity. As General Lauer wrote afterwards:

It was a horrible sight to see these human beings squeezed into the limited area of their open air stockade, digging in the ground with their bare hands, searching, groveling, fighting for grubs and worms to eat. They had gone without food for over a week and were dying like DDT'd flies . . . In the building sheltering the sickest of these prisoners, they were found three in a bed. Their German guards lived in luxury — two soldiers in a room. How so-called human beings could treat other human beings in such an outrageous fashion surpassed all understanding.

When the angry Americans opened the gates, the freed men

streamed out in their thousands and flooded the surrounding countryside in their search for food, women and revenge. They ransacked everything, took what they wanted — and *whom* they wanted. In the end the 99th had to station a full infantry battalion at the camp to restore order and round up those who were pillaging and terrorizing the whole area. But as one young officer later remarked:

The Krauts were funny. They thought they could wander all over Europe in World War Two, doing and taking just what they wanted, and then when they were beaten they expected us, the Americans, to play patsy with them and keep everything nice and sweet for them. They were living in a fantasy world. They simply didn't understand that they were goddam beaten and now they were going to have to pay the price for what they had done in the past!

Whether the German soldiers understood or not, they still continued to surrender in droves: bemedalled officers in smart, elegant uniforms, carrying well-filled suitcases ready for captivity; shabby privates in poor quality, ill-fitting tunics and what looked like boots made out of cardboard, carrying nothing but their *Brotbeutel*, their bread bag, holding half a loaf of hard, brown Army bread, usually with little bits of straw sticking out of it.

That day what was left of the *Panzerlehr*, some 2,000-odd men, prepared to surrender. They blew up their vehicles, spiking the cannon and throwing away the firing pins, as was expected of an elite formation even in defeat. Finally, before the staff marched off to the American prison cages, their commanding officer, Colonel von Hauser, paid a call on Bayerlein, who had founded the division in January 1944, to sign off in the approved Wehrmacht fashion. Then it was the turn of the similarly elite 116th Panzer Division, perhaps 3,000 men now. They had long lost all of their tanks but it was only just in time that a senior officer stepped in to stop them firing the rest of the artillery ammunition at the Americans; instead their shells fell in an empty field as a symbolic gesture, though one did unfortunately slaughter a herd of German cows.

Von Zangen, commander of the shattered Fifteenth Army, reported his position again, then disappeared once more. But this time the Commanding General's disappearance was for good — behind the barbed wire of an American POW cage.

General Bayerlein had now almost completed his own plan for surrender. But he had to be discreet; two of his four divisional commanders were bitterly opposed to giving up. In particular,

General Klosterkemper, Commander of the 180th Infantry Division, wanted not only to continue the hopeless battle, but also to attack! For on this Sunday, 15 April, when the guns were everywhere falling silent, Klosterkemper was planning a counter-attack against the *Amis* on the River Ruhr at Ergste. Bayerlein knew he had to deal with Klosterkemper; otherwise the surrender of his whole Corps was in jeopardy.

Under a pretext, Klosterkemper was ordered to report to Bayerlein's HQ near the town of Iserlohn. There he was placed under immediate house arrest, while Bayerlein himself called the 180th's Chief-of-Staff on the phone and ordered him sharply to stop all further attacks or plans for attack. The war was over, at least for the 53rd Corps.

But even at this late stage, he had trouble with his own Corps staff; both his own Chief-of-Staff and the next senior officer refused to have anything to do with surrender. They were dismissed, and at midday that day, at the head of three divisional generals commanding over 30,000 soldiers, Bayerlein presented himself at the headquarters of General Robert Hasbrouck, who led the US 7th Armored Division. At last Bayerlein had surrendered.

It was an emotional moment for Bayerlein, a real combat soldier who had always led from the front. The Americans remained civil but firmly correct. It was Colonel Ryan of the 7th Armored who conducted the preliminary talks and he told the Germans they had exactly fifteen minutes to make a final decision — *or else*! Only that day, Ryan had seen the terrible conditions at the Hemer POW camp; he had little sympathy with the Germans in the hour of their defeat. Bayerlein's staff surrendered within seven minutes.

Hasbrouck received the four German generals politely enough, concealing his own triumph at being the first Allied general of divisional rank in Europe to accept the surrender of a whole German corps. The 7th Armored had not been a particularly lucky division. Back in the autumn of 1944, in Holland, the Germans had broken through the 7th's lines and penetrated almost to Montgomery's HQ; even Montgomery's clerks and cooks had seized arms and prepared to fight as infantry. As a result the 7th's commander, General Silvester, had been fired., Then in the Ardennes, during its week-long defence of St Vith under Brigadier-General Bruce Clarke, the Division had lost nearly a whole combat command before being forced to withdraw. So it was a proud, though restrained, General Hasbrouck who made polite chit-chat with Bayerlein before sending him off to General Hodges' HQ.

Here Bayerlein was a well-known figure. He had fought the First Army in North Africa and right through the campaign in Europe. Colonel Dixon, Hodges' Intelligence Officer, knew all about him. But Bayerlein was reluctant to talk about battles past. That was already history. He was worried about his family, still in German-held territory; under the terms of the Nazi *Sippenhaft* they could be imprisoned, even executed, if the Party found out he had surrendered. He extracted a promise from Dixon not to reveal the details of the surrender of the 53rd Corps to the media. Dixon agreed, although he, like the men of the 7th Armored Division, felt no sympathy for the defeated Germans. As the 7th's Divisional History says: 'An Army's death is a pitiful sight, but there were no tears shed by the men of the 7th Armored when the once mighty Wehrmacht collapsed.'

On 15 April, while his Army Group fell apart, Model paid a visit to his most reliable Army Commander, Colonel-General Harpe of the Fifth Panzer Army, the same Army that had decimated the US 7th Armored at St Vith the previous December.

There was still some fight left in the Fifth. They had armoured vehicles left and several regiments of flak troops, armed with 88 mm cannon to be used in a ground role. Only two days before, what was left of the Army's 3rd Parachute Division and stationary flak guns east of Cologne had knocked out thirty American tanks of the unlucky 13th Armored Division, much to the annoyance of General Ridgway.

Now Harpe, with Model's agreement, decided to defend the general area of Düsseldorf. His soldiers were to form little pockets of resistance and keep on attacking from behind the Americans' backs until they could do so no more; then they were to break out, eastwards towards the River Weser. Harpe's Chief-of-Staff, von Mellenthin, was in full agreement with this plan. He for one was against surrender (in the end he would break out of the trap himself with a handful of men and escape 250 kilometres northwards before he was finally apprehended). All the same, Model and Harpe's Chief-of-Staff again discussed surrender and again von Mellenthin had a feeling that the 'Boy Marshal', as von Rundstedt had once called him so contemptuously, was wrestling with his conscience, trying to come to terms with some personal anguish.

Von Mellenthin guessed it was the same old problem that faced all senior German commanders this terrible April. Model saw the total hopelessness of the situation. But at the same time he was bound by his oath of allegiance, sworn on the flag of Germany, to stand by not just his superiors but his subordinates too.

Von Mellenthin didn't know it at the time, but Model was also troubled by another reason for not surrendering. When Model left Harpe's HQ an idea was beginning to form in his mind. He personally could not surrender. Nor did he want the men still under his command to surrender, at least not formally as Bayerlein had done. But wasn't there another way, which could make the stigma of surrender unnecessary?

That afternoon, back at his own HQ outside Düsseldorf, he began to toy with this revolutionary idea, one that, as far as he knew, had never been put into practice before. Eventually he sent for his Chief-of-Staff and put the idea to him. Wagener, who was now heartily sick of the whole business, liked the suggestion. Model warmed to it more and more. Together they began to work on the plan, wondering how they could carry it out without arousing the ire of the remaining local *Gauleiters*, who had their own lines of communication with Berlin through Martin Bormann, the Führer's shadowy secretary and reputed grey eminence. For Model, too, feared the consequences of *Sippenhaft*, even though he was a field-marshal. After all, they had arrested Field-Marshal Rommel's son and widow the previous summer — albeit only briefly — after the July, 1944, plot against Hitler which resulted in Rommel being forced to take his own life. And his own wife was still, as far as he knew, in German-held territory. He couldn't let her suffer imprisonment, or worse, on account of his actions.

Not very far from Model's HQ, another Commanding General and his Chief-of-Staff were deep in similar discussions. Early that Sunday morning, General Ridgway of the XVIII Airborne Corps had decided that all the fighting in the Pocket should now come to an end. Model's position was 'hopeless', Ridgway wrote after the war, 'and I knew that so shrewd a soldier as Model was well aware that he didn't have a chance. It seemed to me that here was an excellent opportunity to save many thousands of precious lives.' He decided to present Model with a 'surrender demand'.

But first Ridgway checked with Hodges. He and his Chief-of-Staff drafted the demand and a covering letter which they sent by messenger to the Chief of the First Army for approval. At two o'clock that afternoon, Hodges replied favourably. But, as cautious as ever, the ex-infantryman had several provisos. He wanted the surrender demand to be 'peremptory in character', phrased in English to avoid any later misinterpretation and couched in the form of 'unconditional surrender', as had been laid down by Churchill and Roosevelt at Casablanca in 1943. In short, Ridgway had to be tough with the defeated German commander and not enter into 'deals of any kind' with him. Hodges, at this late stage of the war, was not going to risk any bad publicity back home.

Undismayed by the constraints placed upon him, Ridgway sent off his Chief of Intelligence, Whitfield Jack, and his aide-interpreter, Frank Brandstetter, a fluent German linguist, to find Model's HQ.

And so, carrying a flag of truce, Jack and Brandstetter duly arrived at Haan and conveyed to Model the message from their Corps Commander. Model was in a 'hopeless situation' and 'further resistance could only cause needless bloodshed'. The scene at Model's HQ has never been fully described, either by the two American participants or by any members of the Field-Marshal's staff who were there. But it was unique. For the first time since the outbreak of this war, a *German field-marshal* was actually discussing the possibility of surrendering to the Western Allies! How often in the past had it been British and American generals — such as the British General Fortune in France and the American General Wainwright in the Far East — who had done the surrendering? Now, at last, the boot was on the other foot.

But while Wagener wavered, Model remained steadfast — outwardly at least. He told Captain Brandstetter that he was 'bound still by a personal oath to Hitler to fight to the end'. According to Ridgway, 'It would do violence to his sense of honour even to *consider* my message'.

When his two emissaries returned Ridgway was disappointed by what they had to report. Still, he would try again: he sat down and personally composed a letter to Field-Marshal Model. It was a formal letter, worthy of the man who was steeped in American military history and read Kipling as a relaxation. It read:

Neither history nor the military profession records any nobler character, any more brilliant master of warfare, any more dutiful subordinate of the state than the American Robert E. Lee. Eighty years ago this month, his loyal command reduced in numbers, stripped of its means of effective fighting and completely surrounded by overwhelming forces, he chose an honorable capitulation.

This same choice is now yours. In the light of a soldier's honor, for the reputation of the German Officer Corps, for the sake of your nation's future, lay down your arms at once. The

German people you will save are sorely needed to restore your people to their proper place in society. The German cities you will preserve are irreplaceable necessities for your people's welfare.

The letter was old-fashioned, prosy, but remarkable in the light of the climate of opinion of that time, when America was officially calling for 'unconditional surrender' and the Morgenthau Plan, which would reduce conquered Germany to the status of a third-world agricultural state, was the order of the day.

In addition, Ridgway privately told his Intelligence Officer, Whitfield Jack, that if Model agreed to the surrender, he, Ridgway, would 'give him an excuse for surrendering'. But if Model did not agree, Ridgway warned soberly, Jack was to tell Model that Ridgway 'would attack vigorously and capture him — *dead or alive*'.

Jack and Brandstetter went to Model's HQ once more. To no avail. They returned, accompanied by General Wagener, with bad news. Wagener told Ridgway that the Field-Marshal refused to surrender; 'Model would not consider any plea whatever.' Ridgway gave in. He told Wagener he could return to Model's HQ 'and take his chances in the disaster that was sure to come. Or he could remain in our custody as a prisoner of war.'

Karl Wagener was, as Ridgway stated later, 'a wiser man' than his chief. He decided to stay with Ridgway, and it didn't take him long to come to his decision. He knew Model's situation was hopeless. Ridgway did too, but now he washed his hands of the whole affair. 'That was that,' he wrote afterwards. 'I could do no more. From now on the blood was upon Model's head . . .'

Still the surrenders went on, growing in number by the hour. The entire countryside was a moving grey-blue carpet — the Wehrmacht coming in to give itself up. There were SS, paras, ordinary 'stubble-hoppers' as the infantry called themselves, cavalry still on horses, artillerymen, tankers, Luftwaffe pilots without planes. Column after column of them moving down every road and forest trail, as far as the eye could see.

There was no fight left in them. All they wanted now was to surrender to the first *Ami* they encountered. With dragging feet and slumped shoulders, eyes downcast in defeat, they showed none of that martial arrogance which had awed Europe for these last five years. As General Lauer recorded, watching the dreary columns of men plodding into captivity: 'No bands played, no fanfare, just subdued ranks of troops marching as though they were coming from a big review. On they came, slowly, ceaselessly, doggedly ... Their attitude of finality and resignation cried aloud. These men were conquered. They knew it — we did too.'

The Niagara of prisoners almost overwhelmed the surprised Americans. Here and there, as we shall see, it actually did — and men who thought they were safe at last would die. 'Young men, old men, arrogant SS troops, dejected infantrymen, paunchy reservists, female nurses and technicians, teenage members of the Hitler Youth, stiffly correct monocled Prussians, enough to gladden the heart of a Hollywood casting director' — they arrived in every conceivable manner:

plodding wearily on foot, some in civilian automobiles, assorted military vehicles or on horseback, some pushing perambulators, one group riding bicycles in precise military formation, a horsedrawn artillery unit under faultless control, some carrying black bread and wine, others with musical instruments — accordions, guitars — a few bringing along wives or girlfriends in a mistaken hope they might share captivity. ... Many a German soldier walked mile after mile before finding an American not too occupied with other duties to bother to accept his surrender ... [while] the civilians sought to ingratiate themselves with the conquerors by insisting that they had never been Nazis, that they were happy the Americans had come. There were no Nazis, no ex-Nazis, not even Nazi sympathizers any more.

As one ex-infantry captain, who had been wounded twice in nearly six years of war and had won the Knight's Cross before being captured in the Ruhr, recalled many years later with understandable sarcasm: 'Now I realize that I alone of my whole company had been convinced of our course. The rest of my officers, non-commissioned officers and men had all been secret anti-Nazis, just waiting to be liberated by the freedom-loving Americans.' Even today that same captain will not go to a regimental reunion on account of the fact that his old comrades denied what they had been fighting for in Russia, Greece, France and, in the end, Germany.

A few, a very few, still retained their pride. At the big garrison town of Iserlohn, in barracks which today house British troops, the survivors of the Wehrmacht refused to surrender. The 394th Regiment of the US 99th Infantry Division had surrounded the barracks and now rushed up a tank which had mounted upon it a public address system. Lieutenant Walter Welford, speaking in German, then used the PA to warn the defiant survivors, his voice booming through the town: 'Your situation is hopeless. You are completely encircled. Your commanders have surrendered. Lay down your arms and surrender at once or we will annihilate you with artillery fire. *Los!*'

That did it. One hour after the American attack on the town had started, the garrison troops began to stream out waving white flags, hundreds upon hundreds of them.

A few tried to surrender with military dignity intact. Outside Iserlohn, for example, there was still a detachment of enormous Hunting Panthers. Under the command of Captain Ernst, a hard-looking man who had won the Knight's Cross, this detachment — *Panzerjager-Abteilung 512* (self-propelled gun detachment 512) — decided to surrender. But Ernst wasn't going into the bag just like that. He wanted a formal surrender with due ceremony and military honours — and he got it, though not without some trouble as he led his tanks through the town to reach the American officer who would accept the surrender. As his lead tank-destroyer entered Iserlohn it was surrounded by excited civilians, who evidently thought he was planning to make his last stand in their town. They halted his column and started to throw stones. Ernst drew his pistol; it looked as if there would be firing. But a local parson, Pastor Linde, pushed his way through the angry mob and, holding up his hands for silence, yelled, 'Don't get yourselves killed now. Let him carry on.' So Ernst's tank-destroyers were allowed to trundle on to where the American officer, Colonel Robert Kriz, was waiting for them just outside the town's fire station.

Now a formal military ceremony took place, of the kind the Americans knew from their history books on the Civil War — save that this was not Confederate cavalry surrendering, but massive armoured vehicles whose guns could have devastated whole brigades of Yankee infantry. Watched by some 1,000 civilians and a battalion of the 99th Infantry, Ernst shook hands with each of his men before delivering himself of a bitter little speech; fortunately, most of the American observers did not understand, for it smacked of the old *Dolchlegende* — 'the stab in the back legend' — which the beaten Imperial German Army had spread in 1918: Germany had not been beaten at the front, but had been stabbed in the back by those in the rear. His voice shaking with emotion, Ernst proclaimed:

'My comrades! For six long years we have fought together. We've spent some tough times together. Because of your confidence in me, I have been able to lead you to victory. Now I must lead you to

surrender. The fighting power of our Army is broken. I am doing this because it is the rational thing to do. But you are honourable soldiers, the last fighting soldiers in the Pocket. For days now the others have been breaking up secretly behind our backs and escaping. We have been abandoned and betrayed! Today when we lay down our weapons, remember this. The town and region of Iserlohn are still there. Its citizens have suffered no loss of blood. My comrades, I thank you for your trust and support, which you have always given me. Company — attention! Eyes right!'

It was now time for Colonel Kriz to accept the surrender. He strode forward with his staff, as the German soldiers followed his every movement with the strange wooden turning of the head that dated back to the drill regulations of the eighteenth-century Prussian Army.

Captain Ernst snapped to attention, hand placed rigidly to the brim of his black cap. He repeated the traditional German formula of greeting a superior officer, '*Herr Oberst, ich melde gehorsamst* [Mr Colonel, I report most obediently] that the last fighters of the Pocket, the fighters of Iserlohn, have now decided to stop the senseless fight. They surrender to the mighty opponent and beg for a dignified manner of treatment.'

It was all very gallant and heroic, but oldfashioned and a little pathetic too. One American observer who understood some German thought it was 'a load of crap. They'd fought us to the very last minute and I felt nothing, absolutely nothing, about their feelings. I don't know why the brass tolerated it.'

The brass, in the form of General Lauer, Commanding General of the 99th Infantry Division, who also understood German, reported the formal surrender in more prosaic terms: 'Lieutenant [sic] Ernst shook hands with each of the men, called them to attention, had them count off, delivered a short speech to them, executed an about face, saluted Colonel Kriz and formally surrendered. The Ruhr Pocket was history.'

General Lauer was wrong. The Battle for the Ruhr Pocket was not quite over. On 16 April, the same day that Ernst surrendered, three divisions of Ridgway's XVIII Airborne Corps were still meeting fierce opposition.

The 86th and 78th Infantry Divisions and the 'Unlucky Thirteenth' were engaged in several minor actions in their drive towards the last big city within the Pocket still in German hands, the Rhenish fashion centre of Düsseldorf. And in Düsseldorf itself, German was fighting German!

Düsseldorf that Monday was defended by III Flak Corps, commanded by General von Rantzau; a formation of former anti-aircraft gunners, it was now being used as infantry and ground-role gunners. In a ring around the area of Ratingen—Düsseldorf, von Rantzau had grouped five heavy flak batteries plus a large number of the dreaded 20 mm quadruple flak batteries, which could fire a thousand shells a minute so that it often appeared to unfortunate infantrymen attacking such positions that they were walking into a solid wall of steel.

Von Rantzau had refused to move his guns into Düsseldorf itself, because the once beautiful city on the Rhine had suffered enough from the Allied bombers, but he was prepared to fight 'to the last round before surrendering in a dignified manner'. He was supported in this by Model himself who now believed that von Rantzau's teenage gunners, both male and female, were his steadiest surviving troops. What neither von Rantzau nor Model yet realized was that the danger to Düsseldorf came not only from outside but from within.

Düsseldorf had been a divided city since 3 March, when American troops had occupied the suburbs lying on the west bank of the Rhine. Since then there had been a growing number of prominent citizens within the German-held part of the city who wanted to surrender without any further fighting. These leading citizens, under the leadership of a local lawyer, Dr Karl-August Wiedenhofen, knew they were taking a risk because the political life of Düsseldorf was still dominated by the *Gauleiter* Florian, who, unlike so many of the Party members, had not fled when danger was looming.

Florian was a National Socialist stalwart who never lost his faith in the Führer and the greatness of the German people, even after the war. He had wanted to fight right from the start, even if that fight meant the destruction of his city. Indeed, he had always been the most dominant figure among the four Ruhr *Gauleiters*, and the most bellicose. Now, although surrounded by what he saw as treachery and defeatism, he attempted to bolster up his citizens' flagging courage with the aid of a bunch of SS thugs.

Thus the Wiedenhofen Group knew that they would have to proceed very carefully. The flak gunners outside the city were no real problem; they would surrender to the *Amis* in due course, of their own accord. But within the city there were 4,000 armed policemen under the command of Lieutenant-Colonel Juergens; and, by the very nature of their profession, these admittedly middle-aged policemen would be supporters of the Hitler régime. Wiedenhofen decided that the way to stop them from defending Düsseldorf to the bitter end was to go right to the top and gain the support of Colonel Juergens. If the Colonel ordered his men to lay down their weapons, they would do so.

On Monday, 16 April, therefore, a group of the 'resistance' — as they were now calling themselves, rather late in the day — went with Wiedenhofen to meet the Colonel. Without too much persuasion, Juergens agreed to help them. He furnished them with a pass to get them through the German lines, a vehicle, a white flag — and then, as an afterthought, a set of pistols. The little group was now to drive through the German lines to the nearest US position and offer to surrender the city to the first *Ami* officer they met. Juergens, for his part, said he would personally arrest the local police chief, an ardent National Socialist, *SS Brigadeführer* Korreng.* By detaining Korreng he hoped to break the hold that Florian and his SS thugs still had on Düsseldorf.

Now the plotters set about trying to save what was left of the city, while outside the unfortunate US 13th Armored Division, supported by the 94th Infantry Division, tried to batter their way into the place. Neither side knew that time was running out for Düsseldorf. For over in England, 'Bomber' Harris had decided to take a hand in the Battle for the Ruhr Pocket.

Back in December, 1940, Air Vice-Marshal Harris had stood on the roof of the Air Ministry Building in London and watched the great city burn. By now 30,000 Londoners had been killed with twice that number seriously injured. That night another 700 Londoners lay dead or badly wounded in the smoking ruins. Harris had sworn, there and then, that he would avenge them. Before turning to go back inside, he had told his chief, Charles Portal: 'They are sowing the wind.' Soon he would ensure that they reaped the whirlwind.

In 1942 he had become Chief of Bomber Command. Night after night, for year after year, his brave young bomber crews had sallied out over Germany, losing a staggering 56,000 men in the attempt to devastate the Reich. The Ruhr, in particular, had been Harris's favourite target; he believed that by knocking out

---

*In Nazi Germany it had been policy to give civil servants honorary ranks in the SS. The ranks and the smart black SS uniforms flattered their egos and made them willing and loyal supporters of the régime.

German industrial production he could win the war long before the 'footsloggers' had even stepped on the Continent. On one night alone, 13/14 October, 1944, in Operation Hurricane, he had sent 2,000 Lancasters and Halifaxes to drop 9,000 tons of high explosive and 1,500 tons of incendiaries on Cologne; seventy-five per cent of the town, its factories and inland harbour had all been destroyed.

Well, in the end the footsloggers had had to go in after all. But Harris had supported them with good grace, hammering the Ruhr to the very end. Now he was determined to be in at the kill. If Düsseldorf did not surrender within the next twenty-four hours, 'Bomber' Harris had 2,000 Lancasters, fuelled and bombed-up, ready to raze the Rhenish city to the ground.

For days now, the Red Army's Marshal Zhukov had been preparing for the attack on Berlin. On the River Oder he had massed 4,000 tanks, to be supported by the greatest artillery barrage of the Second World War and three-quarters of a million infantrymen.

Colonel Yurasov, who would one day defect and tell the Americans all about the Russians and Nordhausen, happened to be at Zhukov's HQ when the last briefing before the attack was held. First to speak was General Nikolai Bulganin, a future General Secretary of the Soviet Union. He told the assembled officers: 'The war is not over. We have defeated Hitler, but not Fascism. Fascism exists all over the world, especially in America. We needed the second front and the Capitalists refused to give it to us. And it cost millions of our brothers.' This was the man who Eisenhower would shortly regard as his friend! And no sooner had Bulganin sat down than, one after another, all the other generals got to their feet to echo his words, to denunciate 'the base of the Capitalists', to assert that 'America is now the prime enemy'. But first they had to finish off the German Fascists.

Zhukov's attack began. His men burst forth from the Oder, sending the German Ninth Army reeling back. The 22,000 Russian cannon launched their fearsome barrage. The tanks began to roll.

Signals of alarm and despair were flooding into the German High Command in Berlin. Soon the terrible news reached Model. This, he knew, was the beginning of the end. It was time he put his final plan into action, the plan he had conceived two days before: the plan that would avoid the shame of surrender. Already he had made the first moves; he had ordered that all men born before 1898 and after 1926 should be formally discharged on 16

April. This meant that all his soldiers over the age of forty-seven and under eighteen had been given their papers that day and sent home. This way their lives at least would be saved, and they would be spared the humiliation of surrender. Now Model issued his final order. By the following morning, he decreed, all men still fighting under the command of Army Group B would have three choices. They could go home too; or they could surrender individually (*not* as a unit); or they could try to break out as armed formations and make their way to German lines to continue the fight.

Thus, with a single — albeit somewhat florid — stroke of the pen, Model's unorthodox plan was complete. On the morning of Tuesday, 17 April, the battered remnants of Army Group B would cease to exist.

At last, it seemed, Model had found a way out of the terrible dilemma: he had avoided both the stigma of surrender (and thus saved his family from the malicious backlash of the *Sippenhaft*) and further unnecessary destruction of the Ruhr. Moreover, he could now officially demobilize himself, as he fell into the older-age category. Model's manoeuvre was unprecedented in the history of warfare. Never before had a senior commander disbanded his army *in the middle of a battle*!

But there was one imponderable, one factor that Model — like so many other Germans, both military and civilian — had not taken into consideration. How would the *Amis* react?

For nearly twelve years the Third Reich had dominated the affairs of Europe. For five of those years the Germans had reigned over the greatest empire Europe had seen since the time of the Romans. They had lived in an hermetically sealed world where they gave the orders and everyone else sprang to do their bidding without question. They had long become accustomed to making decisions without consulting non-Germans, without even vaguely considering what the reaction of these lesser, inferior peoples might be.

Now, even in defeat, their country already three-quarters overrun by the enemy, their leaders were still motivated by that old unthinking arrogance, the belief that whatever they commanded would be carried out with the same *Kadavergehorsamkeit* ('obedience of the corpse') that they expected from their own civilians and soldiers. Model had disbanded his army. Now they should go home and resume their former civilian occupations without let or hindrance. That was that. The thought that the Americans might not play ball with him had never even entered Model's head. He had decreed that Army Group B no longer existed. No one could question that, not even the *Amis*.

If he had lived, Model would have been in for a terrible shock.

SIX

'A Field-Marshal does not surrender'

On Tuesday, 17 April, 1945, a heavy brooding silence fell over the Ruhr at last. After six years of war, no cannon boomed, no bomb whined, no aircraft engine snarled as it came into the attack. Instead there was a strange eerie stillness that made the ears tingle. The Ruhr, that workshop of German military might, was at peace.

But the peace was only relative. In besieged Düsseldorf the Wiedenhofen group was running into trouble. Police President *SS Brigadeführer* Korreng had indeed been arrested by Colonel Juergens and thrown into one of his own cells; but Florian's SS men had stormed the place and released him. Juergens and four civilians — Karl Kleppe, Hermann Weill, Josef Knab and Theodor Andresen (their names are worth recording for they were a kind of pledge to the new Germany's democratic future) — were all brutally seized by Florian's thugs. All five were shot that very day. Even as the guns grew silent, Germans were shooting Germans inside Model's last stronghold, Düsseldorf.

Meanwhile, Wiedenhofen and a companion named Odenthal set off through the German lines to reach the Americans. Their task was all the more urgent now, for they knew that Juergens and the others had been arrested; very probably the SS would squeeze them to reveal who else was in the resistance. Halfway to their destination, their driver had an attack of nerves. Thanks to Juergens' pass, they had successfully negotiated the numerous German patrols; but now the driver saw something that jolted him to a halt. An officer had been hanged from a tree, his face purple, his tongue hanging out like a piece of dry leather, while there was a wet stain at the front of his breeches where he had pissed himself in his extreme agony. Around his tortured body hung a cardboard sign which read: '*Defeatist*!' Now the driver, scared out of his wits by the sight, stopped the car and fled.

Neither Wiedenhofen nor Odenthal could drive, so they abandoned the car and set off on foot. Somehow they managed to dodge through the German positions and reached the first American outposts at Mettmann, where they handed in their pistols and asked to be taken to the American '*Kommandant*'. But the American *Kommandant* from the 13th Armored Division did not seem particularly interested in capturing the last remaining German stronghold. Once again the 'Unlucky Thirteenth' was living up to its reputation.

A desperate Wiedenhofen explained that many of his comrades would be shot by the SS if the Americans waited much longer. That moved the American *Kommandant* even less. 'But there are only 4,000 poorly armed policemen left in Düsseldorf to defend the place,' the German pleaded. 'They can cause you little trouble.'

At first the *Kommandant* didn't want to believe the two Germans; his information was that Düsseldorf was defended by over 6,000 soldiers. But the German persisted. In the end the American relented. Orders were snapped. Things started to move. In a matter of minutes a somewhat surprised Wiedenhofen and Odenthal found themselves placed on the turret of the leading American tank, heading a column of eight Shermans and 800 US infantry in halftracks and trucks. The American *Kommandant* was taking no chances; if the two Krauts intended to betray him, they'd be first in the firing line.

Nothing happened. Late that afternoon the Americans entered the city and rolled down the Kölner Strasse watched by crowds of silent civilians, with here and there a subdued soldier, his rucksack already packed for the POW cage. Not a single shot was fired at them. Düsseldorf surrendered without a fight.

Hurriedly 'Bomber' Harris's boys were called off. *Gauleiter* Florian and those of his SS thugs who had not already fled were arrested and sent off to the special camps reserved for hard-core Nazis. But the Americans had come too late to save Juergens and the four brave civilians who wanted to rescue their city. They had already been shot. Florian, for his part, would die of old age decades later, nice and warm in his own bed.

At five-thirty that same afternoon the Commander of Flak Corps III, General von Rantzau, chanced upon Field-Marshal Model and a handful of his staff officers at Düsseldorf's famous race-track. The smoke which the 13th Armored and 94th Infantry had shot into the city to cover the approach of the armoured column had now dispersed and it was a pleasant sunny afternoon. The Field-Marshal and his little staff, so von Rantzau thought, might almost have been taking a stroll before the racing began. They exchanged a few words and then von Rantzau left to meet the Americans; there was nothing more for him to do but surrender.

The Americans' first question to von Rantzau was about Model: where was he? Von Rantzau did not answer.

In fact, by that time Model had left the race-track and very few people knew what his intentions were. Perhaps, on that afternoon when it all ended, Model didn't know himself. After six years of war, he was released from the burden of command at last. Now he had to make some decisions about himself.

Model was travelling around that day in a small convoy consisting of an eight-wheeled armoured car, an Opel-Blitz signals truck and a *DKW Meisterklasse* saloon car (which no less a person than General Bradley, the conqueror of the Ruhr Pocket, would one day commandeer as spoils of war). His little group included several soldiers and three staff officers, all members of the Greater General Staff: Colonel Pilling, Lieutenant-Colonel Michael and Major Winrich Behr, the youngest of the group. It was these three officers who were later able to relate the few facts known about the fugitive Field-Marshal's last days. Pilling, who was to die in the 1950s and was regarded by the Field-Marshal's son as 'somewhat suspect', was the closest to Model. Then came Michael, who later entered the post-war German secret service group, Organization Gehlen, and disappeared on a mission in the East — ironically enough, in the pay of the CIA! Model relied upon him. Then came the young Major Behr, the only survivor into our own time, who provided a pleasant companion for the Field-Marshal, a sounding board for his ideas and plans in these last days.

On that race-course in Düsseldorf the four of them had discussed what Model could do next. For still the Field-Marshal refused to surrender. In a month's time the race track where they stood would be renamed 'Truman Park' by the men of the 94th Infantry Division and would see the start of the 'Flat Racing Season 1945' which featured captured German artillery horses in the fifth race, 'the Workhorse Classic'. But that was in the future. Meantime, as the Americans began to round up what was left of the German Army in Düsseldorf, Model decided they should make a break for it. They'd find a hole in the American defences and hide out in one of the great stud farms or woods which surrounded the city. That night, as soon as it had grown dark, they set off.

A few miles north of Düsseldorf, at Ratingen, they broke through the American lines; tanks were everywhere but the little group saw no infantry patrols. Heading steadily north towards Duisburg, dodging the tanks without much trouble for they could be heard miles away in the still night air, they finally reached a huge stretch of thick woods between the villages of Lindau and Wedau. Here they would hide out for the day while planning their next move. For the time being they had escaped the American net.

Someone remarked that these woods were part of the vast estates belonging to the von Spee family. Model and his three faithful companions would have known the name well, but it is doubtful whether any of them knew the history of the von Spee family in any detail.

Back in the seventeenth century, one of the first public protests against witch-hunting in Western Europe was made by a von Spee, a prelate who dared to raise his voice against the trials being conducted in Trier. His boldness set the pattern for other members of the family to follow. Nearly three centuries later, Admiral Graf von Spee displayed similar courage. After defeating the British in the naval Battle of Coronel, his fleet was trapped off the Falkland Islands in December, 1914, by the British Admiral Sturdee. The British force was superior, but von Spee refused to surrender. He went down fighting with his ship.

Maybe Model did know of Admiral von Spee's valiant last stand. Maybe he also knew that the captain of the pocket battleship, *Graf Spee* – named after the victor of Coronel — had similarly defied a British trap in December, 1939, and chosen instead to commit suicide. Maybe that was what led him to his conclusion.

One thing is certain. It was here, in the forests of the von Spee estate, that Model made his final terrible decision.

At last General Bradley had his 'bag' — and what a bag it was! Bradley's Intelligence staff had estimated, before the Battle of the Ruhr Pocket began, that there were 150,000 German soldiers in the area; in fact the total was more than double that figure. Already his bag contained 317,000 men of all arms. As Bradley himself stated proudly, 'This was a larger German force than the Russians had captured at Stalingrad or than we had captured in Tunisia.' The prisoners included two army commanders, at least four corps commanders, a grand total of twenty-nine German generals — and one admiral, a runty undersized man who also bore a name famous in German naval history: Speer.

At a cost of 10,000 American soldiers of the First and Ninth Armies killed, wounded or missing, Bradley had finally achieved the tremendous 'bag' that he had been dreaming of ever since Normandy and the failure of the trap around the Falaise Pocket.

The American commanders were simply overwhelmed by the huge numbers of prisoners streaming into the cages — soldiers, policemen, postmen, firemen, indeed anyone in uniform, including women and civilians. For Model's demobilization plan had failed. Anyone who looked of military age, even if he was in civilian clothes or possessed official discharge papers issued by Army Group B, was automatically arrested and placed behind barbed wire. 'They're Krauts, aren't they?' was the usual answer given by the GIs when the arrest was queried.

To contain this flood of prisoners, the harassed American staffs set up makeshift cages everywhere and anywhere. Race-courses were favourite sites because they had plenty of central space and accommodation in the stands for guards and other personnel. But schoolyards, gyms, church halls, even open fields, hurriedly sectioned off with barbed wire, were also pressed into service as temporary prisons.

Of course, there was some deliberate brutality. The full accounts of what had happened at Belsen, Nordhausen, Dachau and half-a-dozen other such horror camps were beginning to fill the newspapers. Many of the captives, arriving at a cage, were met by a double line of guards wielding pick handles. Others were punched and beaten; their possessions, medals, watches were torn from them; photographs of their loved ones were sadistically torn up in front of their eyes.

But the suffering, near-starvation and degradation in these camps were mainly due to a breakdown in organization and supplies. In essence, the Americans had not been prepared for so many prisoners and could not cope with them. As for the guards, few of them were real sadists — though there were some — but simply weary young men who had had too much of war and Europe and wanted to go home.* There could be no comparison between these camps and those of the Nazis.

*Eisenhower would soon be confronted by some thousands of US troops filling the streets outside his HQ in the IG Farben building, Frankfurt, demanding to be sent home.

Five months before, in the US prisoner-of-war camp at Hampton Roads, Virginia, one German POW noted that his Christmas dinner consisted of 'turkey filled with sage and onions, turkey giblets in gravy, cranberry sauce, mashed potatoes, candied sweet potatoes, green beans, asparagus tips, fruit cocktail, mixed pickles, rolls and butter, apple pie with cheese, ice cream and coffee'. It was a far better meal than the average GI ever had while fighting in Europe.

That German POW was fortunate in another way, too: he was lucky to be so far away from his homeland. For Germany and all things German were now subjected to all the odium and contempt of the victorious Americans. More than that, the Americans felt they had a score to settle.

Now it was the Germans' turn to suffer. Teenage boys and old men alike were seized by US patrols who ripped off their civilian clothes when they discovered they were really soldiers. Many arrived at the camps wearing only underpants, or pyjamas if they had been arrested while in bed, without boots, without anything but a tin can for whatever food the guards deigned to give them. Yet these Rhine camps, where most of Model's soldiers ended up, were often just fields surrounded by concertina wire, open to the elements. There was no shelter, still less hospital facilities for the wounded or sick.

The prisoners' only refuge from the wind and rain of April and the blazing hot sun of the May that followed were the holes in the ground which they scraped with cans, forks, even with their bare hands. Forced together with as many as 3,000 men to a square hectare, they were hopelessly overcrowded, jostling elbow to elbow in a miserable, heaving mass, slithering and eventually sinking with exhaustion into the sea of watery faeces underfoot; latrines, of course, were nonexistent.

In the American cage at Bad Kreuznach, 'the Hell of Kreuznach' as it soon became known to the men of Model's armies, 56,000 men were eventually packed into an area intended for 4,500. One prisoner there, Marzel Oberneder, later described it to the post-war German Commission of Investigation as just mud: 'Gradually, if one stood around long, one began to sink in the goo, up to the ankles, up the knees.' Another POW at the same camp testified: 'An old man stood next to me, suffering from a high temperature. Finally he sank into the mud. Every time he turned, he slipped deeper and deeper into it until finally his face was covered by it. He must have suffocated in the end.'

Oberleutnant Josef Blome of the 116th Panzer Division later recalled marching into such a camp with a long column of his fellow prisoners from the veteran armoured division:

We thought, according to the rumours which were circulating, that it would only be a matter of days before we were released. Now we learned that that wasn't to be. We came across a huge line of German prisoners waiting for soup. They never got it. Drunken black American soldiers came out and ripped away our last possessions. One black, realizing that I was an officer, tried to punch me in the face. But as he couldn't reach me in the crowd, my poor comrades had to suffer his blows in my place. Thereafter we stood packed together in the ankle-deep mud of an open field for three days without food and drink.

Model's men were learning that the time for parades and gallant surrenders, complete with exchanges of salutes and handshakes, was over. This was the harsh reality of surrender.

Doctor Hans Koch, another of Model's men, found himself in a field near Sinzig on the Rhine; later he found out the area was called locally 'the golden mile'. As he commented sadly, 'For many a comrade it was the *last* mile.' On his second day in the camp he noticed several of his fellow prisoners 'apparently sleeping soundly in the mud'. Upon closer investigation he saw that they were dead: 'They had cut open their wrists with tin cans. In my area there were ten of these unfortunates at least.' Koch also described the rations that he and his companions received — or rather the lack of them:

For every thirty-two men there was one loaf of white bread and a bar of chocolate, broken down so that there was a lump as big as a fingernail for each one of us. With this there was a tin of water, which had been so strongly chlorinated that it burned the throat to drink it. Later we received latrines after the 'thin shits' had broken out. 'Twelve cylinders' we called them because twelve men sat crowded side by side in them, with oftentimes those too weak to take care of themselves slipping off the greasy poles to fall into the horrid mess below.

Another prisoner, an ex-sergeant, later testified to the German Commission of Investigation: 'For the first days the only food was biscuits. Four tarpaulins full of them for every 1,000 men.

Some men got only a handful of crumbs to last them all day.' Another told the Commission that the daily ration at his camp was 'three spoonsful of vegetables, a spoonful of fish, two prunes, one spoonful of jam and four biscuits — and that for weeks on end.'

Next to the great cage of Rheinbach, where Bradley and Eisenhower had once plotted and which was now guarded by the men of the 106th Infantry Division, there had been a field of clover when the camp had opened. The starving prisoners ate it bare. Ex-Lieutenant Willers testified: 'Then we started on the grass next to it — and the hedges. We rubbed the leaves and shoots of the hedges into a powder and ate it. After fourteen days, the hedges looked like skeletons. We did, too.' Willers went on to describe a favourite pastime of his guards at Rheinbach: 'The Americans used to fry steaks and pour the used fat into a hole in the earth, just outside the wire, perhaps to torment us. We made long sticks, stuck them through the barbed wire, and dipped up the fat, which we then licked from the sticks. The *Amis* thought that great fun.'

The prisoners' bellies became bloated. Their teeth fell out. Many of them died of sickness aggravated by malnutrition, just collapsing in the urine-soaked filth and mud. Each morning the burial parties came along to collect those who had died in the night and often they had to dig into the mud to find the bodies. Sometimes they collected those who were not yet dead, as Corporal Kopfermann remembered. He had already lost half his original weight, queuing for up to eight hours simply to collect his daily half tin of water. One morning, as the dead were being picked up, he heard someone say, 'But he's moving. He's not dead yet.' To which someone else replied: 'What does it matter? He'll croak sooner or later, won't he?'

'Every night,' Kopfermann remembered, 'there'd be some poor prisoner-of-war who couldn't stand it any longer. He'd rush the wire, only to be mown down by the machine guns on the towers. The *Amis* used huge searchlights which they'd taken from the German flak batteries. These swept the camps all night. They could see everything. Those who rushed the wire knew they were going to die — and they wanted it. They'd had enough. They *wanted* to die.'

According to American figures, some 3,053 prisoners-of-war taken in the Pocket died in the Rhenish camps alone. The Germans, naturally, place the figure much higher. Ex-Lieutenant Willers, for example, maintains that 200 prisoners died in his camp daily. Even today, over four decades later, local farmers ploughing the fields which were once huge prison camps still find the skeletons of those long-dead prisoners. At Sinzig, as one farmer, Karl Schneider, told the local media in 1981, 'Right to this very day nobody has dared to dig up the original latrine area of the camp because they're scared what they'll find there. My guess is it'll be filled with the skeletons of dead German prisoners-of-war.'

But outside these horror camps, housing the human misery which had once been Army Group B, life was beginning to return to normal. Officer-Cadet Benno Tims, imprisoned at Koblenz-Lutzel, noted bitterly that German civilians hurried past his wire pen as if anxious to forget his existence: 'Well-dressed civilians, women and children and one single man pass without a single glance in our direction.' At another camp, Marzel Oberneder noticed the same phenomenon: 'Girls dressed in white, driving in coaches decorated with roses, hurry to the Corpus Christi celebrations. They didn't look at us.'

Now that the German soldier was virtually beaten, nobody, particularly his own fellow countrymen and women, had much time for him. Why should they care about that half-starved filthy wretch in tattered field-grey uniform? He had lost the war for them. They compared him with the healthy vigorous Americans who guarded him, and that once proud officer of the Wehrmacht was clearly the loser.

Predictably the prisoners from the Ruhr Pocket turned sour. They blamed their defeat on the *Amis'* overwhelming matériel superiority: their tanks, planes, guns. The Allied 'terror raids' had unnerved the conscripts, who were basically just a rabble of old men and young green boys anyway. As always in that nation, divided traditionally even in its own soul (according to Goethe), everyone else was to blame for their misery but themselves. Anything to avoid the plain truth — which was that most of them had simply lost the will to fight and had then tamely surrendered.

But what of Model? It was now 20 April, three days since his Army had stopped the fight and he had fled Düsseldorf. Where was he? Bradley, who was now in Wiesbaden enjoying his 'bag' and the huge headlines he craved in the papers back home, was determined that Model be found. As he recorded in his memoirs: 'Remembering how this chilly Prussian had blocked our advance through the Siegfried Line in September, I told G-2 to give a medal to the man who brought him in.' But no one would ever win that medal.

On the same day that Bradley issued that order, one German sergeant, Walter Maxeiner, a thrice-wounded veteran of the Russian front, was trying to escape from the Ruhr with some comrades. They had discharged themselves under Model's plan and now they were heading 'home to mother', as they put it. On the way they came across a small group of high-ranking officers standing about in a field as if they did not quite know what to do with themselves. Curious, Maxeiner went over to find out who they were. One of them he recognized instantly. Sitting on the barrel of an abandoned 88 mm cannon, swinging his booted legs, that broad-faced officer with jaunty cap and monocle was Field-Marshal Model, his former army commander.

Maxeiner stopped short and stared in awe. But Model beckoned to him and his comrades to approach. As Maxeiner later recalled, Model 'asked where our homes were, our age and military careers. For some time he discussed with me my tour of duty on the Eastern Front. It turned out that I had been in a unit under his command at the time.' Maxeiner plucked up enough courage to ask his former commander what he should do now. Model smiled sadly and said, 'Go home, boys. The war is over for us.' Then, suddenly looking more serious, the Field-Marshal shook hands with the humble sergeant and said, 'Good luck on your trip home and tell your men not to lose courage and continue to remain decent boys.'

Maxeiner saluted for the last time in the war and went off on his journey home. He was one of the last people ever to see Model alive.

Some time later that day the Field-Marshal and his little group gathered expectantly around the radio, as they had done on this day for many years past. For 20 April had been a very special day in Nazi Germany ever since 1933. This was Hitler's birthday and it had always been a day of special announcements and important speeches.

It was Dr Josef Goebbels who spoke that evening to the nation in celebration of Hitler's fifty-sixth — and last — birthday. But Goebbels pointed out that this was not the time for expressing traditional good wishes:

I can only say that these times, with all their sombre and painful majesty, have found their only worthy representative in

*the Führer. We have him to thank — and him alone — that
Germany still exists today, and that the West, with its culture
and civilization, has not been completely engulfed in the dark
abyss which yawns before us.*

Goebbels then acknowledged that the war was nearing its end.
He condemned those who had helped bring the Third Reich to its
knees, including the *'verräterische Ruhrarmee'* (treacherous army of
the Ruhr), before going on to make an amazing prediction. Only
the Führer could lead the way to new victory — and by a most
curious means. 'If history can write that the people of this country
never deserted their leader and that he never deserted his people,
that will be victory!'

To any convinced National Socialist the message was clear.
If the German nation kept faith with the Führer to the bitter
end, his spirit would one day rise triumphant like the phoenix
bird from the smouldering ashes of temporary defeat.

But Model was shocked by Goebbels' speech. That 'treacherous
army of the Ruhr' had hurt him to the quick. Major Behr was
watching him closely at that moment, and, as he later recalled,
Model gave the impression of being someone who suddenly realized
what sort of régime it was that he had served so loyally; what
sort of man it was who had led Germany into this 'dark abyss'.
Certainly Model's face was ashen, his expression grim. But he
made no comment. As always, he kept his thoughts to himself; he
had never been one to broadcast his opinions, except on the few
occasions when he had drunk too much of his favourite Cointreau
or Benedictine liqueur.

However, as Major Behr was only to learn much later, it
was on this day — the last birthday of Adolf Hitler, the very
man who had turned the obscure colonel on the German General
Staff into the legendary Field-Marshal — that Model decided on
his final course of action.

In 1946 when Lieutenant-Colonel Michael, Model's Intelligence
Officer, was being interrogated, he claimed that Model 'chose
death because he had been accused of being a war criminal by
the Russians'. Apparently it was Michael himself who told Model
of the Russians' accusations. Furthermore, Michael informed his
interrogators, he had warned Model that, in his opinion, 'the
Western Powers would hand him over to the Russians'.

But why Michael should have told Model any such thing
is something of a mystery, just as his own death was after
the war; a brave and highly decorated officer, he vanished on

a mission behind the Iron Curtain. In the event, the Western Allies did not hand over any important German officer accused of war crimes to the Russians; the culprits had to stand trial in the Western Allies' own courts. For example, when Model's last chief, Albert Kesselring, was accused of war crimes against the Italians, it was in an Italian courtroom that he was tried — albeit by a British court.

Whatever the truth behind Michael's claims, it is certain that one thought must have been uppermost in Model's mind on that last day of his life: his honour as a Field-Marshal of the Greater German Wehrmacht. He had ruled out the option of surrender, of course. As he had told his own son back in 1943, after Field-Marshal von Paulus had surrendered himself and his Sixth Army to the Russians in Stalingrad: 'A Field-Marshal does *not* surrender! Such a thing is not possible.' But what else could he do?

Just before parting from his Chief-of-Staff, General Wagener, Model had asked if all his orders had been carried out. Yes, Wagener had told him. Whereupon Model had sighed a little and asked: 'What remains for a defeated commander to do?' Then, as Wagener remained silent, Model had said as if to himself: 'In ancient times they took poison.'

And so it would seem that on this Friday, 20 April, as the little group of fugitives sat around a fire in the woods of the von Spee estate, eating their meagre evening meal, Model had already made his final decision. What thoughts must have gone through his head? Did he recall that time when he was a weakly young cadet officer terrorized by the drill sergeant who barked at him, 'Model, you lack hardness!', and regret that he had not become a medical student as once he had been tempted? Did he think back to those dangerous yet carefree days in the trenches of the First World War, before the responsibility of command was thrust upon him? Or those bitter times in this self-same Ruhr when German had fought German and he had been forced to retreat into the British occupied zone and give up his arms to the Tommies? Or those glorious days of 1940 and '41 when Germany's triumph seemed assured, the invincible panzers sweeping everything before them in France, Belgium, Holland, Greece, Yugoslavia, Russia — the whole of Continental Europe under German domination within the short space of one year?

Or was he thinking only of the deed that he must do within the next twenty-four hours?

The next morning, 21 April, was fine and sunny, though with a slight chill in the air. As Model and his companions stretched and yawned after their uncomfortable night in the woods, Major Behr approached him with a suggestion. With the Field-Marshal's agreement, Behr would take his driver, Heinz Crommann, and go off to reconnoitre the area around Wedau, a nearby village, to see if it was safe to proceed or if the *Amis* were there; the round trip would take him, Behr estimated, about three or four hours. Model nodded his approval, but before Behr left he gave the young Major a few personal possessions to deliver to his wife – just in case something happened. It was the last time Behr saw the Field-Marshal.

Around midday Model asked his adjutant, Colonel Pilling, to join him in a stroll around the woods. Neither man made much conversation, until they reached a small glade beneath an oak tree. Then, according to the statement that Pilling made in 1951, Model said to him, 'Anything's better than falling into Russian hands.' He drew his service pistol and added: 'You will bury me here.'

Pilling said nothing. He knew what the Field-Marshal intended to do, but there were no words he could use to dissuade him. He waited, silent and tense.

A soldier knows his firearms. He knows their tendency to jerk upwards when fired. Maybe Model knew that his predecessor in France, Field-Marshal von Kluge, had made a terrible mess of his suicide the previous summer, or that General von Stulpnagel, recalled to Berlin on a charge of treachery, had blinded himself in a similar attempt that same month. Certainly Model knew that the best way to commit suicide was to thrust the barrel of the pistol in one's mouth and grip it firmly with the teeth; then the bullet would tear out the brains. But, sure of himself as ever, the Field-Marshal disdained such a method. He took the traditional 'officer's way out', as it was called by the Imperial Army of his youth. He placed the barrel to his temple, and, while Pilling stood watching, pulled the trigger.

A neat black-rimmed hole at his temple, a sudden stream of blood, and Model had fallen to the ground, the pistol tumbling from his fingers. Field-Marshal Model was dead.

Of all Hitler's field-marshals at the end of the Second World War, Model was the only one to take upon himself the consequences of his loyalty to the Führer and the National Socialist creed that had transported them to such heights and such degrading depths. Back in December, 1944, at the beginning of the Battle of the Bulge, Model had called upon his soldiers not to 'disappoint the Führer and the Homeland'. At the end of the Nazi empire, he knew that his own life must be forfeit. Too proud to suffer the humiliation and recriminations that would be heaped on Kesselring, von Rundstedt and all the rest of Hitler's marshals, Model preferred to end his life by his own hand.

Colonel Pilling fetched Lieutenant-Colonel Michael. No words of explanation were needed for the shot that had echoed round the forest. Together the two men dug a shallow grave beneath the big oak tree that their chief had shown to Pilling, then wrapped his body in a greatcoat and laid it in the ground. After filling the hole once more, they left the scene without any attempt to mark the grave: not even a simple cross made of branches, or an upturned rifle with a helmet hanging from it as once the graves of the dead man's infantrymen had been marked.

But someone — it was never discovered who — later returned to that shadowy glade where Model lay, his grave half hidden beneath branches and fir fronds, and started to carve something on the trunk of the oak tree. It was rather a crude effort; perhaps the unknown carver had only his bayonet for such a task. But it was legible enough. The mark he was carving, which ten years later would lead Hans-Georg to his father's grave, was simply the letter 'M'.

Epilogue

Ende gut, alles gut.'

*German saying**

In a sense Model had died as the victim of two mistakes: one made by his own Führer, who ordered him to defend the Ruhr as a fortress; the other by the enemy Supreme Commander who had insisted on attacking into the Ruhr Pocket. But Model had chosen the soldier's way out, for in his soldier's heart he must have known that he had made a mess of his last battle. He had been indecisive, waiting too long before he launched the Bayerlein counter-attack, which had gone in at the wrong place anyway. He had failed to keep control of his armies and, in the final analysis, he had lacked the courage to make his own decisions independently of the Führer.

But Eisenhower's mistake in making the Ruhr his primary objective that April, instead of Berlin, was disguised — for the time being, at least — as victory. No one could dispute that Bradley had finally achieved his 'bag', that the Ruhr Pocket had fallen to the Americans. The jubilant coterie of high-ranking US generals considered that they had won the war in Europe; never mind the fact that the Red Army had seized Berlin on 21 April.

And now the US Army's senior generals were all busy turning their victory to personal advantage. They were world-famous now, feted everywhere they went both in Europe and America, pursued by newspaper reporters and photographers who would relay their every move and utterance to an admiring public back home. Most of all, it was Eisenhower who prospered.

Those who had scoffed at General Patton, back in March 1945, when he claimed that Eisenhower would one day run for president, were soon to realize he had been right. But Patton himself did not

*Literally 'End good, all good'; i.e. 'All's well that ends well.'

live to see his prophecy fulfilled. By an irony of fate, the man who had urged his one-time chief Bradley to stand up to Eisenhower and teach Montgomery a lesson — and who thus was a prime instigator of the change in strategy — was sacked by Eisenhower in September 1945 and died before the year was out, killed in a car crash. Neither Bradley nor Eisenhower attended his funeral.*

Eisenhower returned to the War Department in Washington, still Chief of Staff of the US Army but with his eyes already drifting towards the White House. Suddenly, one day in 1946, his progress was threatened by scandal. Kay Summersby walked into the War Department and demanded to see 'the boss'. She plumped herself down on a sofa in his secretary's office, stroking her Scottie dog Telek. Once, when she and Eisenhower shared a 'hideaway cottage' outside London, the dog had been a great favourite of the Supreme Commander; around its neck it wore a collar with a disc inscribed 'Telek. This dog belongs to Kay and Ike'. That disc was what had got Kay past the War Department guards.

Cora Thomas, Eisenhower's secretary, stared at Kay pop-eyed. She could not have chosen a worse moment. Mamie Eisenhower was due at the office any moment to meet Ike and go to the airport with him; Montgomery, now Chief of the British Imperial General Staff, was arriving in Washington on an official visit. And Cora was not the only one to be horrified.

'Get her out of here!' one of Eisenhower's aides screeched at Cora. So she took Kay to another office, safely out of the way while Mamie collected Ike and left the building. As Cora later recalled, 'I'll never forget how panic-stricken Ike's aides were at the thought that Mamie might see her.'

Kay Summersby waited for hours, but in vain; eventually she left, disappearing from his life to become just another foot-note in history.

Gradually, as the months and years passed, it became increasingly obvious that Eisenhower was going into politics. As a result, his wartime career started to come under close scrutiny. But, although there was outright criticism in some quarters of his decision not to take Berlin, no one outside that tight little circle — Eisenhower himself, Bradley, Marshall and Ike's former chief-of-staff, Bedell Smith — really knew what lay behind it. And they, of course, were too smart to be provoked on the subject.

*Not one single US president has ever visited his grave, even Reagan who was only twenty-five miles away when he made his controversial visit to Bitburg, Germany in 1985. Surprisingly enough, the only senior statesman ever to visit the grave was Churchill in 1946.

In the end it was Marshall who suffered the harshest criticism. After the war, he served in Truman's cabinet as Secretary of State for Foreign Affairs, and as such became a prime target for the Republicans squaring up for the 1952 elections. Marshall was accused by that arch rabble-rouser, Senator McCarthy, of being a traitor. He had tricked America into the Second World War and then, as Truman's henchman, succeeded in losing China and Korea to the Communists. Marshall, now over seventy, remained silent, perhaps hoping that Eisenhower as Republican candidate for the presidency would come to his defence. When it was announced that Eisenhower would share a platform with McCarthy at a rally in the latter's home state of Wisconsin, everyone was expecting him to refute his fellow Republican's accusations. Indeed, before the rally, the text of Eisenhower's speech was circulated in advance to reporters, and it contained a spirited defence of his old chief. But in the event, Eisenhower omitted that section of his speech. Marshall went undefended.

Marshall bore no grudge against his former protégé, even writing to congratulate him when Eisenhower won the presidency. But his wife Katherine never forgave him for what she regarded as his cowardice. Just as Eisenhower had dropped Patton when he was no longer needed, so he dropped Marshall.

In 1959 Marshall died. But still those men who had once been part of his 'old boys network', at Fort Benning and the War Department, continued to thrive and prosper. Bedell Smith became head of the CIA. Ridgway was appointed commander in the Korean war, and later became head of NATO. 'Lightning Joe' Collins took over the position of Chief-of-Staff of the US Army and later advised Kennedy and Johnson on Vietnam. Omar Bradley was promoted a five-star general. Post-war America did them all proud.

Eisenhower survived until 1969, his reputation as a military commander untarnished. Kay Summersby refused large sums of money to tell her story; at least until after his death. Bradley died in 1981, followed one year later by 'Big Simp' Simpson and four years on by 'Lightning Joe'.

Now they are all gone, those old men who had sent their young soldiers into the Ruhr Pocket. Soldiers like Gavin's paras, trapped beside the Rhine; Sergeant Petersen of 'the Big Red One', fighting to the bitter end; Rose's tankers, trapped and beaten on the road to Paderborn . . . and a whole host of others.

All those young GIs had fought and died for their Top Brass, not knowing that the sweat, pain and sacrifice had been in vain.

The battle they should have fought, the battle for Berlin, was a Soviet victory — but it should have been theirs. If Eisenhower and Bradley had followed the original strategy Berlin would not be a divided city today. In the end, the battle for the Ruhr Pocket was not worth one red cent.

Bibliography

Atwell, Lester: *Private* (Popular Books)

Blair, C.: *Ridgway's Paratroopers* (Doubleday, New York, 1985)

Bradley, Omar: *A Soldier's Story* (Doubleday, New York, 1951)

Bryant, Arthur: *Triumph in the West* (Collins, London, 1959)

Brynes, L.: *The History of the 94th Infantry Division in World War II* (Infantry Press, 1948)

Butcher, Harry C.: *Three Years with Eisenhower* (Heinemann, London, 1946)

Churchill, Winston S.: *The Second World War, Vol. VI: Triumph and Tragedy* (Cassell, London, 1954)

Davis, F.: *Across the Rhine* (Time-Life Books, 1980)

Dornberger, W.: *V-2 — der Schuss iss Westall* (Esslingen, 1952)

Eisenhower, David: *Eisenhower at War 1943–45* (Random House, New York 1986)

Eisenhower, Dwight D.: *Crusade in Europe* (Doubleday, New York, 1948)

Essame, H.: *The Battle for Germany* (Batsford, London, 1969)

Euler, H.: *Die Entscheidungsschlact an Rhein und Ruhr* (Automotorsport Verlag, 1979)

Fuermann, G.: *The 95th Infantry Division History 1918–1946* (Atlanta, 1948)

Gavin, J. M.: *On To Berlin* (Bantam, London, 1979)

Goebbels, Josef: *Tagebucher* (Berthelsmann, Gütersloh, 1977)

Gorlitz, W.: *Strategie der Defensive — Model* (Limes Verlag, 1982)

Goudsmet, S.: *ALSOS* (Morrow, 1964)

Hamilton, Nigel: *Monty — The Field Marshal, 1944–1976* (Hamish Hamilton, London, 1986)

Hoegh, and Doyle,: *Timberwolf Tracks: The History of the 104th Infantry Division* (Infantry Press, 1947)

Houston, D.: *Hell on Wheels* (Presidio Press, 1977)

Irving, David: *The War between the Generals* (Allen Lane, London, 1981)

Kesselring, Albert: *A Soldier's Record* (Morrow, 1954)

Knickerbocker, H.: *Danger Forward: The Story of the 1st Division in World War II* (Infantry Press, 1947)

Longmate, Norman: *Hitler's Rockets* (Hutchinson, London 1985)

MacDonald, Charles: *The Last Offensive* (Office of Chief of Military History, 1973)

Mellenthin, F. W. von: *Panzer Battles 1939–45* (Cassell, London, 1955)

Minott, R.: *The Fortress That Never Was* (Holt, 1964)

Mittelman, J.: *Eight Stars to Victory: A History of the Veteran 9th US Infantry Division* (Infantry Press, 1948)

Montgomery, Bernard Law: *Normandy to the Baltic* (Hutchinson, London, 1947)

Mosley, L.: *Marshall, Organizer of Victory* (Methuen, London, 1982)

Mues, W.: *Der Grosse Kessel* (Mues, 1986)

Paper, F.: *Der Wahrheit eine Gasse* (Bechtle, 1952)

Patton, George S.: *War as I Knew It* (Houghton Mifflin, Boston, 1947)

Peukert, K.: *Die Amis Kommen* (Hagen, 1969)

Ryan, Cornelius: *The Last Battle* (Simon & Schuster, 1966)

Shulman, Milton: *Defeat in the West* (Ballantine, 1947)

Speer, A.: *Erinerungen* (Propylaen Verlag, 1969)

Summersby Morgan, Kay: *Past Forgetting* (Collins, London, 1977)

Toland, John: *The Last Hundred Days* (Random House, 1966)

Wagener, C.: *Kampf und Ende der Heersgruppe B* (Wehrwissenschaftlice Rundschau, 1957)

Weber, R.: *Als Düsseldorf Front Wurde* (Stadt Düsseldorf, 1952)

Westphal, S.: *The German Army in the West* (Cassell, London, 1951)

Spearhead in the West: The 3rd Armored Division 1941–45 (Nashville, 1980)

First US Army Report of Operations 23 February–8 May 1945 (Commanding General First Army, 1946)

Conquer: The Story of the US Ninth Army (Infantry Press, 1948)

Ninth US Army Report after Action against Enemy, 1 March–30 April 1945 (Army War College, 1945)
Tornado: The Story of the 8th Armored Division
Lightning: The History of the 78th Division (Infantry Press, 1947)
The History of the 5th Infantry Division
The 35th Infantry Division in World War II

INDEX